Jane Asher's

Complete Book of

Cake Decorating Ideas

WITHDRAWN

JANE ASHER'S

COMPLETE BOOK OF

CAKE DECORATING IDEAS

BBC BOOKS

BBC Books would like to thank the following for their kind permission to reproduce the various licensed characters in this book:

Tessie Bear and Noddy © Darrell Waters Ltd; *Peter Rabbit*™, *Jemima Puddle-duck*™ and *Tom Kitten*™ figures © Frederick Warne and Co.; *Tintin* © Hergé: the character from *Hergé's Adventures of Tintin*; *Crunchie* logo © Cadbury Ltd; Lonsdale Sports Equipment Ltd; Heron Suzuki; *Classic Citroën 2CV*, Citroën UK Ltd; *Sooty*™ Matthew Corbett Ltd (authorised by Patsy B Marketing Ltd); *Spot* © Ventura Publishing Ltd; *Pingu* © Editoy/SRG 1992 licensed by BBC Enterprises Ltd

Published by BBC Books,
a division of BBC Enterprises Limited,
Woodlands, 80 Wood Lane
London W12 0TT

First Published 1993

ISBN 0 563 36492 0
Designed by Bill Mason
Illustrations by Kate Simunek
Inside photographs by Chris Turner
All cakes made by *Jane Asher Party Cakes*

Set in Garamond by Goodfellow & Egan, Cambridge
Printed and bound in Great Britain by Butler & Tanner Ltd
Colour separation by Technik Ltd, Berkhamsted
Jacket printed by Lawrence Allen Ltd, Weston-Super-Mare

For Ara, as sweet as the cakes

ACKNOWLEDGEMENTS

When I started cake decorating as a child, many years ago, I had no idea it would eventually become such an important part of my life. In those days I saw it simply as an enjoyable hobby, and when I wrote my first cake decorating book, over ten years ago, I made all of the cakes on my kitchen table at home.

Now it has become a business – although remaining as enjoyable as ever – and I no longer have to produce every decoration on my own. The cakes in this book have been made by my wonderful team at my shop *Jane Asher Party Cakes*, who have also contributed to many of the ideas. Their professionalism, enthusiasm and brilliance of technique are a constant inspiration to me and I would particularly like to thank Lydia Patrice, Julie Reynolds, Justine Lord and Louise Summers-Brown.

My special gratitude goes to my wonderful manageress, Ruth Clark, who organised and contributed to the making and photographing of the cakes, remained calm while having to produce the 78 cakes in the book *as well* as taking all the usual orders for the shop, and who encouraged and supported all of us.

My thanks also to Suzanne Webber (who was brave enough to ask me to write *yet another* cake book), Anna Ottewill and Frank Phillips at BBC Books. Also thanks to Chris Turner for photographing the cakes so patiently and beautifully, to Bill Mason for his design, to Kate Simunek for the clear step-by-step drawings and to John Jefford for the cover photograph.

And thank you to everyone who enjoys making, eating or buying these extraordinary confections, for sharing my love of such a frivolous and happy branch of cookery and for ensuring it will continue to delight and entertain children and adults now and in the future.

CONTENTS

INTRODUCTION

If I'd known you were coming I'd have . . . decorated a cake to look like the Albert Hall and covered it in sugar flowers. Don't let your celebration cakes be boring! However limited you feel are your skills as a decorator, there is always a way of achieving an unusual, dramatic or beautiful effect. It's the *idea* that counts, and that's where you can really let your imagination run wild.

I'm quite sure that if you look through the pages of this book there'll be something that will jump out at you and feel right. Does Uncle Fred like gardening? Try the garden cake on page 63, or the flower pot (page 72). Little Susie's keen on Sooty and Sweep? The Castle (page 151) or The Spider-Man cake (page 161) with Sooty's face instead of Spider-man would be perfect. Don't ever feel you have to follow the characters and shapes I have given you: even if you start by copying the designs exactly I'm sure you'll soon want to adapt them to suit yourself.

Start – always – with the person or occasion for which the cake is intended. That's far better than deciding in limbo on a complicated design which might have no relevance to the event in question and which if it went wrong or didn't quite live up to the image you had in mind would be disastrous. A cat cake specially made for a cat lover, however amateur and home-made looking, will be far more appreciated than a fancily piped creation that just hasn't quite worked.

There's always a suitable theme – don't ever give up on thinking of something just right, however difficult it seems. A lady came into my shop recently to order a cake for an eightieth birthday. 'I simply don't know what to choose,' she confessed, so I started the usual tactful questioning. Was it for a man or woman? A woman. Did she have any hobbies? No. What, not even knitting or watching television? No, her sight wasn't too good. Any adored grandchildren? No. Pets? No. Favourite flowers? Gone off gardening since confined to her chair. Becoming just fractionally desperate I ventured 'What's her name?' 'Olive.' 'Ah ha! A simple white cake with a large, clear olive branch on top with leaves and green olives and her name added in icing!' 'Perfect.' And it looked lovely.

And of course you can send many interesting messages on your cake. A very smart elderly lady from Chelsea ordered a cake with 'Sod off, birthday boy' piped on it. 'He's been telling me to sod off for years; I thought it was my turn,' she cheerfully explained. You needn't even pipe the words in icing; you can be far more subtle and use symbols and codes to put across your feelings. The language of flowers opens up endless possibilities: apart from the classic red roses for love you'll find that by combining several flowers on to one cake you can convey a huge array of sentiments, from 'be mine for ever' to 'lend us a fiver' (well, perhaps not quite).

You'll find techniques and ideas in the book that can be adapted very easily to fit every possible theme and all the information on recipes and techniques is at the back of the book. None of the cakes needs any great skill; I've kept the piping to a few simple shapes and all the cakes are covered with roll-out icing which is much easier to use than royal icing and gives a smooth, even finish. Obviously if you prefer royal icing you can use it instead. Some of the modelling is quite difficult, and if you feel a bit daunted by it then choose the run-out or painting method instead. But I can't stress enough how it's worth having a go – some of the most uneven, strange and quirky-looking models have by far the most charm, and if the children think your model of Bugs Bunny looks like a dinosaur then so be it . . . give him a name tag if you feel a little insecure about the likeness.

Be bold and adventurous: if you feel like making a purple caterpillar then do it – one of the joys of cake decorating is that you needn't be authentic or even tasteful and that you can create animals, buildings and situations that couldn't possibly exist in real life. Fulfil your favourite person's fantasy: perhaps modelling a husband catching a giant fish, or a boyfriend driving a Ferrari, or a mother sitting in an armchair surrounded by Champagne and chocolates.

People often tell me that they don't know how I can bear the thought of the cakes being sliced into and eaten, but for me that's part of the fun. I like the craziness of spending hours on something that will face imminent destruction, and it's comforting to remember when your planned cake of a yacht is looking more like a rusty barge that before too long it will be inside somebody's stomach.

Good luck with the decorating – enjoy yourself and please don't get frazzled if they don't turn out exactly as you want. If I'm trying something new and difficult, taking it all far too seriously and find myself shouting at the children or having to give Gerald baked beans on toast for supper – again – I do try to pull myself up short and remind myself . . . they're only cakes!

Children's Stories

It's very satisfying to see a child with his nose buried in a good book – quite a rare sight in this age of TV and videos – and it is probably partly because of its rarity that it seems so worthwhile. Perhaps when books were first around parents worried just as much about their bad influence as we do about television ('Marcus, for goodness sake get your nose out of that papyrus and go out and hunt something'). What is very pleasing is the way some of the old stories have survived so long and remain so popular. Beatrix Potter (see page 18) sells as well as ever, because we all like to pass on such delightful stories and pictures to the next generation, and many of the old fairy stories (I loved the coloured fairy story books with their strange, magical and often gruesome stories) are enjoyed as much as ever.

Tessie Bear

I've always assumed that Tessie Bear is Noddy's girlfriend, although it's never made completely clear. Certainly he seems very fond of her and often talks admiringly of her pretty clothes and bonnet. Teddies of all kinds are always popular – I still have my much-loved Oswald, who has survived over forty years of life with me and still doesn't complain – but once you've mastered this method of building up a large seated figure you could use it for many different characters.

Serves 35

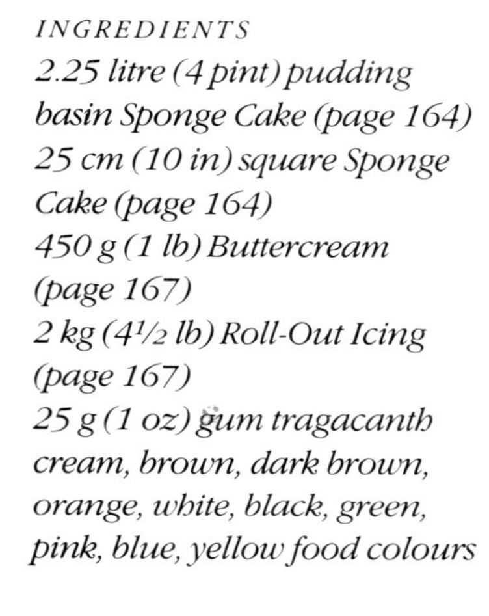

INGREDIENTS

2.25 litre (4 pint) pudding basin Sponge Cake (page 164)
25 cm (10 in) square Sponge Cake (page 164)
450 g (1 lb) Buttercream (page 167)
2 kg (4½ lb) Roll-Out Icing (page 167)
25 g (1 oz) gum tragacanth
cream, brown, dark brown, orange, white, black, green, pink, blue, yellow food colours

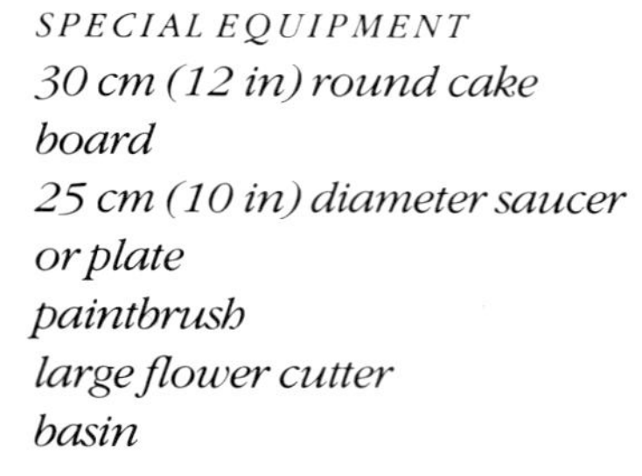

SPECIAL EQUIPMENT

30 cm (12 in) round cake board
25 cm (10 in) diameter saucer or plate
paintbrush
large flower cutter
basin

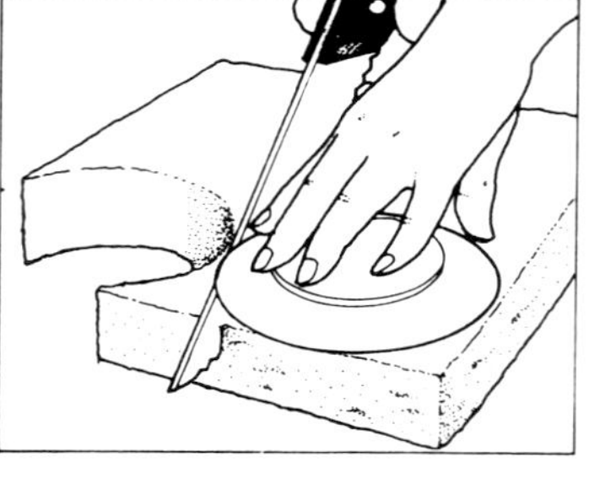

1 Using a saucer or small plate as a guide, cut 2 circles 13 cm (5 in) diameter from the side of the square cake for the head. Cut two legs from the remaining piece.

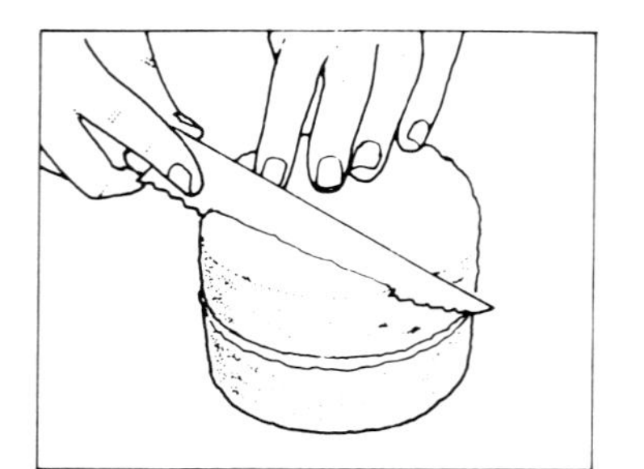

2 Stick the head shapes on top of each other with a little buttercream. With a serrated knife, trim them to a head shape, allowing for a nose at the front.

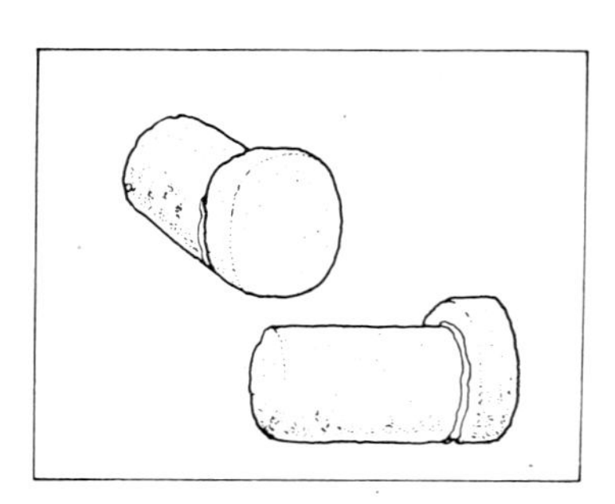

3 Trim the legs to rounded shapes and stick a larger disc of cake to the end of each with buttercream to make feet. Cut the pudding basin cake in half horizontally and sandwich it together with about 175 g (6 oz) of the buttercream.

4 Stick the cake to the board and stick the head to the body. Colour 900 g (2 lb) of roll-out icing with cream and brown to make a light tan. Roll out a thick strip and stick it round the neck.

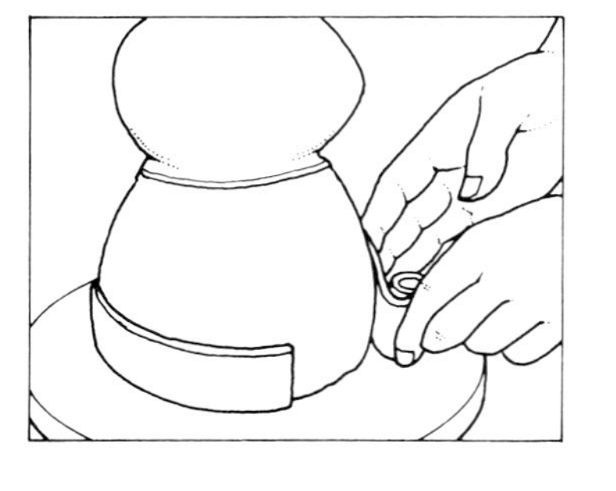

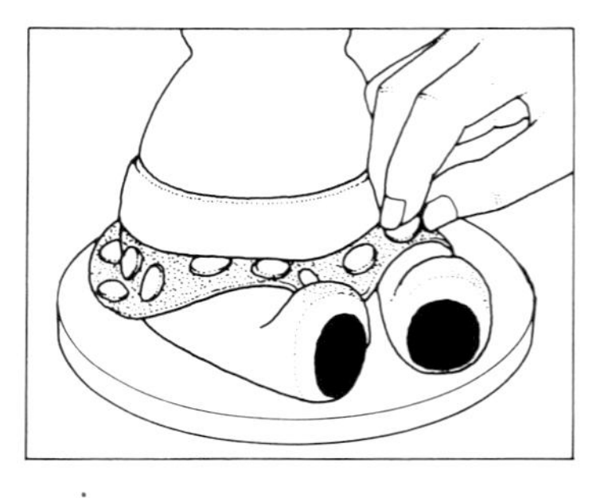

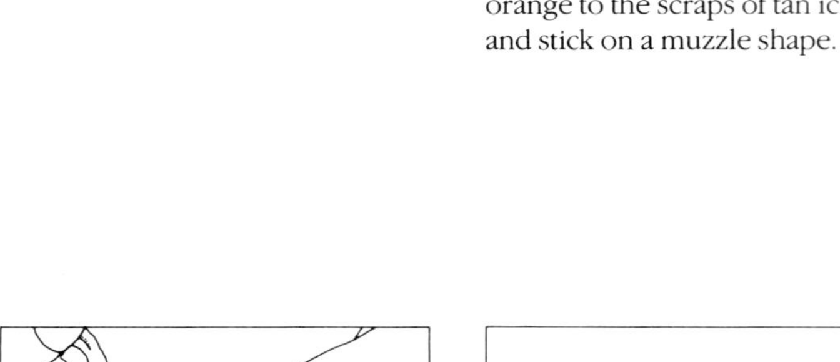

5 Spread the head and the top of the body with buttercream. Roll out about a third of the remaining tan icing and cover the head and neck as shown. With another piece of tan icing, cover the upper body. Add a strip round the bottom of the cake.

6 Roll out half of the remaining tan icing and cover the legs and feet. Stick the legs to the body. From the trimmings make two ears and stick them to the head with a little water. Colour about 50 g (2 oz) of icing dark brown. Add small brown pads to the bottom of the feet and brown insides to the ears. Add a little orange to the scraps of tan icing and stick on a muzzle shape.

7 Add the markings to the muzzle. Cut eye shapes out of the icing and fill with white, then add a black nose, mouth and pupils. Colour about 350 g (12 oz) of roll-out icing light green and 550 g (1¼ lb) light pink. To make the skirt, roll out a strip of green icing then stick a strip of pink on top then stick to Tessie's waist. Cut out a few white spots and stick them to the skirt.

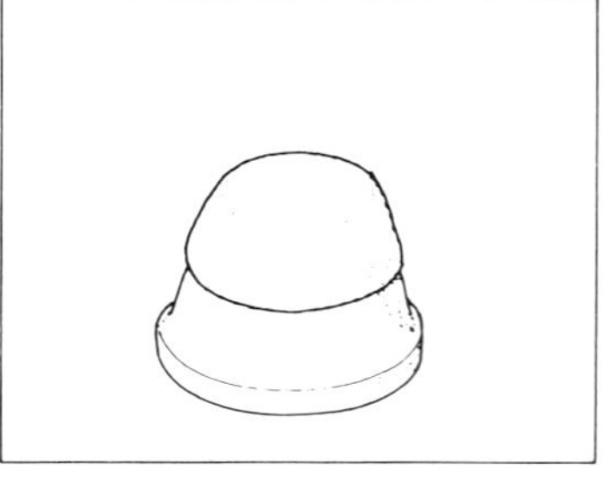

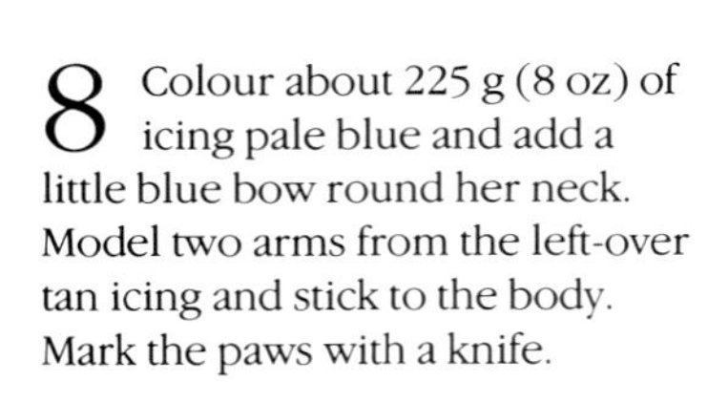

8 Colour about 225 g (8 oz) of icing pale blue and add a little blue bow round her neck. Model two arms from the left-over tan icing and stick to the body. Mark the paws with a knife.

9 Using the rest of the pink icing cut a circle about 25 cm (10 in) diameter and stick it to the head. Fold the edge over slightly to make a brim. Add a little gum tragacanth to the left-over pink icing and roll out enough to make the crown of the hat at the back of the head, drying it over a basin to make a rounded shape.

10 Roll out the remaining light blue icing and cut out 6 flowers with a large flower cutter. Leave them to dry, then add yellow centres and paint dark blue on to the petals. Stick the bonnet crown onto the brim adding the flowers. Add a thin blue ribbon of icing to cover the join of brim and crown.

The Mermaid Lagoon

My favourite scene from Peter Pan is the Mermaid Lagoon. Those strange, fascinating, half-fish, half-woman creatures used to make me feel quite creepy as a child, and there's no doubt they have quite sinister powers. They certainly don't leap to Peter's defence when he is threatened with extinction by the rising tide, but, of course, if they did we would miss one of the great theatrical lines of all time: 'To die will be an awfully big adventure!'

Serves 20

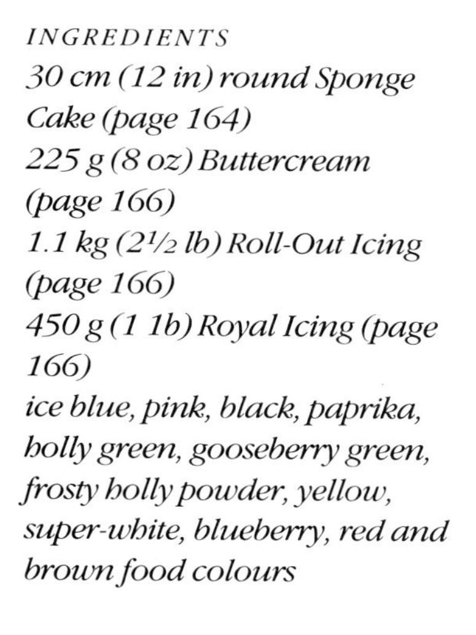

INGREDIENTS

30 cm (12 in) round Sponge Cake (page 164)
225 g (8 oz) Buttercream (page 166)
1.1 kg (2½ lb) Roll-Out Icing (page 166)
450 g (1 1b) Royal Icing (page 166)
ice blue, pink, black, paprika, holly green, gooseberry green, frosty holly powder, yellow, super-white, blueberry, red and brown food colours

SPECIAL EQUIPMENT

1 35 cm (14 in) round cake board
straw
paintbrush
piping bag with no. 44 nozzle
modelling tool
non-stick baking parchment

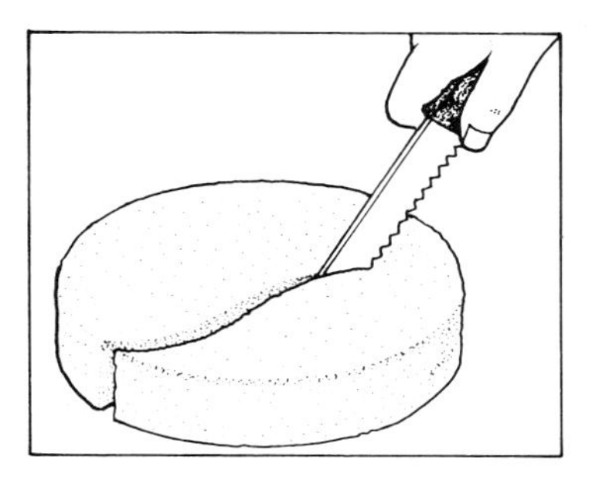

1 Cut off about one-third of the cake in a wavy line, using a sharp serrated knife.

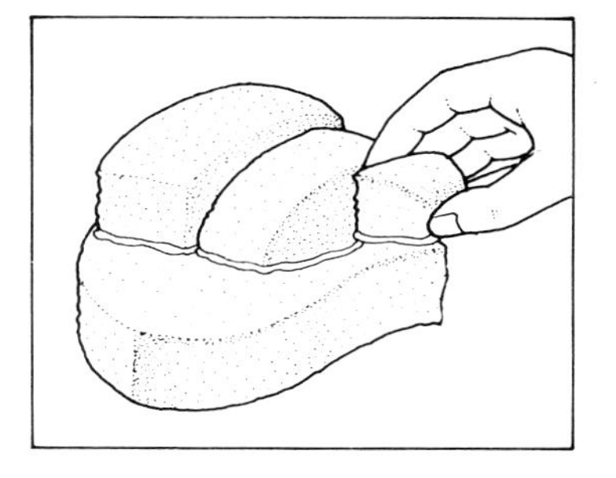

2 Break the smaller piece into 2, and cut a further chunk off the main cake. Stick the broken pieces on top of the cake with about 50 g (2 oz) of buttercream to build up the rock.

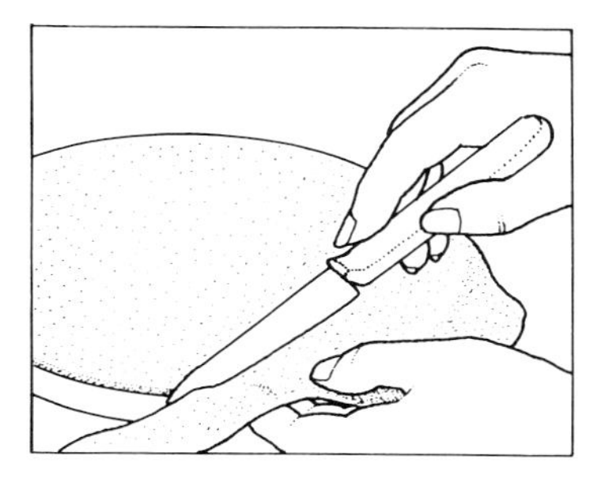

3 Colour 100 g (4 oz) of roll-out icing ice blue and roll out and cover the board.

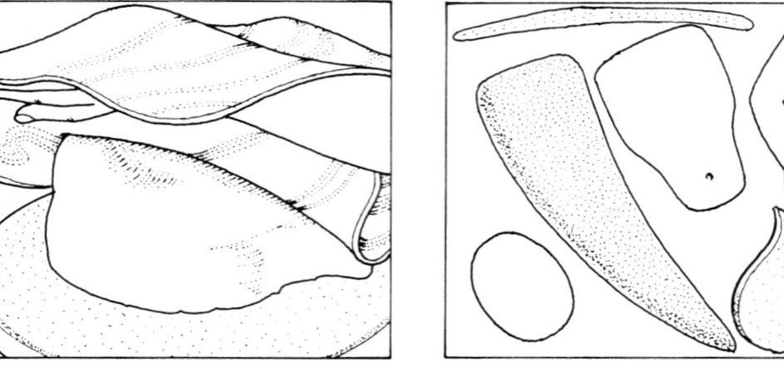

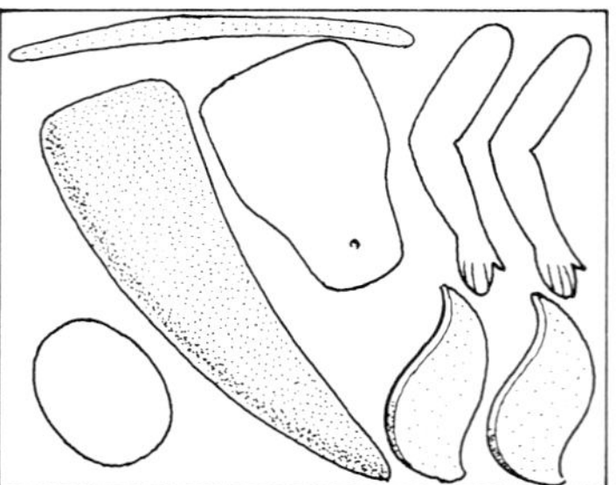

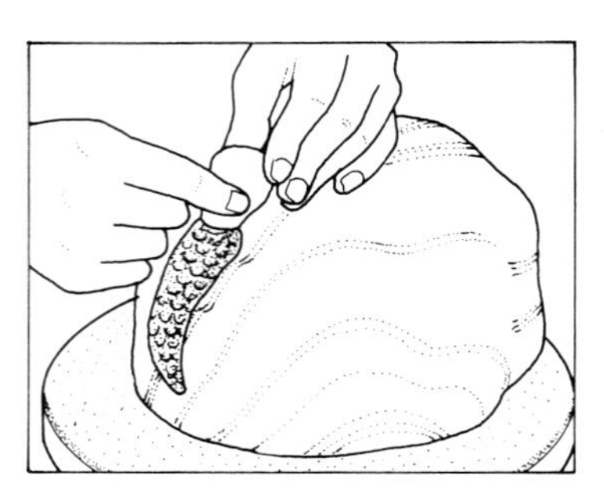

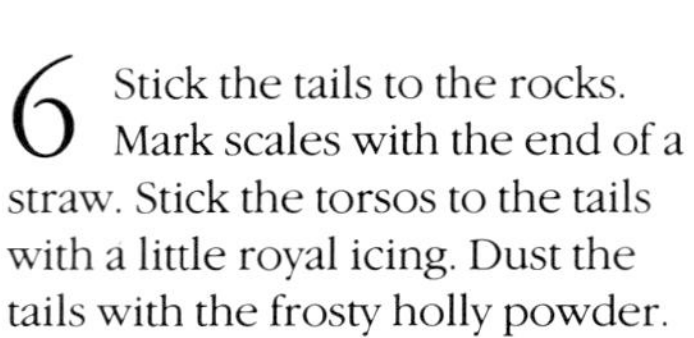

4 Colour 75 g (3 oz) of roll-out icing pink. Knead a tiny amount of black food colour into a further 350 g (12 oz) of roll-out icing, stopping before it is mixed in so that you achieve a mottled 'stratified rock' effect, then knead it together with the pink icing to give a grey/pink mottled effect. Stick the cake to the board with a little buttercream and spread the remaining buttercream all over the cake. Roll out the grey icing and cover the cake completely, moulding the icing round the shapes well and trimming it at the base with a sharp knife.

5 Colour about 175 g (6 oz) of icing with a tiny amount of paprika to make it flesh colour. Model a head, torso and two arms for each mermaid. Colour about 275 g (10 oz) of icing holly green and make the tails, and colour 150 g (5 oz) gooseberry green to make a waistband and fins for each.

6 Stick the tails to the rocks. Mark scales with the end of a straw. Stick the torsos to the tails with a little royal icing. Dust the tails with the frosty holly powder.

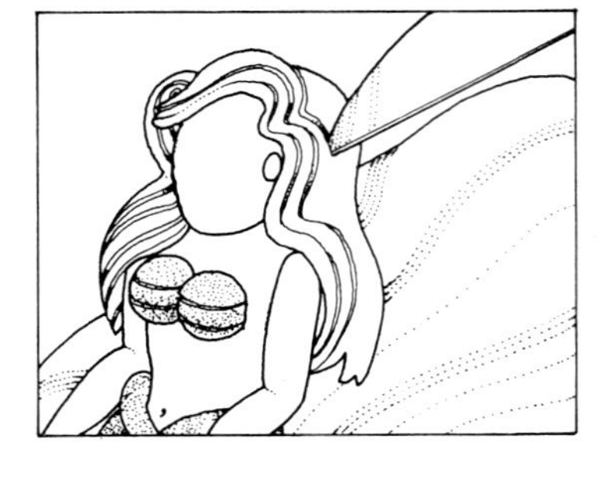

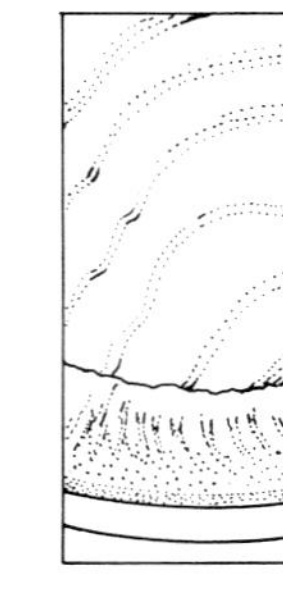

7 Add the fins and waistbands, heads, tiny ears and stick on the arms. Add bikini tops made from icing coloured with pink. Colour a small amount of icing yellow and add some hair. Mark it with the end a knife.

8 Paint the faces using super-white, blueberry, black, red and brown.

9 With a no. 44 nozzle and an icing bag pipe a continuous line of white royal icing around the rocks on to the board. Using a wet brush, stroke the white icing outwards into a wave effect.

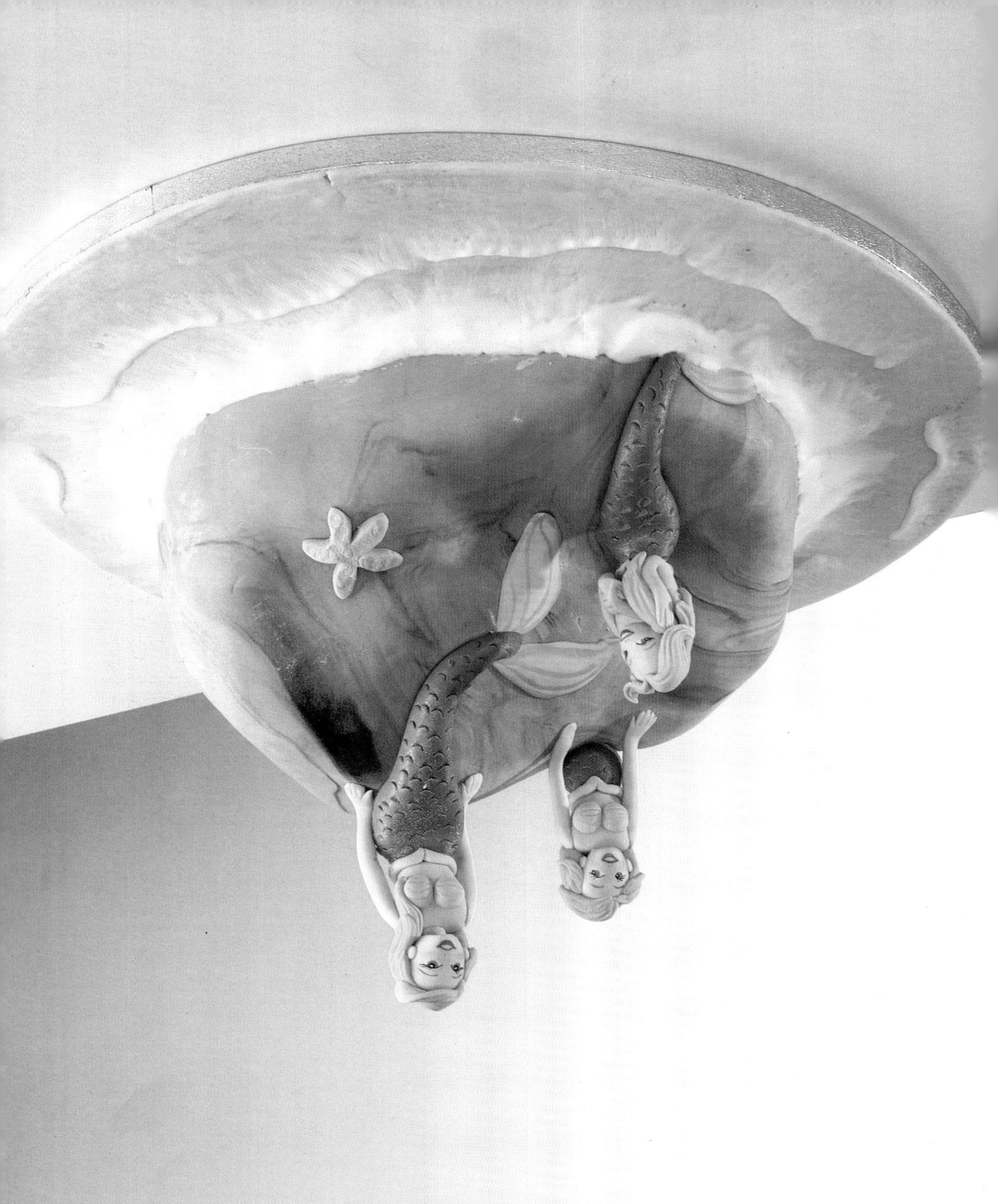

Peter Rabbit and his Friends

Build up these charming models piece by piece just as for Fun in the Font (page 77). Keep looking at the original, being very careful to reproduce the colours as accurately as possible, so as to keep as close to Beatrix Potter's 'look' as you can.

Robin Hood and his Merry Men

Once again I've avoided standing up characters in order to make this easier, but because they are sitting round a fire it's perfectly acceptable. It's always worth thinking your design out carefully before you start, so you don't come across any unexpected problems!

Alice in Wonderland

This shows how very effective a black-and-white 'drawing' can be. Either copy a picture freehand, using a paintbrush and food colouring or an icing pen, or enlarge or reduce a picture to exactly the size you need at your local photographic shop and trace it on to the cake.

Tintin Goes to the Moon

This shows how much a painted board can add to the drama of a cake. Cover it in white and give it plenty of time to dry before painting it. The rocket is built up from two layers of cake and shaped.

FUN AND FOOD

This is one of my favourite sections. No, I don't quite know why the boy scout is included, but he didn't seem to fit in anywhere else and I'm fond enough of him not to want him to be left out. I suppose scouts have fun when they're putting up tents or bob-a-jobbing and whatever else they do so that can justify his being here. And the violin's connection is a bit tenuous too, but let's assume a very jolly violinist owns this one and has great fun while playing.

Stereo System

Nowadays sound systems become out of date extremely quickly, and it could well be that in a few years time this type of stereo will look like a period piece, but it makes a wonderful cake for a music lover and you can always adapt it to be a CD player or hologram producer or whatever the latest thing may be . . .

Serves 25–30

INGREDIENTS
20 cm (8 in) square Fruit Cake (page 166)
sieved jam
1.5 kg (3 lb) marzipan
1.5 kg (3¼ lb) Roll-Out Icing (page 166)
100 g (4 oz) Royal Icing (page 166)
black, light grey, green, red, and silver (page 164) food colours

SPECIAL EQUIPMENT
40 × 35 cm (16 in × 14 in) cake board
piping bag with no. 1 nozzle
paintbrush
non-stick baking parchment
crimper

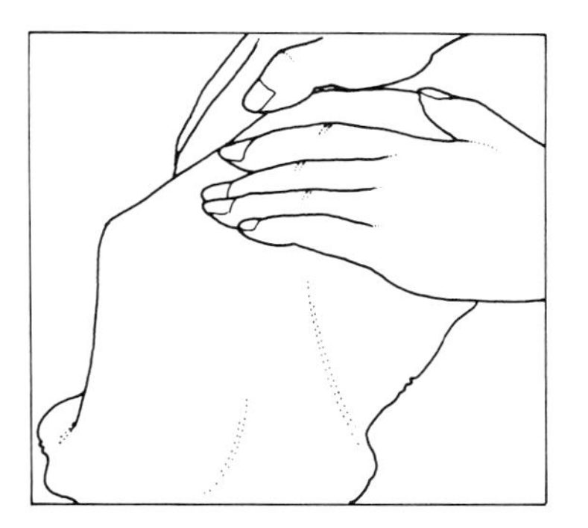

1 Cut the cake into one box shape about 20 × 10 × 7½ cm (8 × 4 × 3 in) and two further shapes of 10 × 5 × 5 cm (4 × 2 × 2 in). Spread the cakes with jam. Roll out the marzipan and cover all three cakes, getting the edges as sharp as possible.

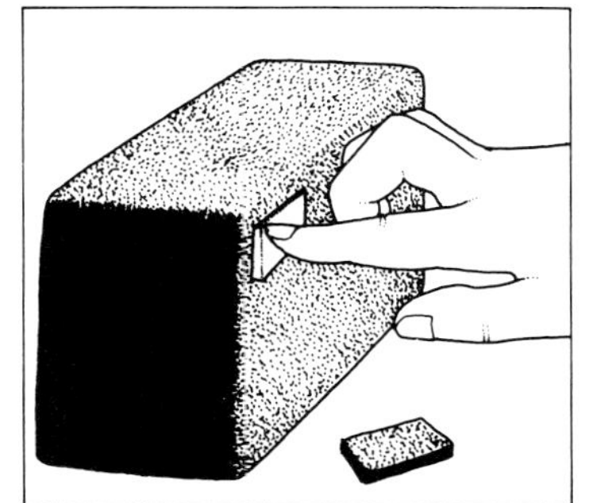

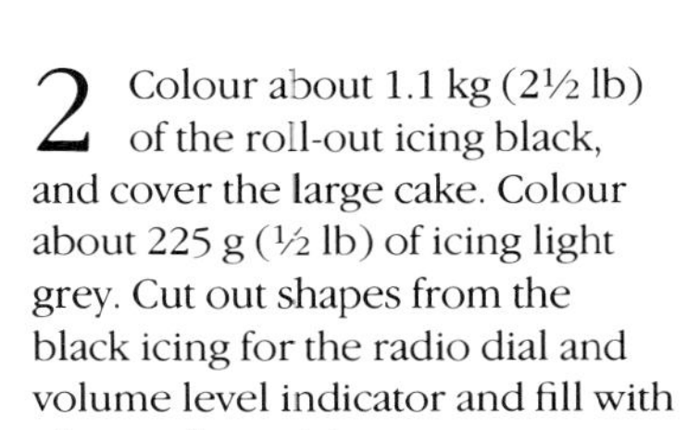

2 Colour about 1.1 kg (2½ lb) of the roll-out icing black, and cover the large cake. Colour about 225 g (½ lb) of icing light grey. Cut out shapes from the black icing for the radio dial and volume level indicator and fill with pieces of grey icing.

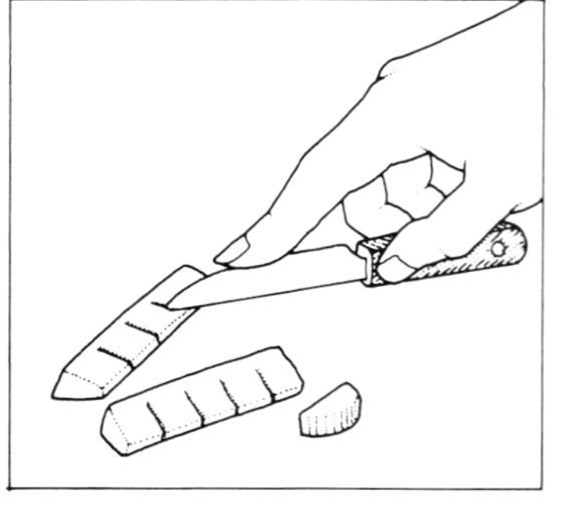

3 Roll and cut out of grey icing two pieces about 7.5 cm (3 in) long to make the operating buttons. Mark them suitably with the back of a knife and stick in position. Colour about 50 g (2 oz) of icing green and remaining 50 g (2 oz) red. Cut out A and B cassette panels and rectangles and stick in position. Add a red button. Cut and stick grey cassette middles and radio tuner knobs. Paint them silver.

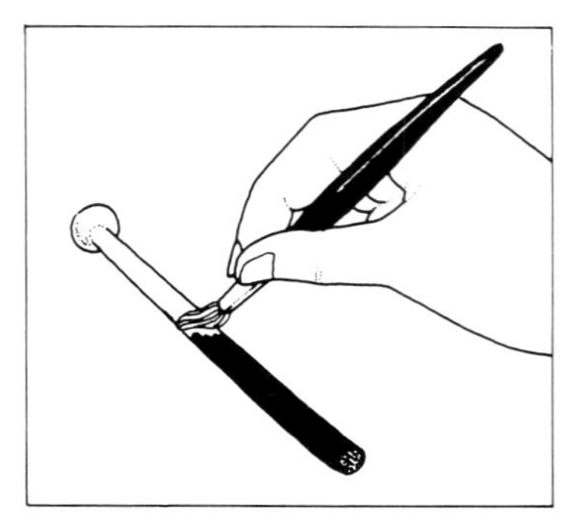

4 Paint on the radio dial, noise level dial and A and B on the tape deck using black and red colouring. Roll out a small piece of any left over icing into an 18 cm (7 in) long sausage and add a ball at one end to make the aerial. Leave it to dry for 2 hours then paint it silver. Add a small black handle to the stereo.

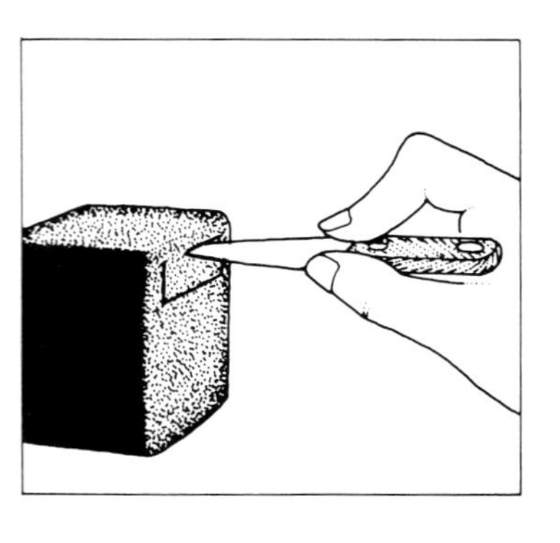

5 Cover the speakers in black icing. Cut out the shapes as shown on the finished cake and fill with grey icing.

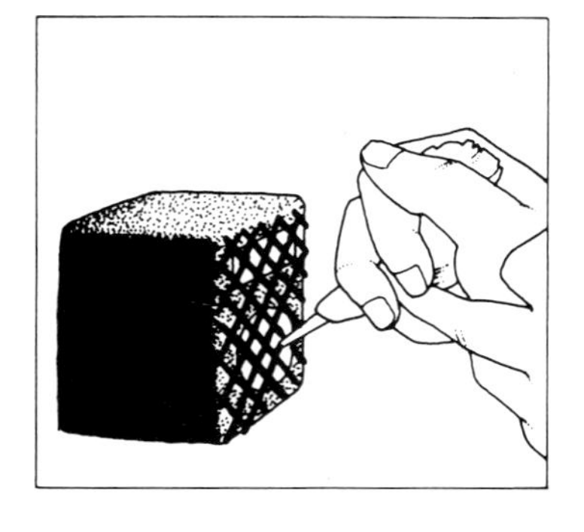

6 Colour the royal icing black. Pipe criss-crossing lines over the front panel of each speaker.

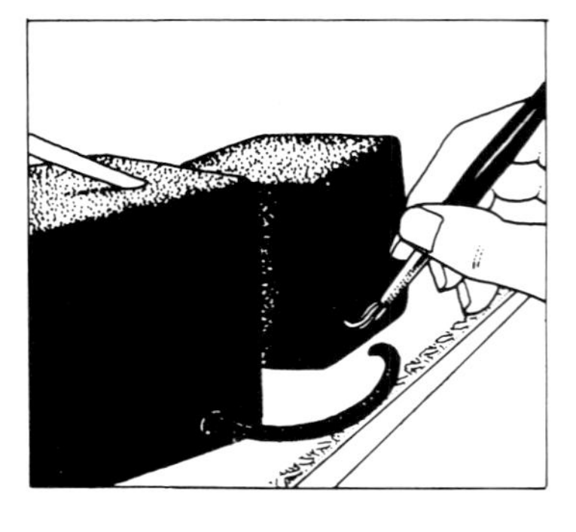

7 Cover the board in white icing and crimp the edge. Stick the stereo and speakers on to the board with a little water and add some rolled out black icing wires. Stick the aerial in position with a little royal icing.

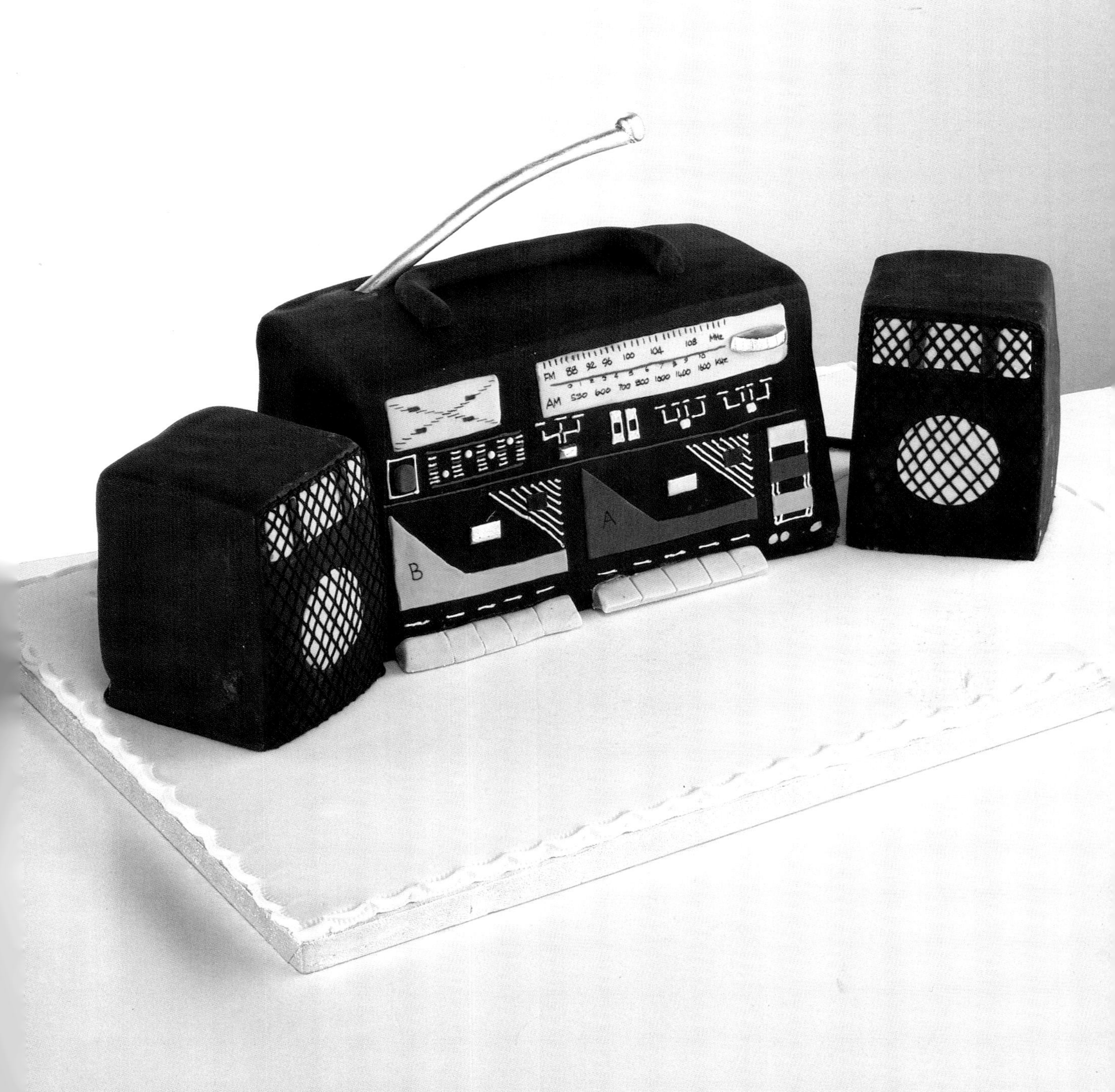

FM 88 92 96 100 104 108 MHz
AM 530 600 700 800 1000 1400 1600 KHz
A
B

VIOLIN

If you include the music and the chin cloth as I have with this cake, it will obviously mean you have a large amount of icing. It does look wonderful, I think, but the violin on its own would be very attractive, too. If you decide to do the music you could choose a piece suitable for the occasion – 'Happy Birthday' or 'Congratulations', for example.

Start 2 days before

Serves 15

INGREDIENTS

20 × 15 cm (8 × 6 in) Fruit Cake (page 166)
350 g (12 oz) marzipan
1.4 kg (3 lb) Roll-Out Icing (page 166)
175 g (6 oz) gum tragacanth
50 g (2 oz) Royal Icing (page 166)
brown, cream, black and red food colours
sieved jam

SPECIAL EQUIPMENT

46 × 30 cm (18 × 12 in) cake board
picture of violin to copy
scissors and card
non-stick baking parchment
paintbrush
florists' wire

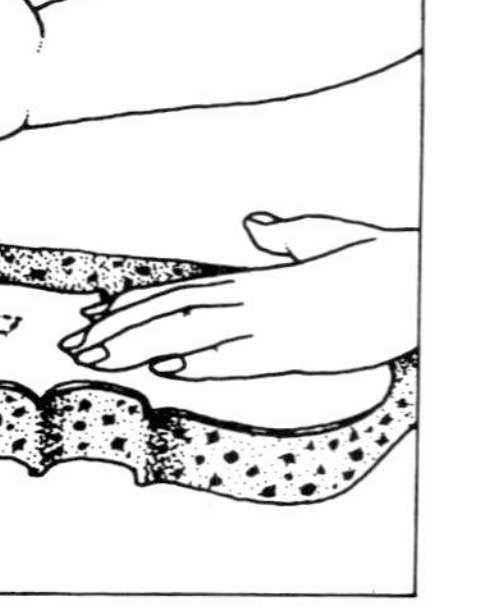

1 Using the template on page 178 as a guide, cut a violin shape out of card. Place the card template on the cake and cut round it with a sharp serrated knife.

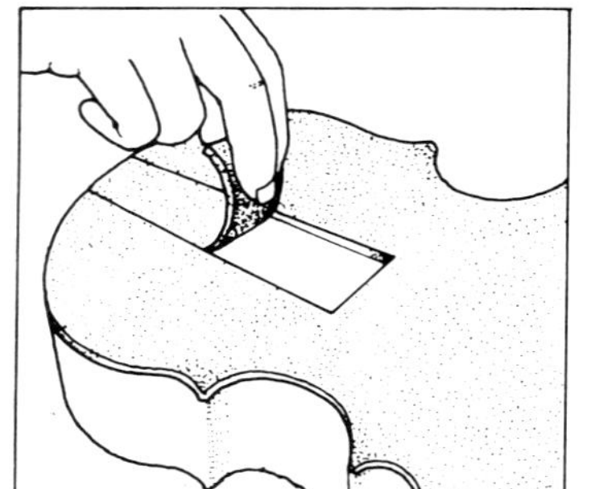

2 Roll out the marzipan. Cut a strip for the side of the violin first. Stick it to the cake with jam. Use the template to cut a shape from the marzipan to fit the top. Stick it to the cake with jam. Colour 350 g (12 oz) of roll-out icing brown. Roll it out and again use the template to cut a shape for the top. Dampen the marzipan slightly with water and stick the icing top in place (leave the side uncovered for the moment). Cut out and remove a shape from the top (from the layer of icing only, not cutting through the marzipan) as marked on the template for the neck to fit into.

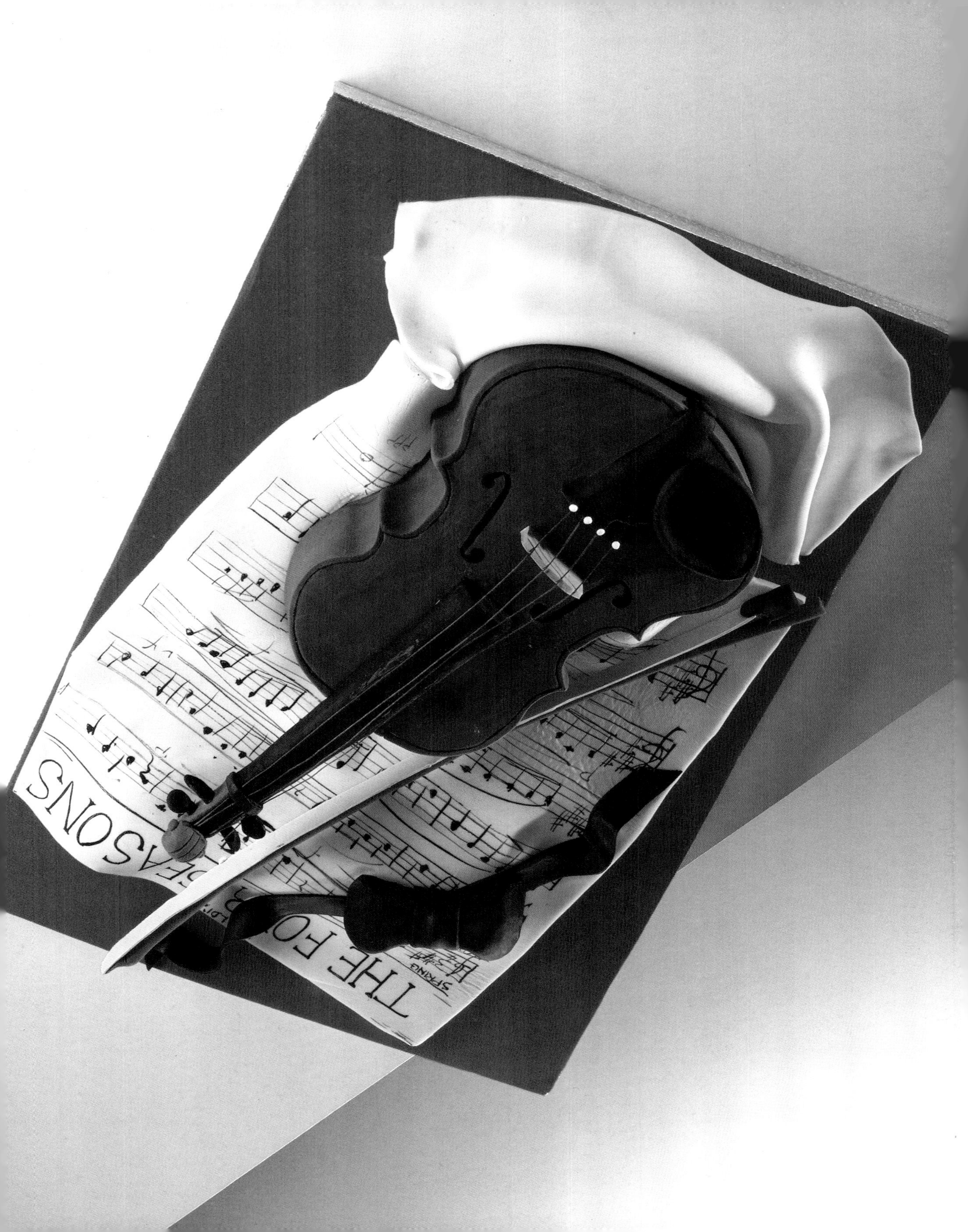

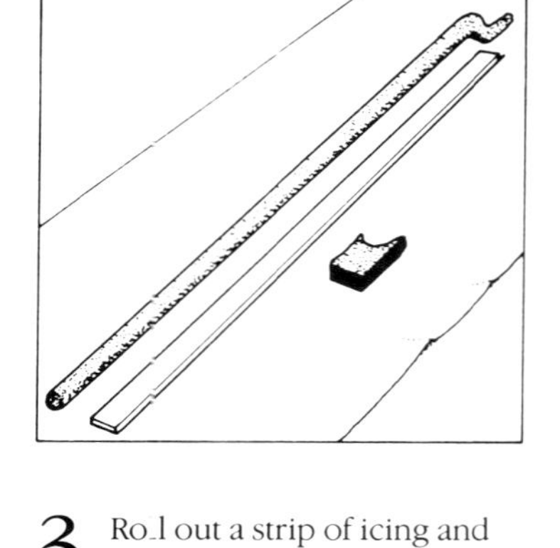

3 Roll out a strip of icing and cover the side. Knead 25 g (1 oz) of gum tragacanth into the trimmings. Roll the gummed icing into a sausage shape about 38 cm (15 in) long to make the bow. Pinch one end flat and lie it carefully to dry on non-stick paper. Colour about 25 g (1 oz) of icing cream. Knead in a pinch of gum tragacanth and roll it to the same length as the bow. Flatten and trim it to a strip. Colour 350 g (12 oz) of icing black. Use a piece to make the end of the bow.

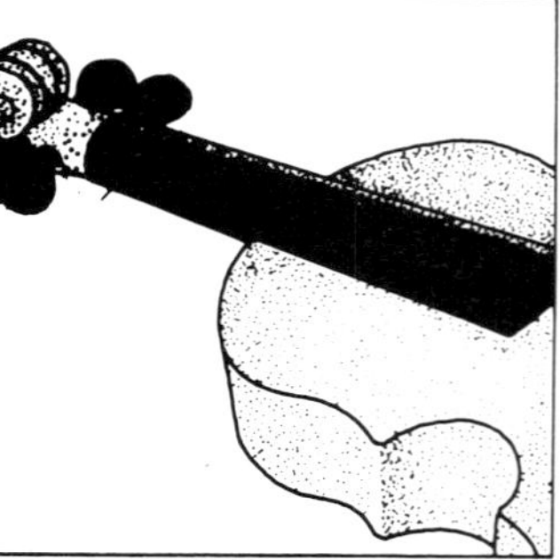

4 When dry, stick the 3 bow pieces together with a tiny amount of royal icing. Leave it on non-stick paper. Knead the remaining gum tragacanth into about 225 g (8 oz) of black icing. Roll out just over half the black icing into the shape of the neck to fit the gap on top of the violin and to protrude by 10 cm (4 in). Model a scroll from the brown trimmings, make tuning knobs and stick to the top of the finger board with royal icing. Finish off the join with small black pieces.

5 Cut a bridge 4 cm (1½ in) wide and 2 cm (¾ in) high from the cream trimmings. Make 4 tiny grooves in one side. Model a chin rest and lower string holder out of black icing. Dry on non-stick paper for 24 hours. Meanwhile, colour 350 g (12 oz) of roll-out icing red. Roll it out and stick it to the cake board with a little water. Stick the violin in position with a tiny amount of royal icing about 20 cm (8 in) from the top of the board.

6 Using 225 g (8 oz) of white icing, roll out a rectangle 30 × 25 cm (12 × 10 in). Using the template as a guide, cut the shape of the upper three-quarters of the violin body from the edge of the icing. Dampen the iced board and drape the white icing on to it, making little folds as if it were paper. Let it dry for 30 minutes.

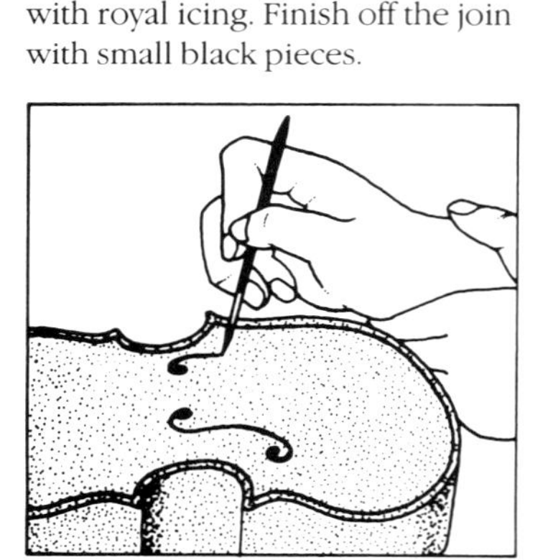

7 Paint the details on to the violin with the brush and black colour. Paint some music on to the white sheet. Colour the remaining white icing pale pink with a small amount of red colour. Roll out the icing and cut out a chin cloth. Dampen the board and drape the cloth round the bottom of the violin.

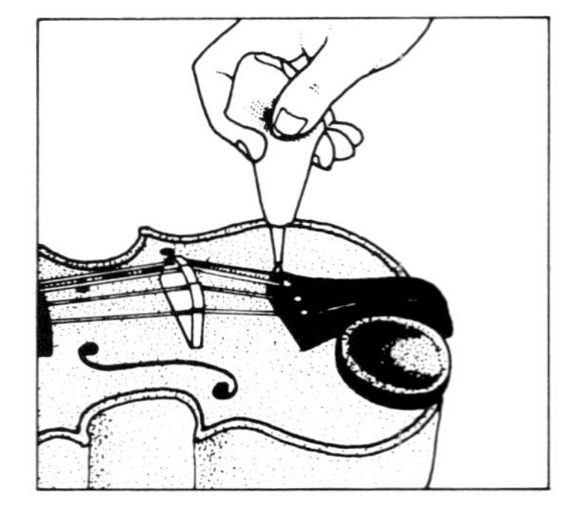

8 With the remaining black icing, model a bow tie and 2 strips. Stick them to the music. Stick the thoroughly dry remaining pieces to the top of the violin with royal icing. Cut 4 strings from florists' wire to fit the neck. Position them on to the neck and over the bridge and secure them with a strip of icing at the top and 4 dots of royal icing at the bottom.

Egg and Chips

There's something very silly and satisfying about making one type of food look like another – especially when it's something savoury made out of something sweet. This one is modelled entirely from icing and is to be used on top of a large cake – perhaps draped with an icing tablecloth like the china breakfast tray (page 109). Mould the plate as for Wimbledon Strawberries (page 65).

Pizza

A very easy cake to make, and very popular. Just cover a round cake with white icing, brush unevenly with watered-down brown colouring and decorate as desired. The 'cheese' is coloured royal icing dribbled on from a piping bag.

CRUNCHIE BAR

Start with a large rectangular cake, cut a corner off then cover two-thirds with yellow icing and one-third with brown. The pulled back piece can be added separately – and don't forget if you use silver colouring as I have that you must remove it all before cutting the cake (see page 164).

Boy Scout

You can either use an extra round piece of cake for the head or something like a doughnut. I've used this design for several different ideas – from a schoolboy to a witch – but I particularly like this jolly scout. You could add some intricate knots round the side to finish it off.

SPORT

A very rich subject indeed for inspiration: people become quite fanatical about their favourite sport or about the team they support. The wonderful thing about cake making is that you can fulfil somebody's wildest dreams – I made a cake for a young friend of mine last year in which he was scoring the goal that won the World Cup. The principle of reproducing the central piece of sports equipment, as in the rugby cake (page 34), is very useful. Try a cricket ball, football, tennis ball, beach ball, bowling ball and so on. A pitch, as in the cricket cake (page 41), can also be the basis of many sports cakes: football, of course, but also tennis (with the bonus of only two players), hockey, netball, baseball and rounders. A running track would be fun: add a strip of red icing round the edge of the cake and pipe on some white lines for the lanes.

Rugby Ball

A rugby ball is much easier to make than a football because whoever originally designed it was thoughtful enough not to construct it from all those hexagons and octagons. A few yellow stitches is quite a different proposition, and extremely effective.

Serves 20

INGREDIENTS
25 cm (10 in) square Fruit Cake (page 166)
550 g (1¼ lb) marzipan
550 g (1¼ lb) Roll-Out Icing (page 166)
100 g (4 oz) Royal Icing (page 166)
sieved jam
brown, yellow and green food colours
225 g (8 oz) caster sugar

SPECIAL EQUIPMENT
30 cm (12 in) round cake board
modelling tool (optional)
2 piping bags with nos. 1 and 23 nozzles

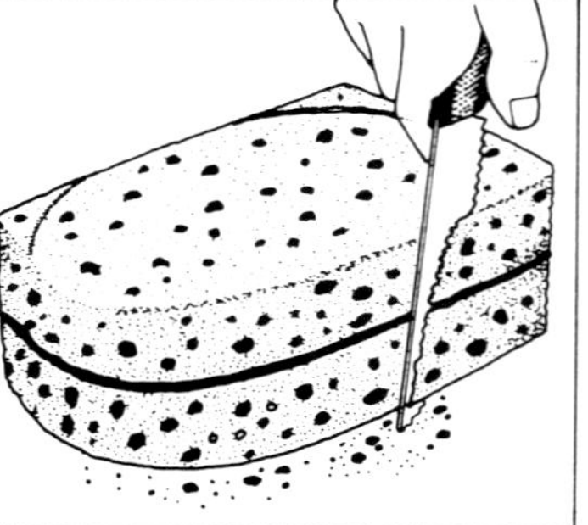

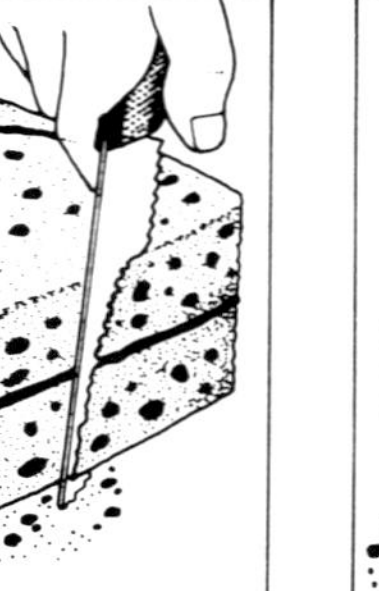

1 Cut the cake in half vertically. Stick one half on top of the other with jam, with or without a thin layer of marzipan between. Mark an oval shape on top of the cake with a knife. With a sharp serrated knife cut out the oval through both layers of cake.

2 Using the serrated knife shape the top and underneath, graduating the cake into a rounded rugby ball shape.

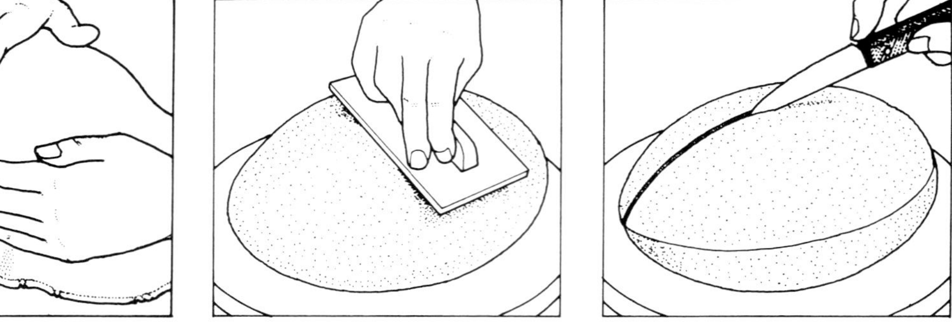

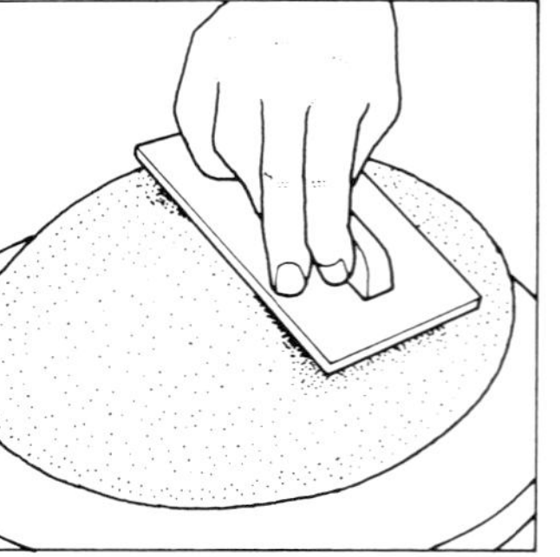

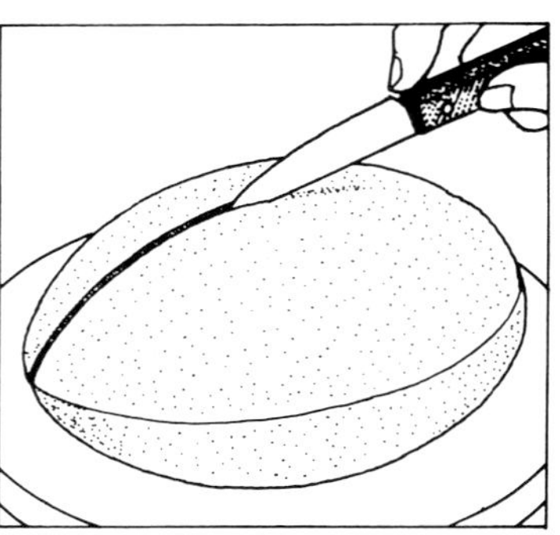

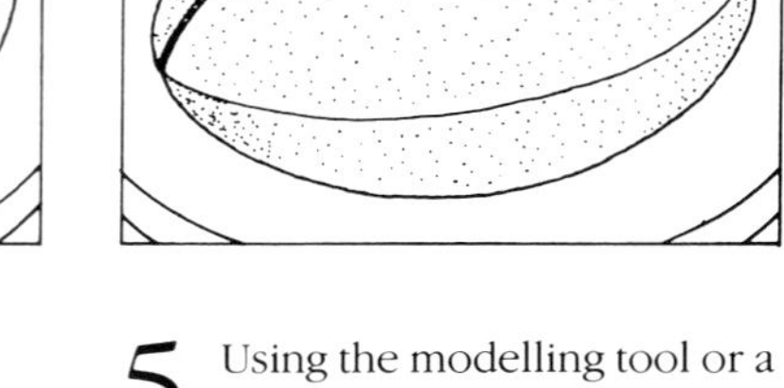

3 Roll out the marzipan. Spread the cake with jam and cover it with the marzipan in one piece, smoothing well.

4 With a tiny amount of royal icing, stick the cake to the board. Colour the roll-out icing brown and roll it out. Dampen the cake and cover with the icing, again smoothing well.

5 Using the modelling tool or a suitable implement, mark a crease round the side of the cake and across the top.

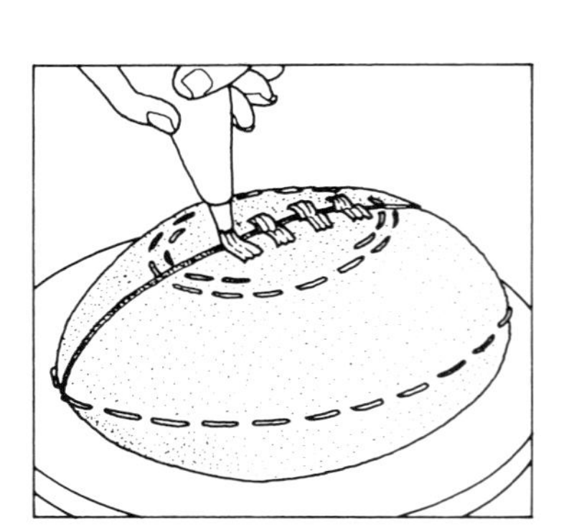

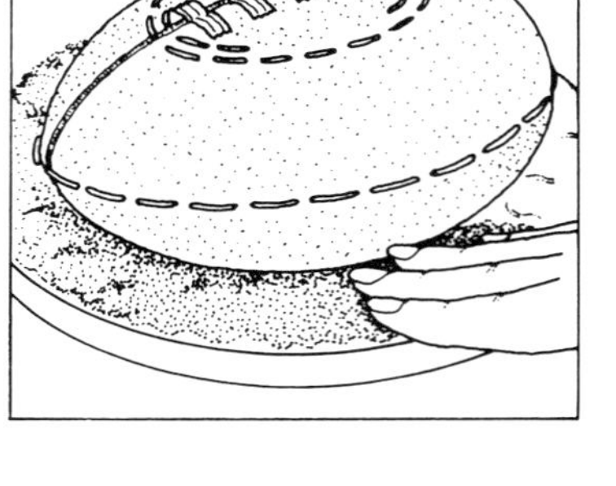

6 Colour about one-third of the royal icing yellow. Using a no. 1 nozzle, pipe stitches onto the top and round the side.

7 Using a no. 23 nozzle, pipe the lacing on to the top.

8 Colour the caster sugar green. Spread the board with the remaining royal icing and press the sugar into it.

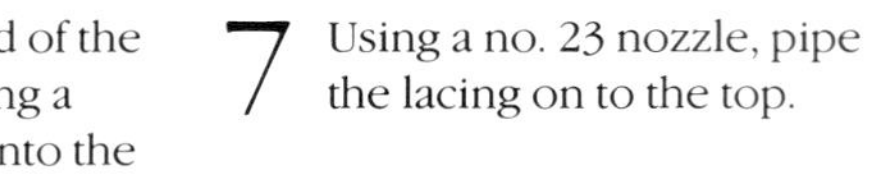

Golf Bag

People seem to become quite obsessed with golf. I've never seen the fascination but I admire it for being a very gentle sport – you don't often hear of golf hooligans. It's also interesting that although you could really play golf in anything, it has developed its own particular brand of uniform. Where else would you see those extraordinary hats, checked trousers and white shoes?

Do remember that if you use the silver food colouring it must not touch any part of the cake that will be eaten (see page 164) – pull the clubs and other decorations off before you cut it. Or you could always make 'wooden' clubs instead, with brown colouring.

Start the day before

Serves 20

INGREDIENTS
25 × 20 cm (10 × 8 in) Fruit Cake (page 166)
450 g (1 lb) marzipan
900 g (2 lb) Roll-Out Icing (page 166)
75 g (3 oz) gum tragacanth
75 g (3 oz) Royal Icing (page 166)
green, blue, red, silver and black food colours
sieved jam

SPECIAL EQUIPMENT
40 × 30 cm (16 × 12 in) cake board
non-stick baking parchment
paintbrush
piping bag with no. 2 nozzle

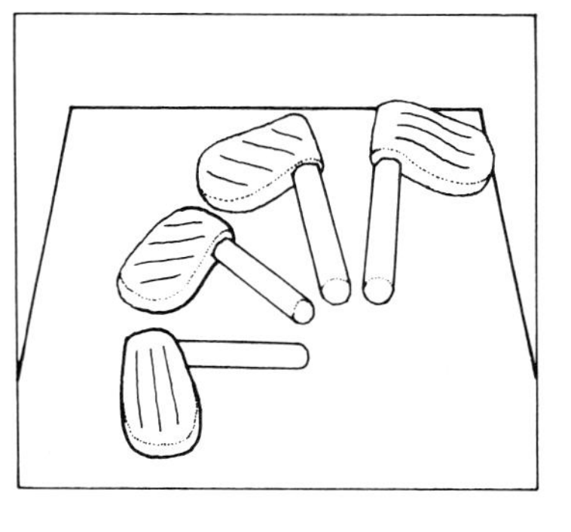

1 Knead most of the gum tragacanth (keep back about 5 ml (1 tsp)) into about 175 g (6 oz) of the roll-out icing. Roll half of the gummed icing into a long sausage shape roughly 35 cm (14 in) long and cut it into 4 lengths of about 9 cm (3½in). Cut out the heads of the clubs from the remainder and mark them with the back of a knife. Stick the heads to the handles with a little water and leave them to dry for 12 hours or so on non-stick paper. (If you're a golf fan then no doubt you will make them no. 2 irons, or drivers or chippers or whatever . . . I'm afraid mine are completely anonymous.)

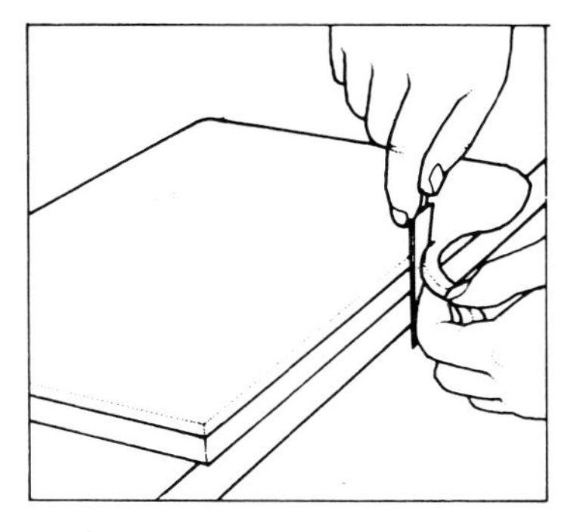

2 Colour about 225 g (8 oz) of roll-out icing green. Dampen the board, roll out the icing and cover the board, smoothing well. Trim the edges.

3 Using the template on page 179 and with a sharp serrated knife, cut a golf bag shape from the cake.

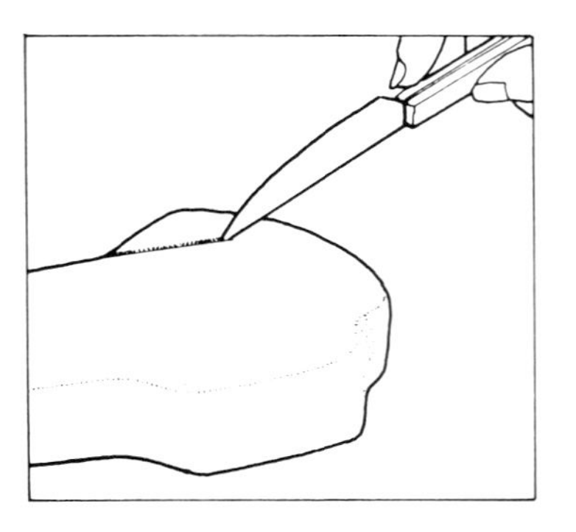

4 Spread the cake with jam. Roll out the marzipan and cover the cake. Colour about 450 g (1 lb) of roll-out icing blue. Dampen the marzipan slightly, roll out the icing and cover the cake, smoothing well. Mark an indented line with the back of a knife, as shown by the dotted line A on the template.

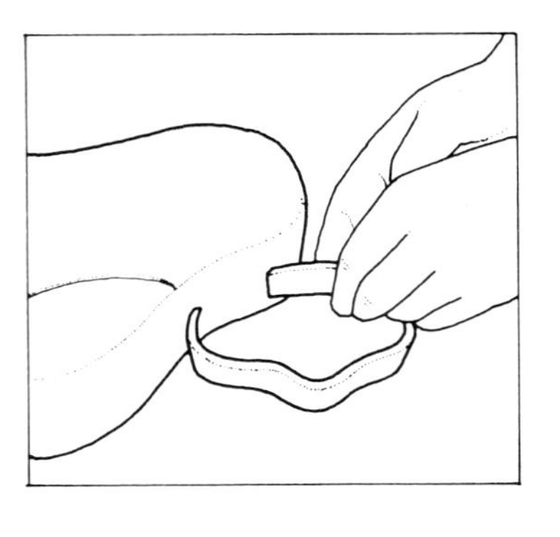

5 Knead the remaining gum tragacanth into the trimmings and cut a long strip for the carrying strap. Stick it to the cake with a little water.

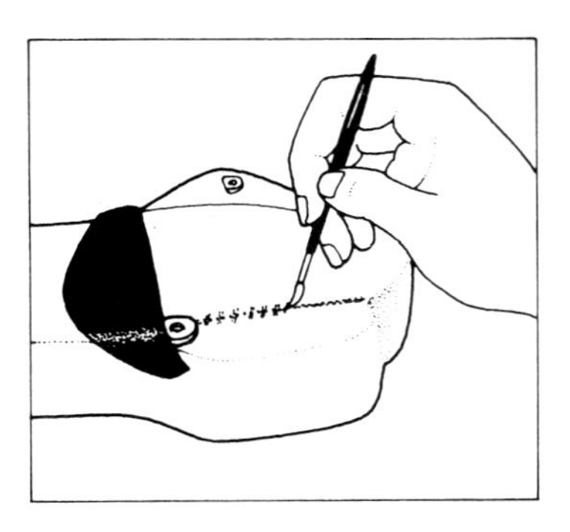

6 Colour about 50 g (2 oz) of roll-out icing bright red. Roll out and cut a shape as on the template allowing extra for the sides. Stick it to the bag with a little water. Cut two tiny 'clips' from white icing and stick them to the bag. Paint them silver. Paint the golf clubs silver. Paint the zip on to the bag.

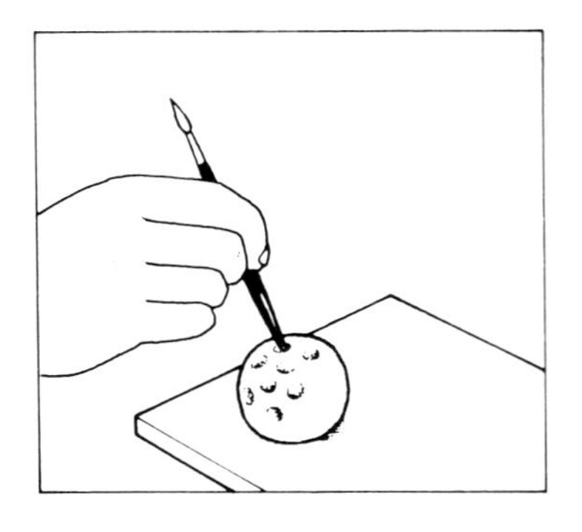

7 Roll a small piece of white icing into a ball and indent it with the end of the paintbrush into dimples.

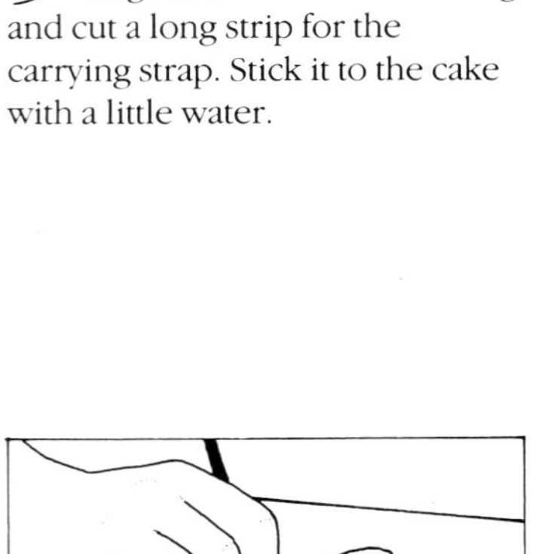

8 Stick the cake to the board with a little water. Stick the clubs on to the end with a little royal icing and let them dry for 30 minutes. Colour the remaining royal icing red and pipe the trimmings on to the bag. Paint black round where clubs 'enter' the bag. Stick the ball to the board with a little water.

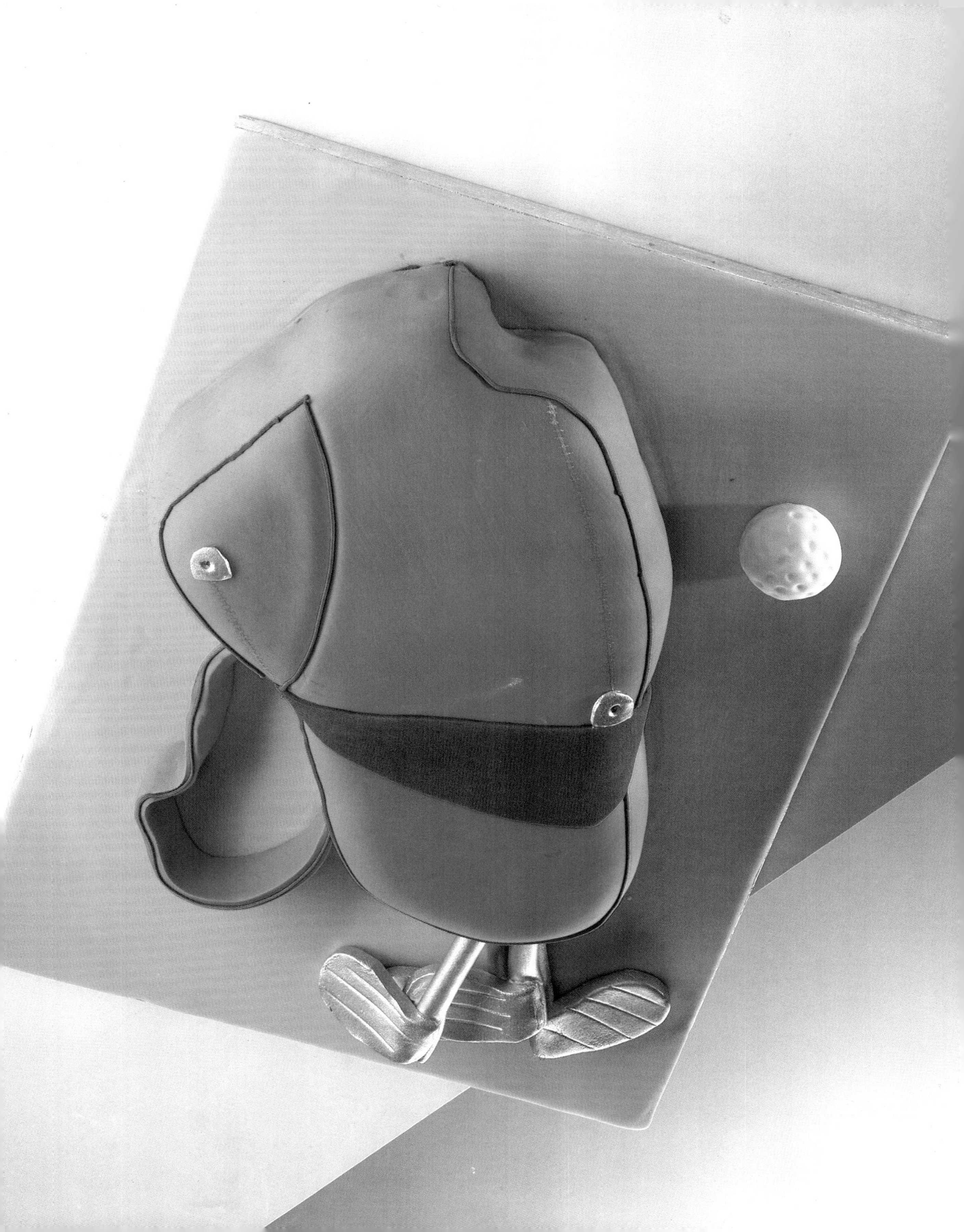

Ski Boot

I love skiing, and just looking at this cake makes me want to drop everything and get out on the slopes. Start with one large rectangular cake and a small round one. If you copy a real boot and build up the icing layer by layer you won't find it difficult. Stand by to make a white iced 'broken-leg-in-plaster' cake . . .

Cricket Pitch

I've just noticed this batsman is playing left-handed and they're certainly a little short of men. If you are keen it would look wonderful to make all 13. Model them very simply like the naked ladies (page 144) then add little white clothes. Obviously a football field could be made in a similar way, and even if your men aren't perfect they'll have much more charm than the little plastic ones.

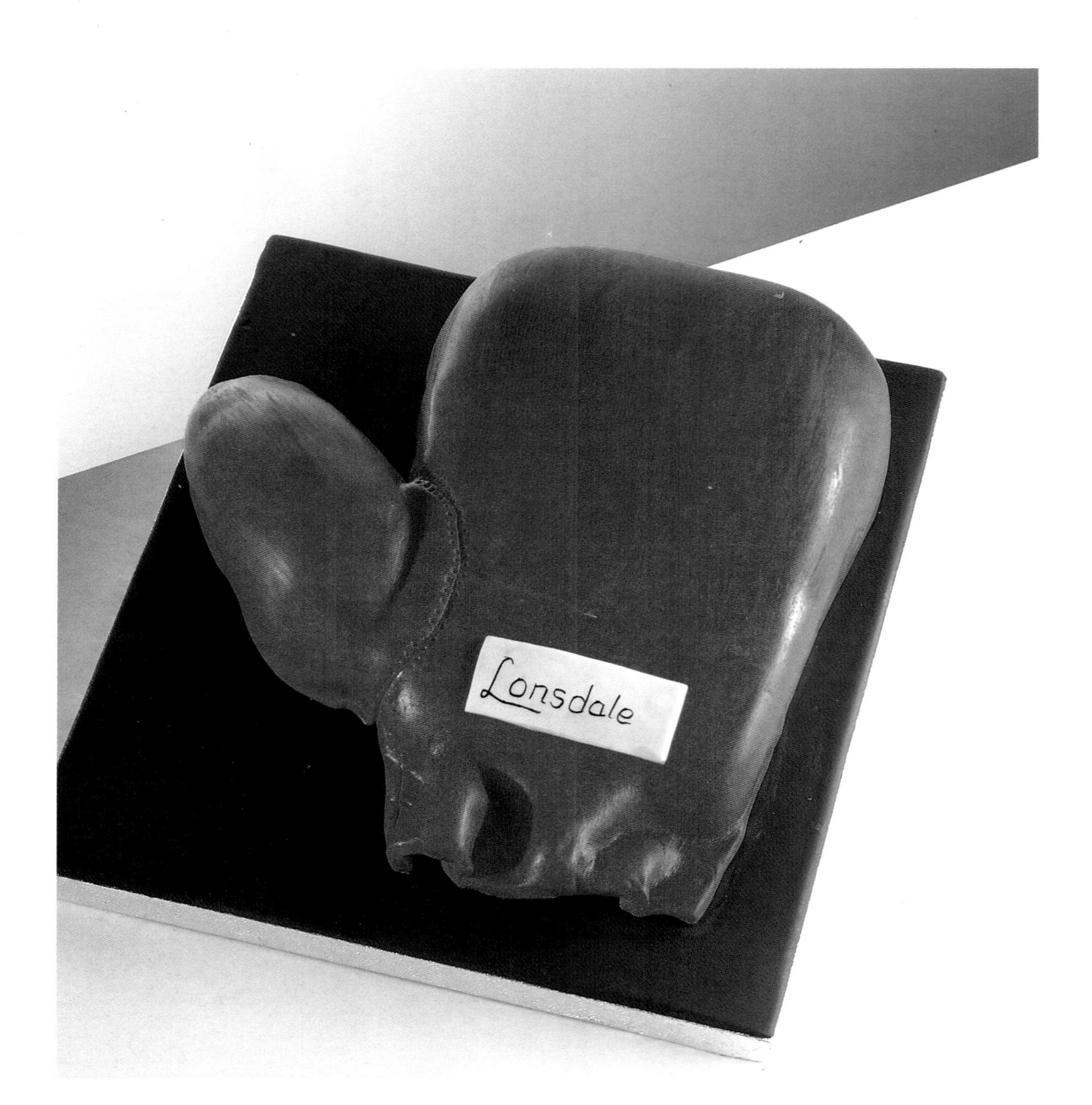

BOXING GLOVE

Simple dramatic use of colour makes this cake. Start with a large square cake and use the trimmings after you have shaped it to build up height and to add the thumb piece. It's a very popular cake with young boys, but I like to think this is the nearest they'll ever get to a boxing glove.

Pigs Keep Fit

I'm sure all of us who ever try to work out feel a bit like this at times. It would make a very good cake for someone who takes it all a bit too seriously. The pig at the front is dreaming of food, and the technique of using a cartoon bubble in this way could be used for all sorts of other ideas.

PETS AND ANIMALS

We've always had pets of one kind or another in our house, from a couple of goldfish to a much loved retriever, and, as in every household, they become part of the family.

I am asked to reproduce many pets in cake. Treasured photographs of Muffy, Tiddles or Rover are brought into the shop and are painstakingly translated into icing. It's very important to try to maintain the character – you don't want granny's beloved, gentle old beagle to come out like the hound of the Baskervilles – and if you find it too difficult to model the animal in icing there are other ways round it (see Cut-Out Jungle, page 48). Big bold animal faces make good cakes for young children. Start with a round cake iced in the main colour. You don't necessarily have to be realistic – a pink cat or blue mouse can go down very well.

Comfortable Cat

A bed is a very useful shape cake-wise – all sorts of inhabitants can be used for every type of occasion: Father Christmas, a witch at Hallowe'en, Sleeping Beauty, teddies and so on. Dare I even suggest *people*? Far apart or closer together, depending on how innocent you wish your cake to remain . . . Don't be put off this one by the patchwork quilt, it is much quicker and easier to reproduce than it looks. If it still seems a bit tricky then just paint a few little flowers on the quilt – or even make it in a plain, pretty colour.

Serves 12

INGREDIENTS

20 × 15 cm (8 × 6 in) Sponge Cake (page 164)
800 g (1¾ lb) Roll-Out Icing (page 166)
75 g (3 oz) gum tragacanth
225 g (8 oz) Buttercream (page 167)
25 g (1 oz) Royal Icing (page 166)
various food colours, including brown

SPECIAL EQUIPMENT

25 × 20 cm (10 × 8 in) cake board
heart plunger cutter (optional)
non-stick baking parchment
paintbrush
straight frill cutter (optional)

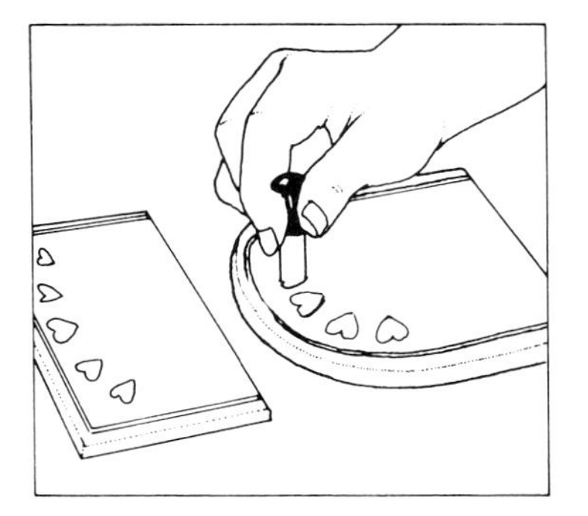

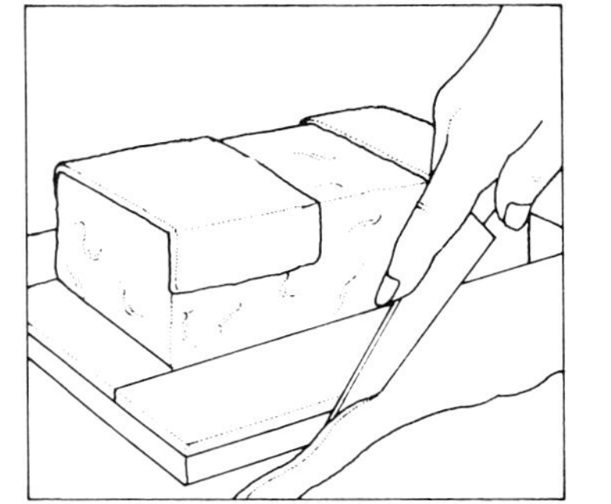

1 Knead brown food colour into 175 g (6 oz) of the roll-out icing. Knead in the gum tragacanth. Roll out just over half and, using the template on page 177 cut a headboard about 16.5 cm (6½ in) wide and 11.5 cm (4½ in) high, depending on the height of your cake. Cut a base from the remaining brown icing about 16.5 cm (6½ in) wide and 6 cm (2½ in) high. Mark each with a line and a plunger cutter, if you have one. Leave both to dry on non-stick paper.

2 Trim the cake to a neat rectangle. Split it in half horizontally and sandwich it together with half the buttercream. Stick the cake to the board with a little buttercream and spread it with the remainder. Roll out 50 g (2 oz) of roll-out icing and cover the end of the bed. Roll out a further 75 g (3 oz) and cover the top of the bed, covering at least 5 cm (2 in) down the bed. Roll out some strips of icing very thinly, dampen the remainder of the board and cover it with the icing and trim the edges.

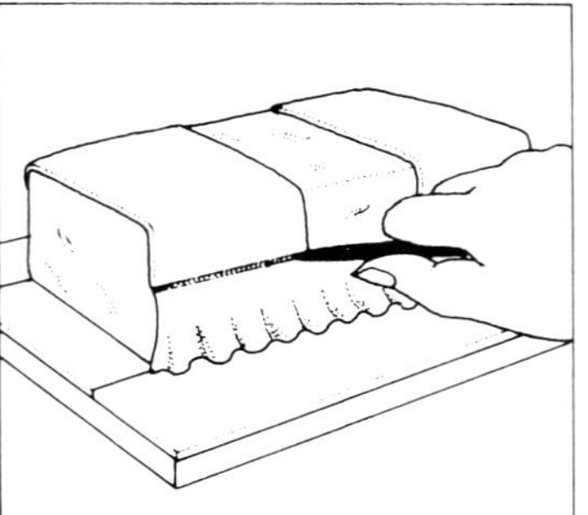

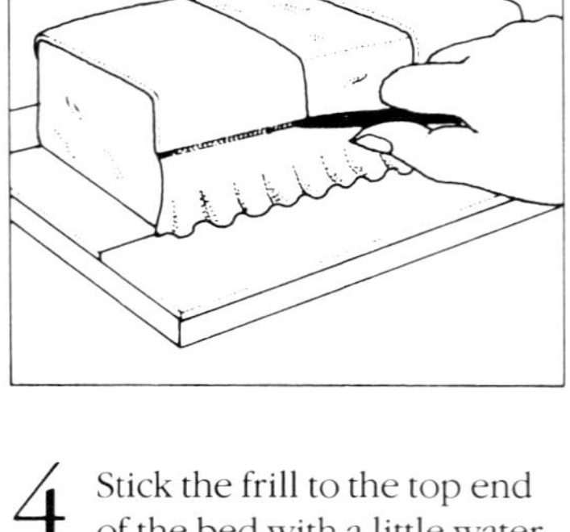

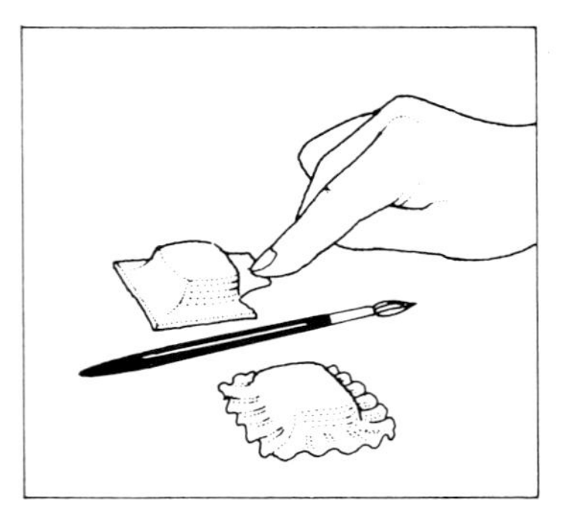

3 Roll out about 25 g (1 oz) of roll-out icing into a strip about 6 cm (2½ in) long and 2.5 cm (1 in) wide. Frill the strip by rolling the edge with the end of the paintbrush.

4 Stick the frill to the top end of the bed with a little water to make a valance. Mark the join with the end of a paintbrush.

5 Take 50 to 75 g (2 to 3 oz) of roll-out icing and cut out 2 pillows about 6 × 4 cm (2½ × 1½ in). Pinch out the edges then frill them.

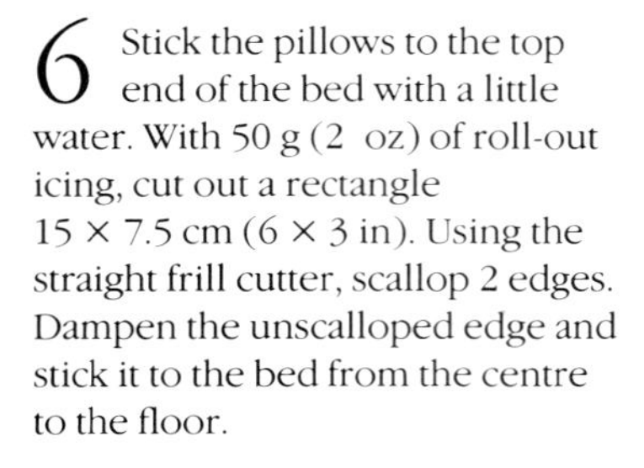

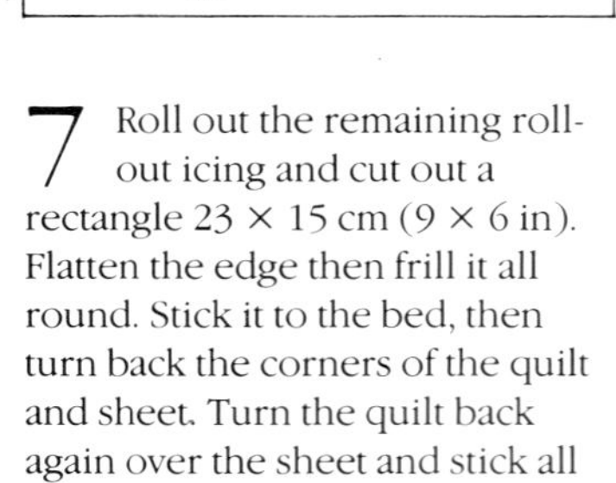

6 Stick the pillows to the top end of the bed with a little water. With 50 g (2 oz) of roll-out icing, cut out a rectangle 15 × 7.5 cm (6 × 3 in). Using the straight frill cutter, scallop 2 edges. Dampen the unscalloped edge and stick it to the bed from the centre to the floor.

7 Roll out the remaining roll-out icing and cut out a rectangle 23 × 15 cm (9 × 6 in). Flatten the edge then frill it all round. Stick it to the bed, then turn back the corners of the quilt and sheet. Turn the quilt back again over the sheet and stick all the corners with a little water.

8 Paint the bedcover as desired! With the icing trimmings model a little cat. Let it dry for about 30 minutes then paint it. With the royal icing, stick the headboard, base and cat to the bed.

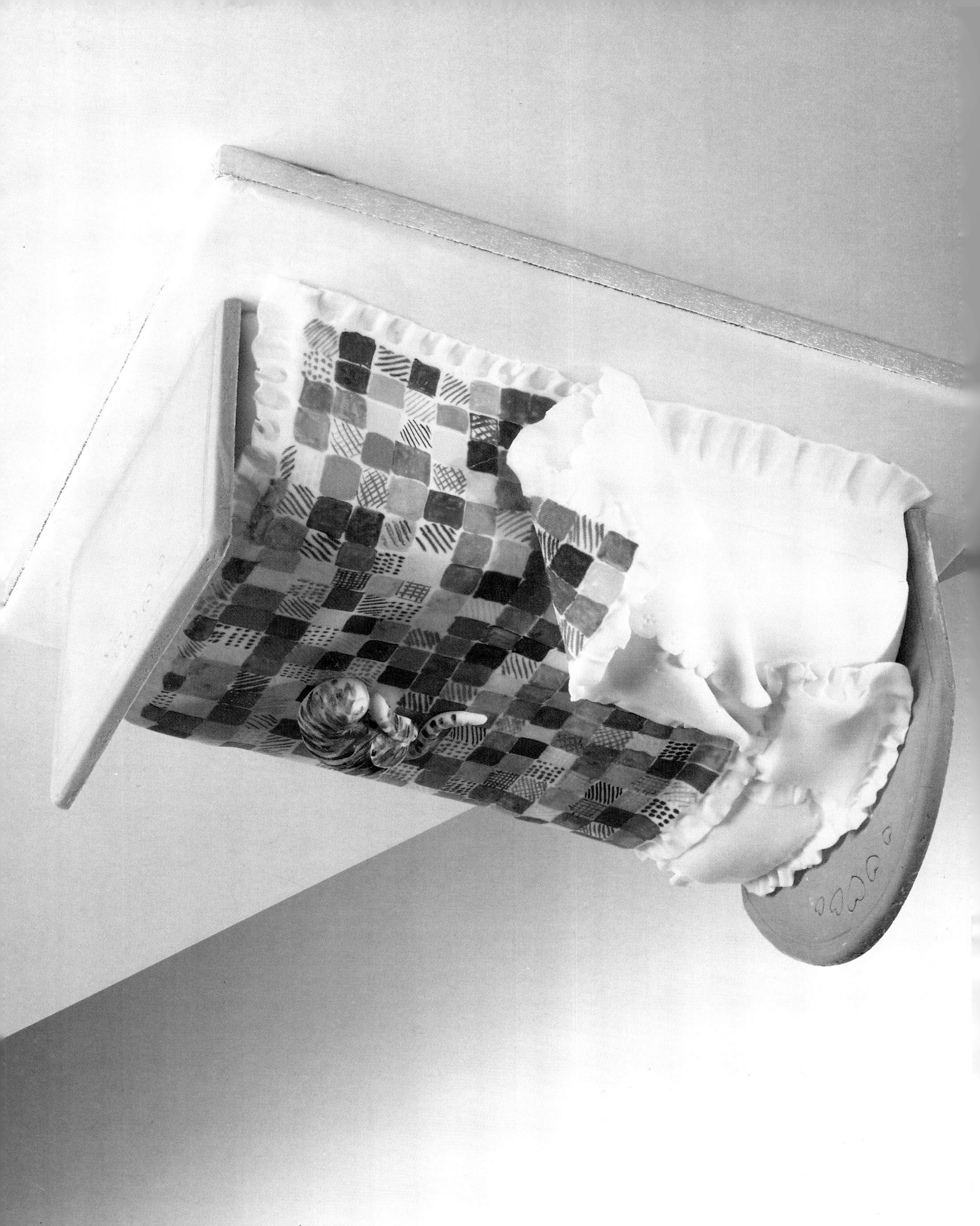

Cut-Out Jungle

Another very useful technique. Modelling in three dimensions can be quite difficult, but this method of cutting out flat shapes from rolled-out icing is easy and effective. You could trace pictures from books and magazines to use for all sorts of different occasions.

Start the day before

Serves 15

INGREDIENTS

20 cm (8 in) square Sponge Cake (page 164)
1.4 kg (3 lb) Roll-Out Icing (page 166)
175 g (6 oz) gum tragacanth
225 g (8 oz) Buttercream (page 167)
225 g (8 oz) Royal Icing (page 166)
various food colours, including green

SPECIAL EQUIPMENT

30 cm (12 in) square cake board
scissors and card
pencil
non-stick baking parchment
piping bag

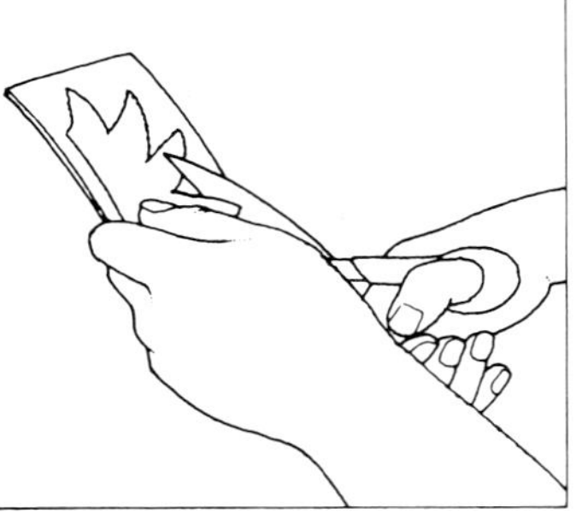

1 Using the templates on page 180–1 as a guide, cut animal and leaf shapes out of the card.

2 Knead the gum tragacanth into 675 g (1½ lb) of roll-out icing. Allowing about 50 g (2 oz) per animal, colour pieces of icing one at a time. Roll out each piece and cut round one of the card shapes with a sharp knife. Cut further smaller pieces for the elephant's ear, lions' heads etc. Cut out a few strips to use as struts. Let everything dry on non-stick paper for 24 hours.

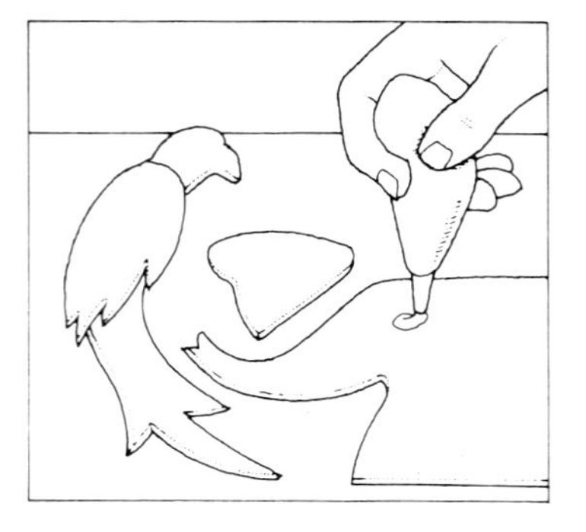

3 Assemble the pieces with a little royal icing. Let them dry for an hour or more.

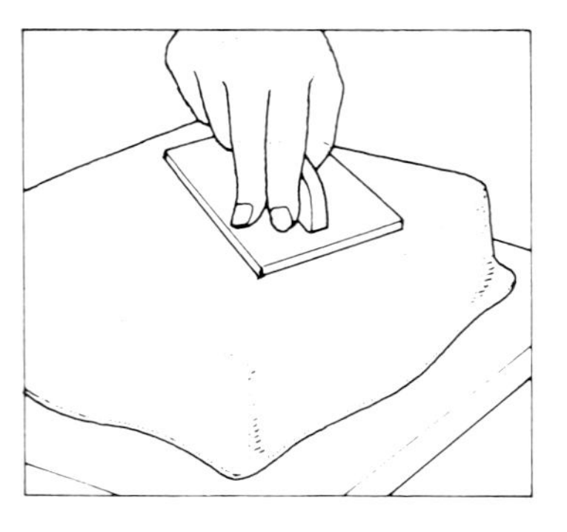

4 Meanwhile split the cake horizontally and sandwich it together with half the buttercream then spread the entire cake with the remainder. Colour the remaining white roll-out icing bright green. Roll it out and drape it over the cake, smoothing well. Trim the lower edge.

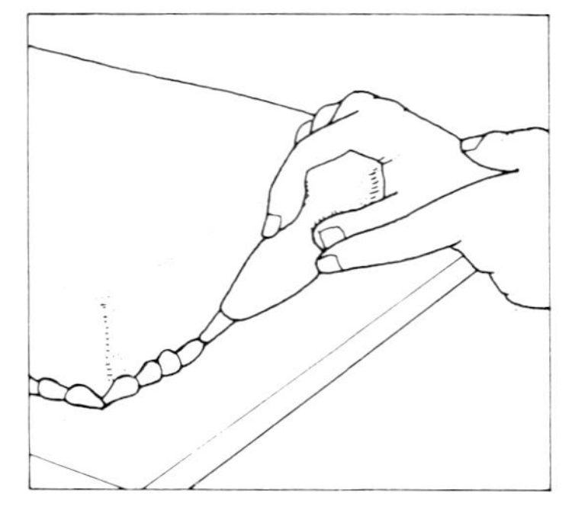

5 Colour the remaining royal icing green. Using the piping bag with the end snipped off, pipe a snail's trail round the base of the cake.

6 Cut slots in the icing and insert the animal and grass shapes. Stick struts where necessary with some royal icing to support the animals. Add some lumps from trimmings of roll-out icing to support the smaller shapes. Stick the crocodile and grass to the front of the cake and the parrot to the large bush.

Hedgehog

A hedgehog is often the first cake attempted – usually with lots of little chocolate buttons pressed in to make the spines. This way uses royal icing cones made with a no. 3 nozzle – just pull the bag away from the cake while you give a short, sharp squeeze. It's worth mastering, as it's a useful technique for fur of all types – and for the kind of decoration used on the Pretty Primroses wedding cake (page 99).

Dog

Another easy way of making fur, this time by marking with a sharp knife while the icing is soft. Start with a rectangular cake and use the trimmings to build up the head. The back legs are made entirely from icing. This shows again how much a covered and decorated board can add to the look of a cake.

ADULT HOBBIES

When anyone asks me what my favourite hobbies are I go a complete blank. As a child, my hobbies were collecting things and sending off for everything I could find. I started numerous collections – of badges, china cats, stamps (briefly), milk bottle tops (for guide dogs for the blind, a connection that always puzzled me) – and sent off for information on anything and everything, for free samples, for lucky charms (did anyone else send for Joan the Wad?) and for beauty tips and courses. As an adult, business, pleasure and family seem to be so enmeshed in a confused jumble that it's hard to separate hobbies from everything else. I could hardly describe my children as a 'hobby', but in effect they have indeed taken over the obsessive interest once shown in the milk bottle tops. But of course everyone, including myself, has interests that they enjoy, from gardening to skiing, from music to cookery, and a little gentle questioning will eventually throw up a good subject for a cake. All the categories I have used in this section can be explored almost infinitely.

Basket of Fish

The only times I have stood watching fishermen they never seem to catch anything at all except the odd tiddler (never the old boot as seen in comics – that would be *far* more entertaining). Much as I hate to see the poor old things flapping about and gasping, there is something magnificent about a pile of gleaming silver fish, and I can guarantee this particular catch will taste delicious.

Serves 30

INGREDIENTS

2 × 20 × 15 cm (8 × 6 in) Fruit Cakes (page 165)
900 g (2 lb) marzipan
2 kg (4½ lb) Royal Icing (page 166)
1.1 kg (2½ lb) Roll-Out Icing (page 166)
brown, black, blue, violet, 2 different greens, red, yellow and gold (page 164) food colours
sieved jam
silver petal powder (page 164)

SPECIAL EQUIPMENT

25 cm (10 in) square cake board
20 × 15 cm (8 × 6 in) thin cake card
piping bags with nos. 23, 4 and 1 nozzles
modelling tool
paintbrush
non-stick baking parchment
wooden skewers
small plunger flower cutter

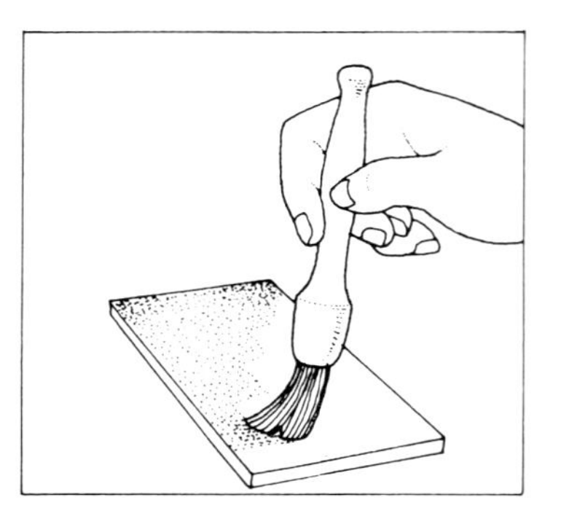

1 Sandwich the cakes together with jam to make one tall cake. Spread the cake with jam. Roll out the marzipan and cover the cake entirely. Stick the cake to the board with a little royal icing. Paint the underneath of the spare cake card with brown colour. Let it dry.

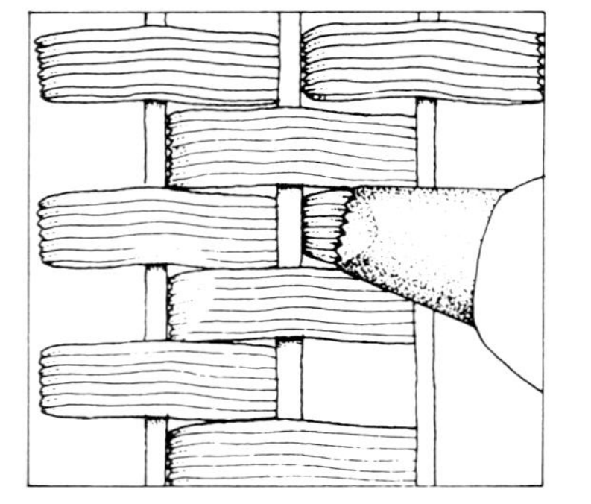

2 Colour about two-thirds of the royal icing dark brown, and one-third of the remainder medium brown. Using 2 piping bags with no. 23 nozzle and dark brown in one and no. 4 and medium brown in the other, pipe a basketweave pattern round the sides of the cake.

3 Pipe basketweave on top of the spare cake card. Let it dry. Colour about 225 g (8 oz) of roll-out icing light brown. Roll out half of it, and cut a strip to go around the top of the basket. Damp and stick.

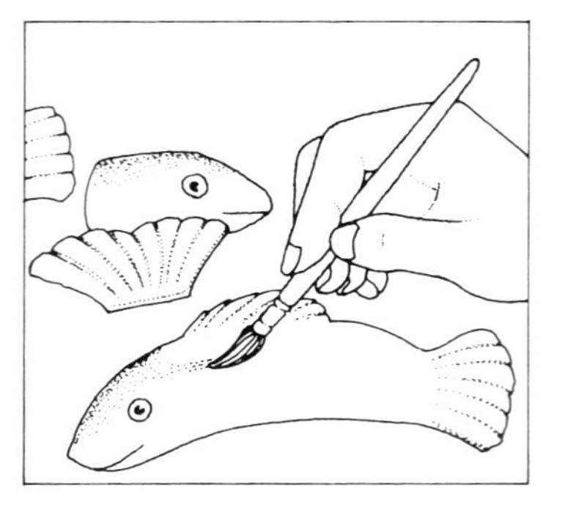

4 With about half the remaining white roll-out icing, model 3 complete fish, 3 extra heads and 3 tails. Paint them with watered-down black, violet and blue colours. Let them dry on non-stick paper.

5 Stick the fish to the top of the cake with a little royal icing. Dust them very carefully with the silver petal powder, not letting any spill on to the basket. Colour 75 g (3 oz) of royal icing dark brown and pipe a thick line round the edge of the basket lid.

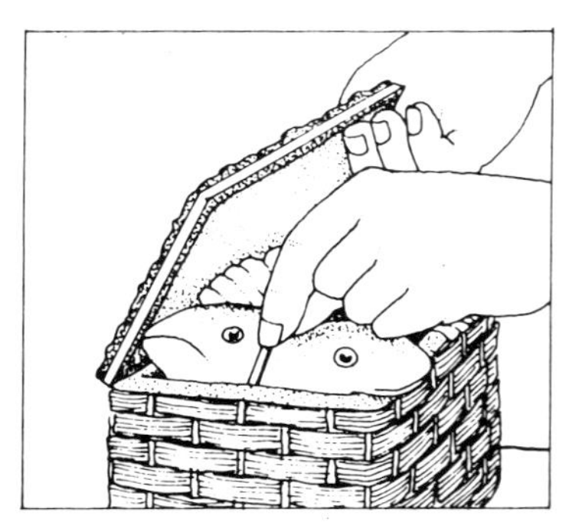

6 Keeping back about 225 g (8 oz), colour the remaining roll-out icing green and cut strips to cover the edges of the board, sticking with water. Stick the lid in position with royal icing and support with 2 wooden skewers, cut to length as necessary.

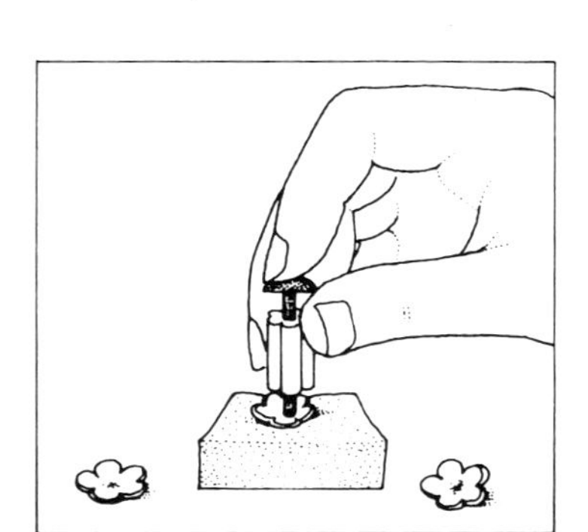

7 Cut 2 straps from the remaining light brown icing and stick them to the lid and basket. Colour pieces of the remaining roll-out icing in various colours and roll and cut out some plunger flowers.

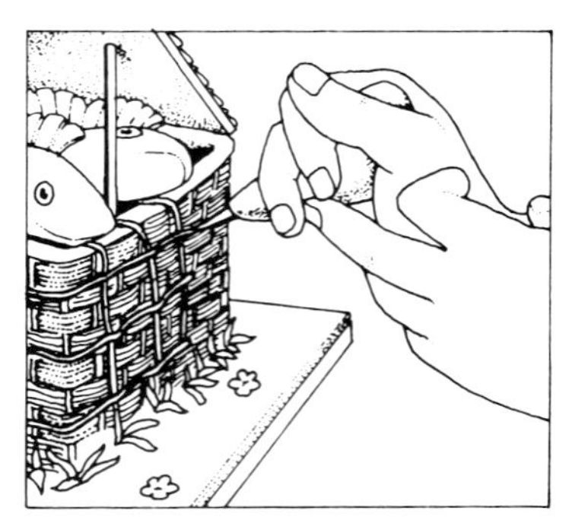

8 Colour half the remaining royal icing pale green and using a no. 4 nozzle, pipe some grass round the basket and a buckle on to the strap. Pipe more grass on to the board and stick the plunger flowers on to it. Paint the buckle gold. Colour the remaining royal icing dark green. Using a no. 1 nozzle, pipe a net on to the basket.

Sewing Machine

Very few people will have a machine like this one nowadays, but it has much more charm than a modern machine and will certainly be a very nostalgic cake for the right person. My mother had an old sewing machine almost exactly like this one, but it did at least have a motor – I don't think I'd like to go back to all that handle turning. Not that I sew much in any case – I've found the best technique with mending is to keep the torn trousers and clothes in a drawer where they get completely forgotten until the children have grown out of them.

Serves 25

INGREDIENTS
25 cm (10 in) square Fruit Cake (page 165)
675 g (1½ lb) marzipan
900 g (2 lb) Roll-Out Icing (page 166)
25 g (1 oz) Royal Icing (page 166)
brown, black and gold (page 164) or yellow food colours
sieved jam

SPECIAL EQUIPMENT
35 cm (14 in) square cake board
paintbrush

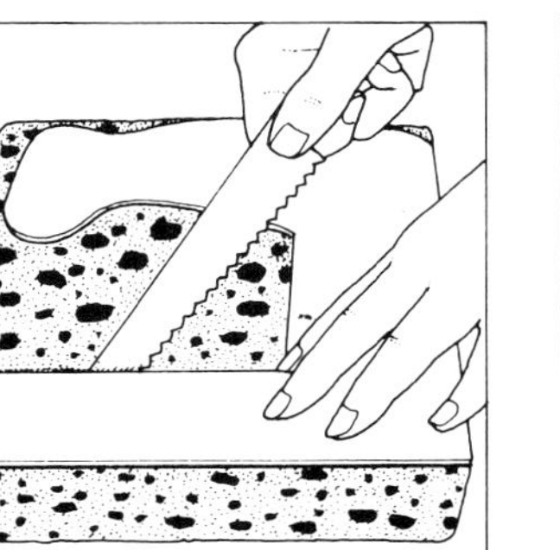

1 Using the template on page 182, cut out a sewing machine shape from the cake, using a sharp serrated knife.

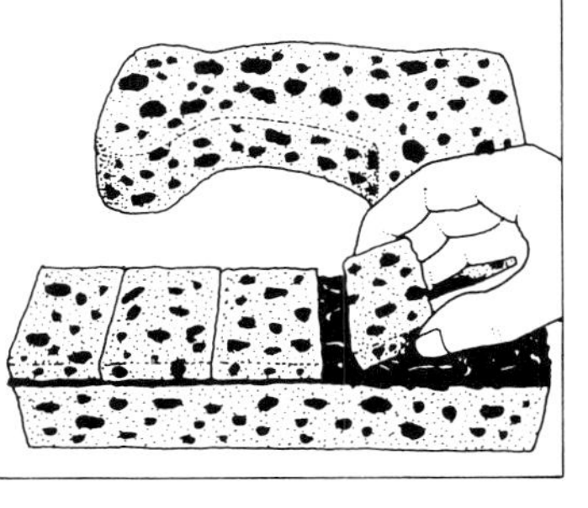

2 Slice the piece you have cut off into strips and stick them to the lower half of the machine with jam to build height.

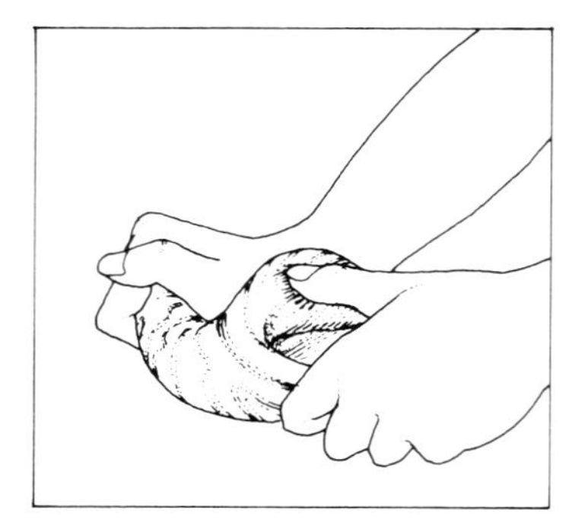

3 Spread the entire cake with jam. Roll out the marzipan and cover the cake. Colour about one-third of the roll-out icing brown, stopping before it is well mixed to achieve a grainy, wood effect.

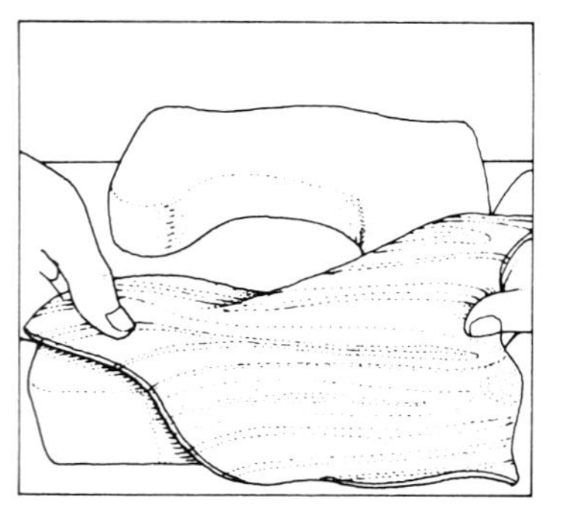

4 Stick the cake to the board with a little royal icing. Keep back about 75 g (3 oz) of brown icing, then cover the base of the machine with the remainder, dampening the marzipan first slightly with water to make it stick.

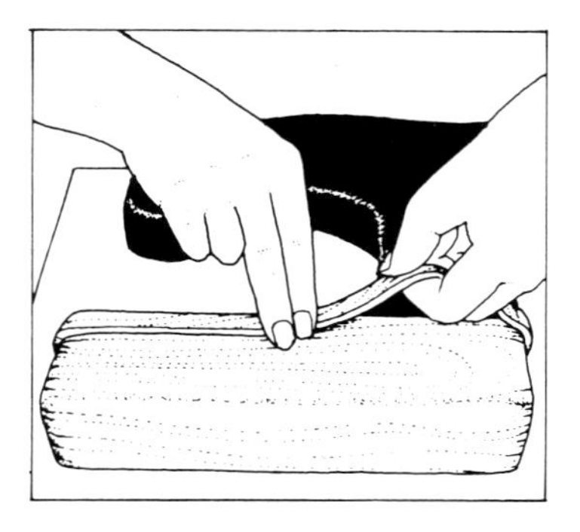

5 Still keeping back the 75 g (3 oz) of brown icing, colour the trimmings and the remaining icing black. Cover the rest of the machine. Add a brown strip over the join.

6 Add a needle holder, needle, cotton reel holder, wheel and handle. Leave to dry for about 30 minutes, then paint the needle and holder and add a pretty design. If you use the gold colour you will be unable to eat the black icing, so if you want it all edible use a golden yellow instead.

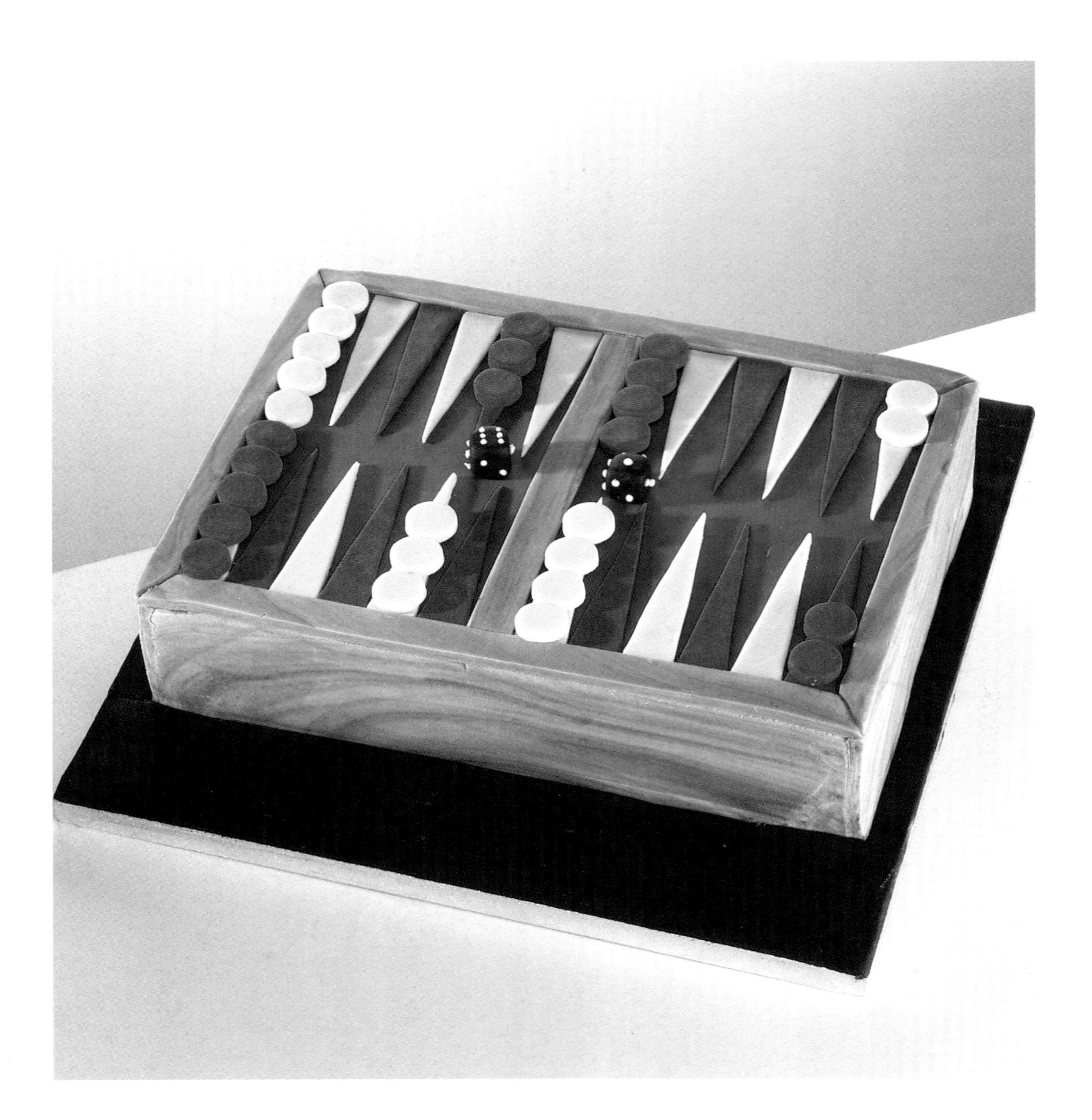

Backgammon Board

A very popular game, and a satisfying cake to produce. Base it on a rectangular cake and knead the brown colour unevenly into the icing for the sides to achieve the wood effect. Use cut out shapes of coloured icing to make the points and a small round cutter for the playing pieces.

A Brazilian Journey

A map can be a good idea for a 'Bon Voyage' cake, or even just for somebody particularly fond of travelling. The cake is cut from a large rectangle, and the lady made entirely out of icing.

A GAME OF BRIDGE

Card games always make good cakes, and the hands bring a bit of life to it. Of course you can give the birthday person a winning set of cards if you wish. Base it on a square cake and once more leave the brown unevenly mixed to look like wood.

GARDENERS' WORLD

Use a square cake and paint on the basic greens and browns of the garden. Model the rest, and build up the shed from tragacanth icing in a similar way to the toy box (page 74).

THE ENGLISH SEASON

Even if most of us never get near Ascot or Henley I'm very glad they are there . . . they represent something so very English and summery. In any case these four cakes could be used for all sorts of other occasions and show you various techniques that you will find very useful. The bowl of strawberries could be used for many different types of food and the flower pot is a particularly easy and effective cake that adapts to many different ideas – think of a bucket filled with sugar 'sand' for instance.

Wimbledon Strawberries

A summer without strawberries just wouldn't be right – or a summer without the usual newspaper reports of the shocking price of strawberries at Wimbledon. Why not make your own and get much better value! As it stands, this design contains very little cake (and you can't eat the bowl), so you may want to stand it on top of a square cake (perhaps iced with a draped 'tablecloth'). You could omit the cake in the bowl altogether, in which case you could keep it for several months as a decoration.

Start the day before

Serves 4

INGREDIENTS

10 cm (4 in) round Sponge Cake (page 164)
350 g (12 oz) Pastillage (page 167)
350 g (12 oz) Roll-Out Icing (page 00)
100 g (4 oz) Royal Icing (page 166)
red, green, yellow and blue food colours
cornflour
sieved jam
1 teaspoon castor sugar

SPECIAL EQUIPMENT

bowl to use as mould
paintbrush
calyx cutter (optional)
piping bag with no. 0 nozzle

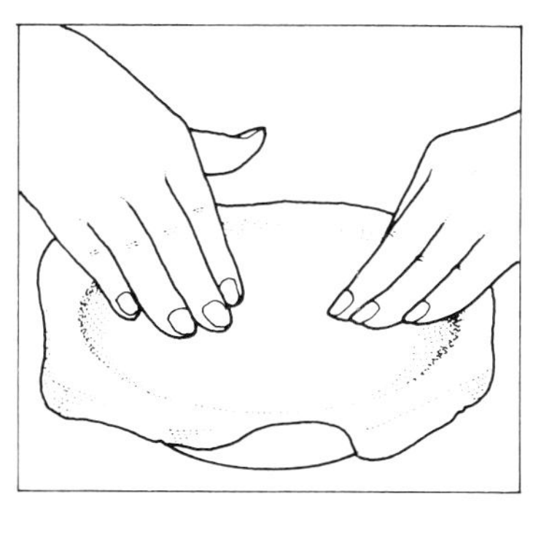

1 Dust the inside of the bowl with cornflour. Roll out the pastillage to a thickness of about 3 mm (⅛ in) and line the bowl, smoothing carefully well down into the shape.

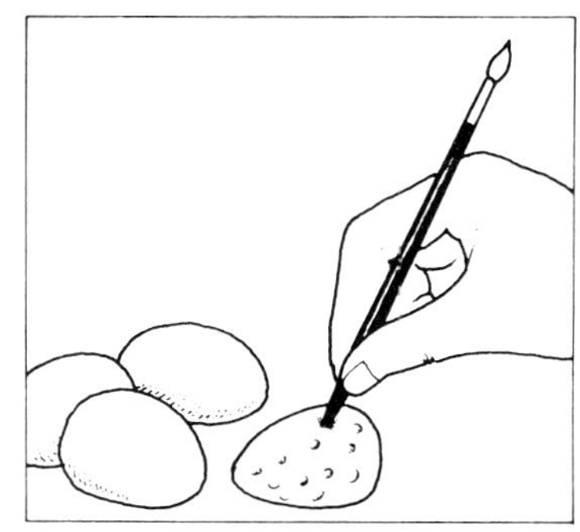

2 Trim the top edge and leave the bowl to dry for 24 hours. Colour about 225 g (8 oz) of roll-out icing red and model about 18 strawberries. Make tiny indentations with the end of the paintbrush for the seeds.

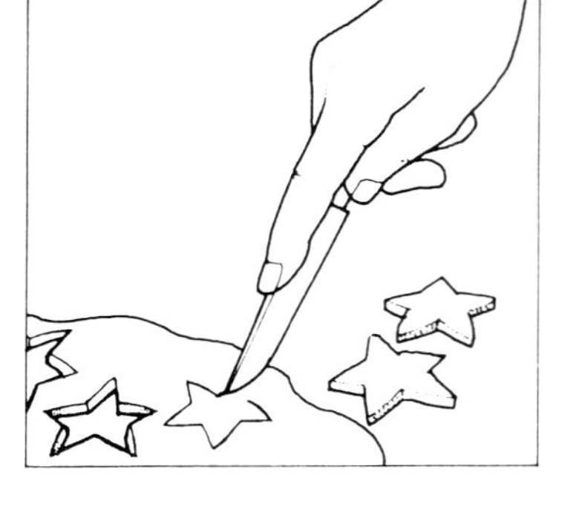

3 Colour about 50 g (2 oz) of roll-out icing green. Roll it out and cut out 18 calyxes with the cutter or a sharp knife.

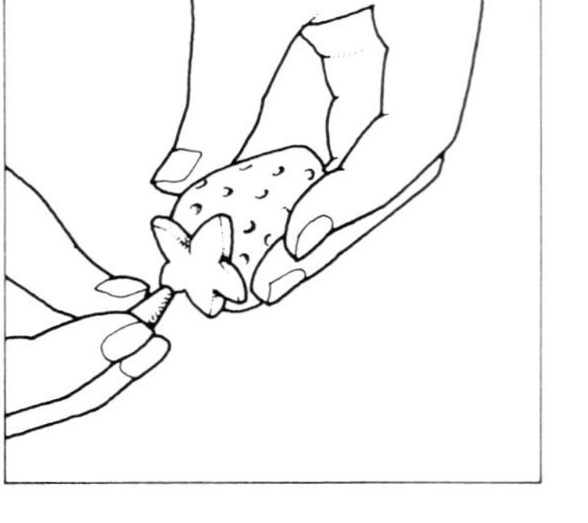

4 Damp and stick the calyxes to the strawberries and add tiny green stalks.

5 When the strawberries are dry enough to handle, colour a small amount of royal icing yellow and pipe tiny seeds into the identations, using the no. 0 nozzle.

6 Gently remove the icing bowl from the mould. Dust off any excess cornflour. Paint a decorative edging on to the bowl with blue food colour. Place the sponge cake into the bowl. Roll out the remaining icing. Spread the cake with jam and cover it with a disc cut from the icing.

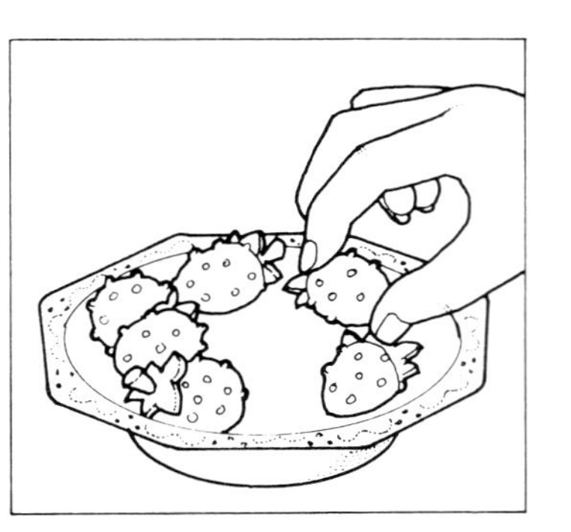

7 Dampen the icing disc slightly with water and arrange the strawberries on it.

8 Check that the royal icing is of a slightly runny consistency, adding a little water if necessary. Fill the piping bag (without a nozzle) with the remaining royal icing and flood it over the strawberries. When it is dry, sprinkle with the castor sugar.

ASCOT HAT

Usually a hat cake is made in the shape of a traditional straw boater – a swirl of yellow buttercream decorated with a few sugar flowers. Very pretty, but not quite Ascot. I think this more elegant and high fashion hat works very well, and would be a perfect birthday cake for any well-dressed lady. Try to buy ready-made black icing to save time (or of course you could make it in any other colour combination you like).

Serves 8

INGREDIENTS

2.25 litre (4 pint) pudding basin Sponge Cake (page 164)
225 g (8 oz) Buttercream (page 167)
900 g (2 lb) Roll-Out Icing (450 g (1 lb) black, 450 g (1 lb) white) (page 166)
black food colour

SPECIAL EQUIPMENT

30 cm (12 in) round cake board
string
28 cm (11 in) round board or plate for template
paintbrush

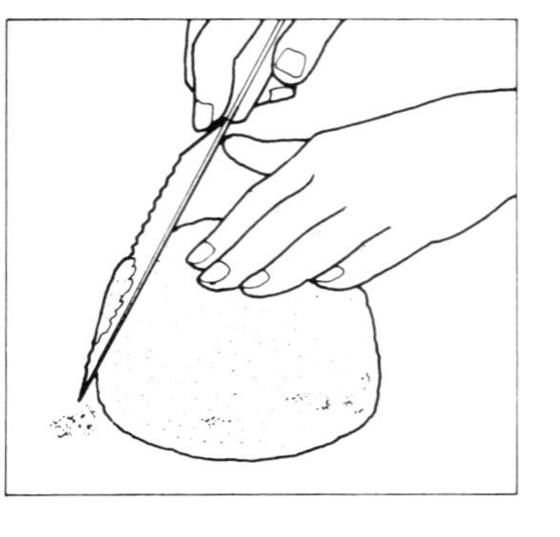

1 If you are using a pudding basin cake, trim it to a round dome shape with a sharp serrated knife.

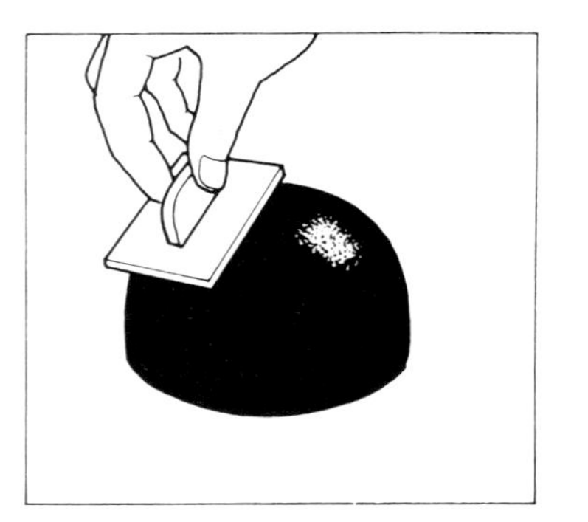

2 Cut the dome in half horizontally and sandwich it together with half the buttercream. Knead some black food colour into 450 g (1 lb) of the roll-out icing if you are colouring your own. Spread the cake with almost all the remaining buttercream, keeping a tiny amount back. Roll out the black icing and cover the cake, smoothing it well. Trim the bottom edge.

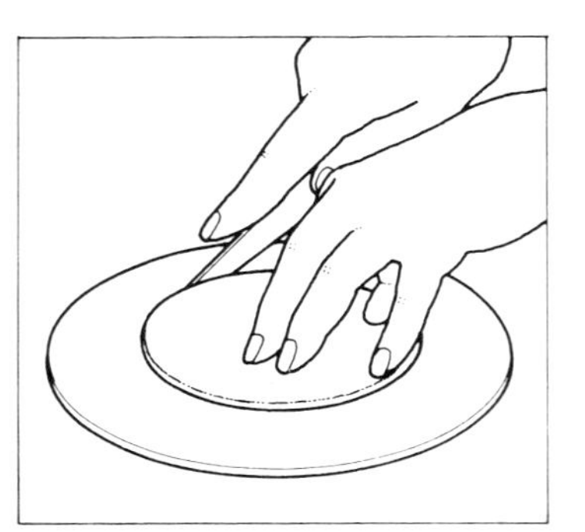

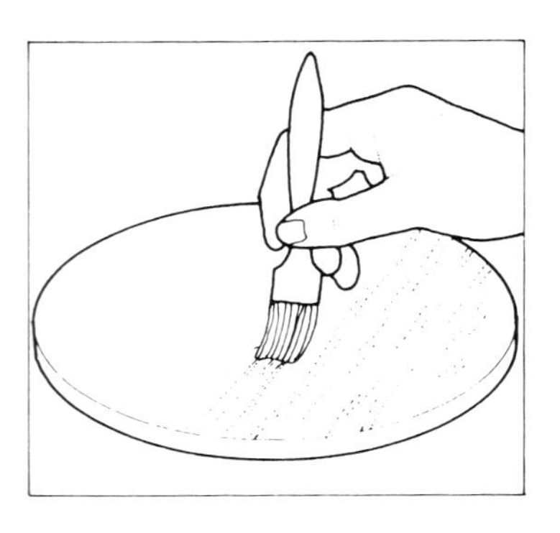

3 Measure round the base of the cake with the string. Roll out a strip of white icing about 1 cm (½ in) wide and the length of the string. Stick to the lower edge of the cake with a little water.

4 Roll out the remaining white icing into a 28 cm (11 in) diameter disc, using a cake board or plate as a guide. Using the bottom of a cake tin or pudding basin, cut a circle out of the centre slightly smaller than the cake.

5 Dampen half the board only (so you will stick half the brim to the board but still be able to lift up the rest. Stick the white brim to the board.

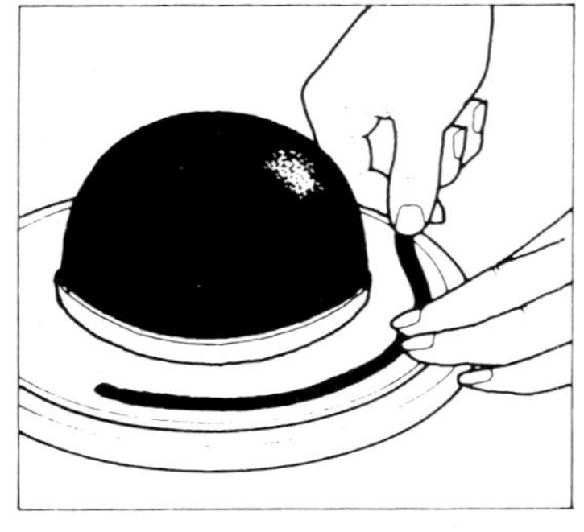

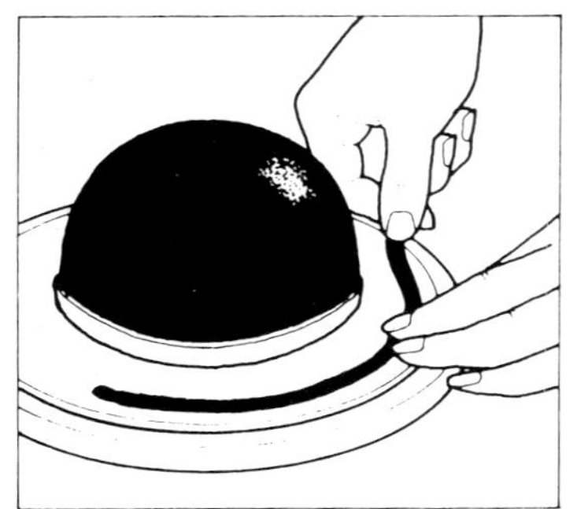

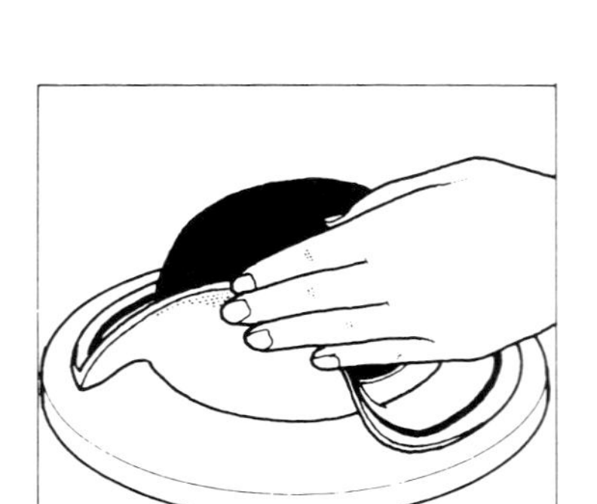

6 Stick the cake on to the centre of the board with the remaining buttercream, overlapping the brim. Working quickly so that the icing does not dry out, roll out the black trimmings into a long sausage, flatten it with a rolling pin and stick it to the edge of the brim with a little water.

7 Lift the part of the brim that is not stuck to the board and stick it to the side of the hat with a little water, holding it until firm.

8 Cut 4 bow pieces from the white trimmings. Assemble them on to the hat, sticking them with water. Let them dry for about 30 minutes then paint the bow with black stripes.

Henley Rowing Boat

If you don't want to attempt a three-dimensional boat as on page 143, you can just make half of it like this one. It's much easier to build things up from the side in this way, and you can create quite complicated scenes by working in layers. I rather hope this smug-looking young man falls in.

Chelsea Flower Show

I love this simple pot, and it can be filled with all sorts of different flowers, including holly, ivy and white roses at Christmas time. Line a pottery flower pot with greaseproof paper and bake the cake mixture in the pot, just as in the old-fashioned way of baking flower-pot bread. Finish it with a little brown coloured sugar round the flowers.

CHRISTENINGS

This is about the only instance when it's no good asking the person for whom the cake is designed for his or her hobbies, interests or favourite colours. You can always try, but I don't think the delightful gurglings and cooings of a very young baby are going to give you much of a clue! If there is already a toy or rattle that the baby seems to respond to you can always include that, but otherwise choose something sweet and pretty with perhaps a part that can be kept as a souvenir, like the toy box (page 74). If you're making it for your own baby do choose something simple – unless you're far more organized than I ever was you'll surely be too busy to spend much time fiddling about with icing.

Toy Box

This sweet cake is one of my favourites. Most babies are given some lovely toys when they are born and to copy some of them in sugar and put them in this little toy box would make a very special cake – just make sure you don't leave anything out, or you might have a very offended grandma if her carefully chosen rattle wasn't included.

Serves 20

INGREDIENTS

20 cm (8 in) round Fruit Cake (page 166)
450 g (1 lb) marzipan
900 g (2 lb) Roll-Out Icing (page 166)
50 g (2 oz) gum tragacanth
225 g (8 oz) Royal Icing (page 166)
pink, green, violet, yellow and black food colours
sieved jam

SPECIAL EQUIPMENT

25 cm (10 in) round cake board
piping bags with nos. 1 and 2 nozzles
paintbrush

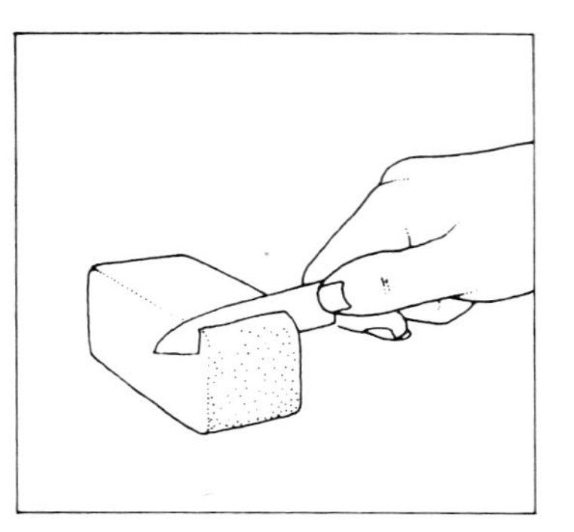

1 Spread the cake with jam. Roll out the marzipan and cover the cake. Stick the cake to the board with a tiny piece of dampened icing. Roll out half the roll-out icing, dampen the cake and cover with the icing, smoothing well. Roll out a strip of icing from the trimmings. Dampen and cover the remainder of the board. From some white icing, using more than the trimmings as necessary, make a rectangular block about 9 × 5 cm (3½ × 2 in) and 4.5 cm (1¾ in) high.

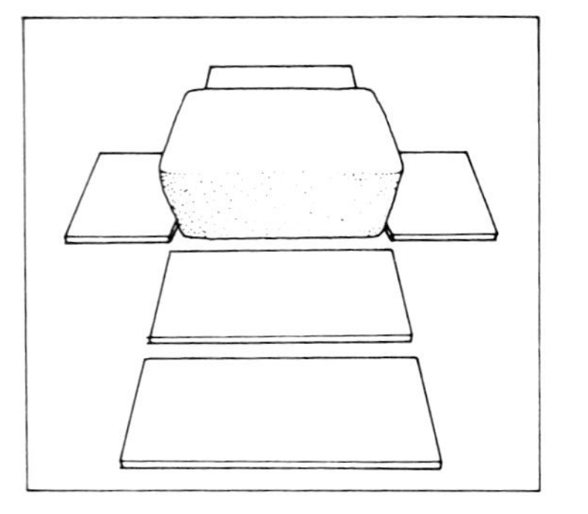

2 Knead the gum tragacanth into about 100 g (4 oz) of roll-out icing. Roll it out and, using the block as a guide, cut 4 sides and a lid, making them 6 cm (2½ in) in height and fractionally longer than the sides of the block so they will fit neatly round it.

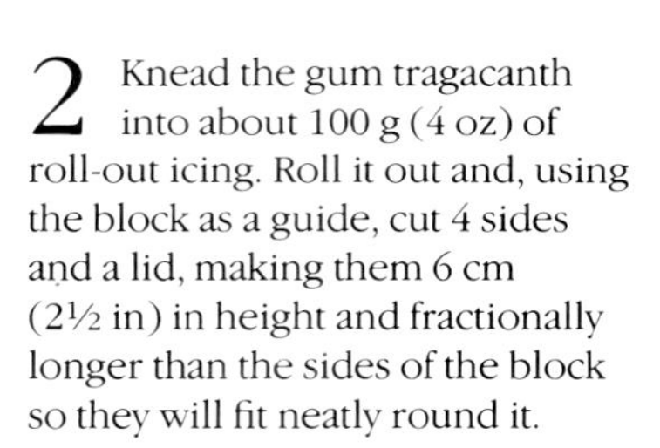

Julie Anne
8th Sept

3 Colour a tiny amount of royal icing pink and, using no. 1 nozzle, pipe decorations round the edges of the sides and lid, adding the word 'TOYS' on the lid. Pipe some tiny white flowers in the centres. Paint some leaves and stalks with green food colour. Leave it to dry.

4 Model some toys from coloured scraps of icing, building up figures as shown. Make some extra toys to go outside the box.

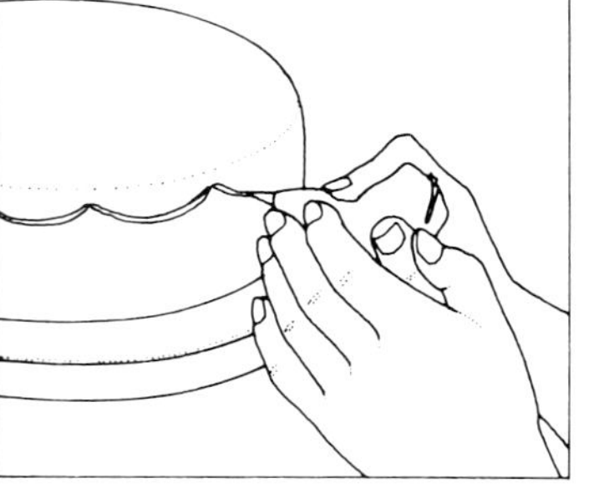

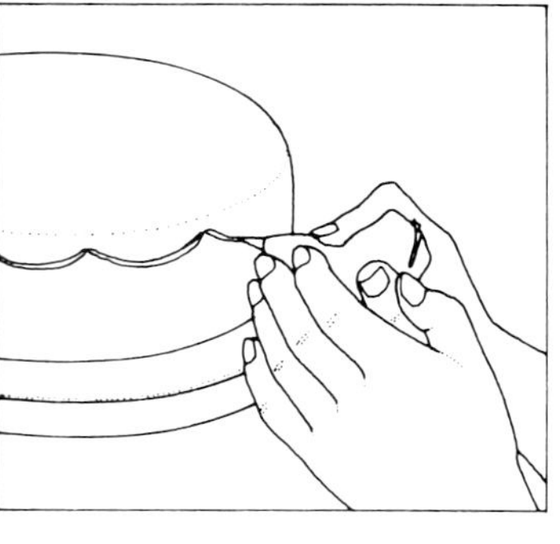

5 Colour about 175 g (6 oz) of roll-out icing pale pink and model 8 rosebuds (see page 94 but only make 2 or 3 petals for each). Divide the side of the cake into 16 (see page 171). Using white royal icing and a no. 2 nozzle, pipe 3 looped lines on to it.

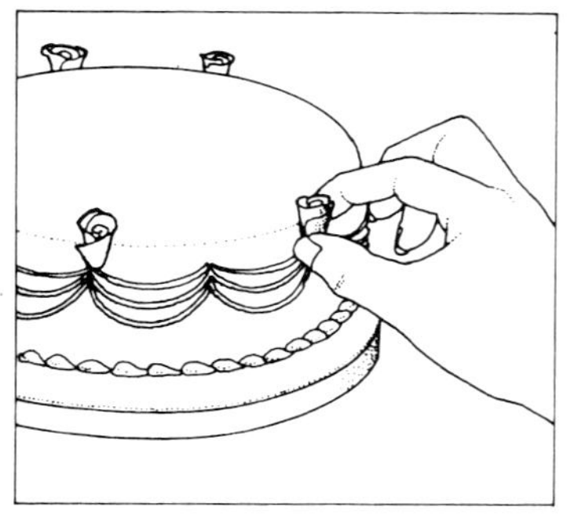

6 Using a no. 2 nozzle, pipe a snail's trail round the bottom edge of the cake. Stick a rosebud at the top of every other loop. Pipe tiny white flowers at alternate loops. Paint some leaves and stalks with green food colour.

7 Stick the sides of the box to the block with royal icing. Position the toys in the box. Stick the lid on to the box, letting it rest on the toys. Leave everything to dry. Stick the toy box on to the cake and add the extra toys and blocks at the base. Using a no. 1 nozzle, pipe some decorations and an inscription on the top.

Fun in the Font

Well I know this wasn't *quite* what the font was intended for but I'm sure God wouldn't mind it being borrowed for a bath with a favourite duck. It would be very special if you copied the font from your church – and if the vicar is coming back for tea after the service I'm sure it'll make him smile.

Start 2 days before

Serves 30

INGREDIENTS

2 × 15 cm (6 in) round Fruit Cakes (page 166)
450 g (1 lb) marzipan
1.4 kg (3 lb) Roll-Out Icing (cream or white) (page 166)
175 g (6 oz) gum tragacanth
175 g (6 oz) Royal Icing (page 166)
paprika, yellow, blue, brown, black and cream food colours
sieved jam

SPECIAL EQUIPMENT

25 cm (10 in) square cake board
modelling tool
non-stick baking parchment
10 cm (4 in), 3 cm (1¼ in) and 2.5 cm (1 in) round cutters
cocktail stick
paintbrush
turntable
piping bag with no. 44 nozzle

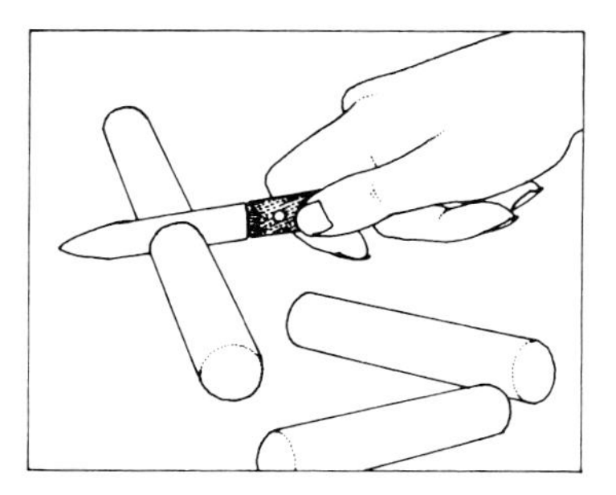

1 Knead the gum tragacanth into 450 g (1 lb) of the roll-out icing. Roll out a long sausage about 2.5 cm (1 in) diameter and 51 cm (20 in) long, keeping any left over in a plastic bag. Cut the sausage neatly into 4 × 12 cm (4½ in) long pillars, trimming the ends.

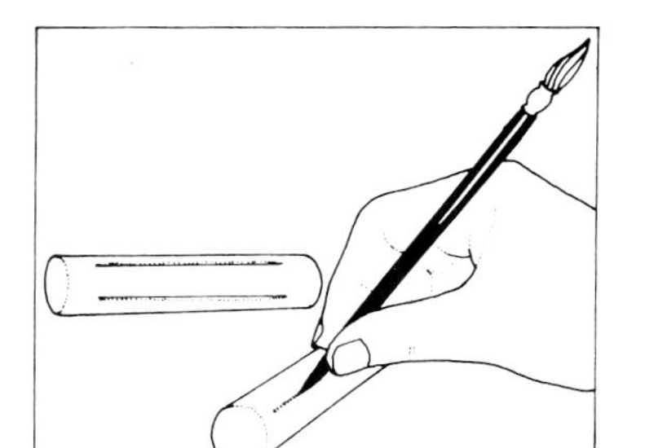

2 Mark some long grooves with a modelling tool or the end of a paintbrush. Leave the pillars to dry on non-stick paper for 24 hours.

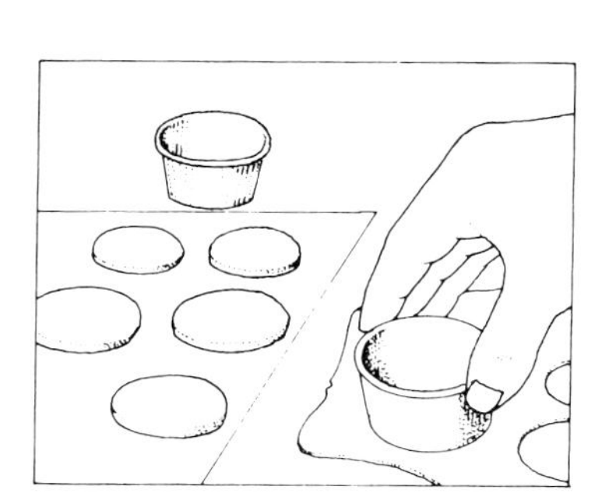

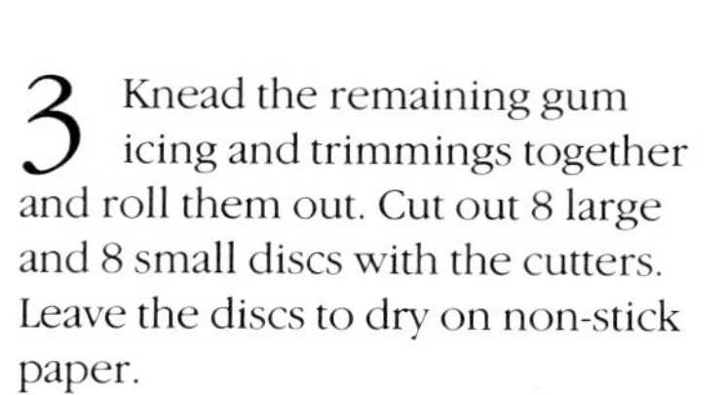

3 Knead the remaining gum icing and trimmings together and roll them out. Cut out 8 large and 8 small discs with the cutters. Leave the discs to dry on non-stick paper.

4 Colour about 100 g (4 oz) of roll-out icing pink using a little paprika food colour. Model the baby in 6 pieces.

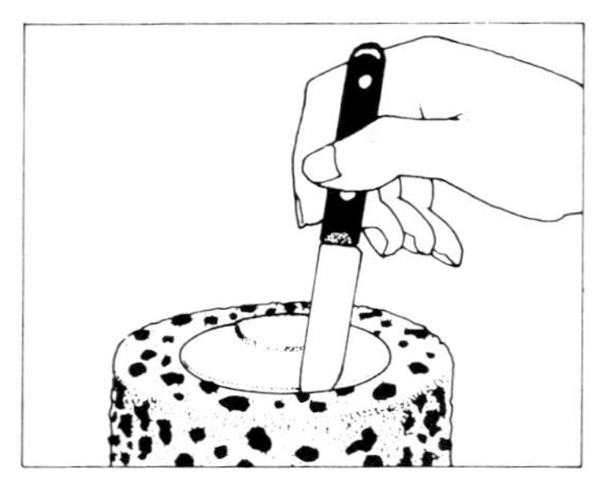

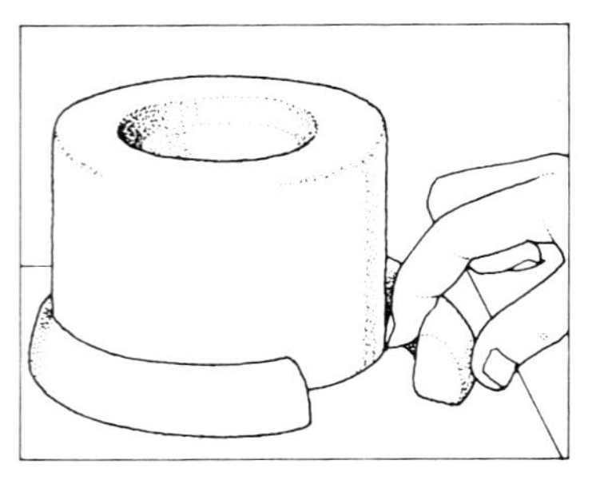

5 Stick the baby together with a tiny amount of royal icing, using a cocktail stick to secure the head to the body. Colour a scrap of icing yellow and add some hair. Model a tiny duck. Cut out and stick eyes, nose and ears on to the baby. Model and stick on a bow.

6 Let everything dry for 30 minutes then paint eyes, lashes, brows, mouth and cheeks on to the baby. Paint the duck's eyes and beak and paint the ball. Stick the 2 cakes together with jam. Using the large cutter or a saucer mark the centre and scoop out to a depth of about 2 cm (¾ in).

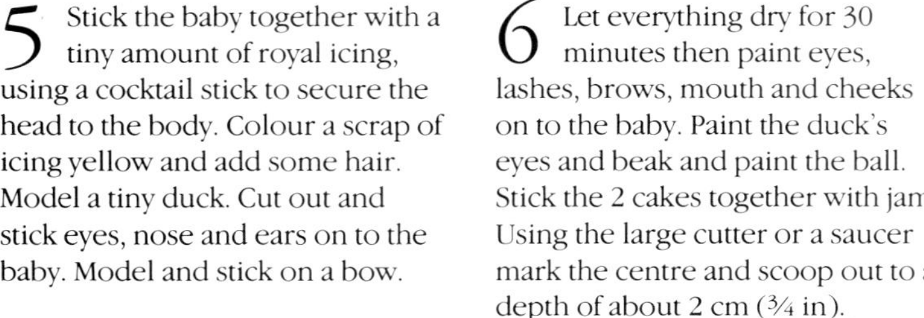

7 Stick the cake to the board with a little royal icing. Spread the cake all over with the remaining jam and roll out the marzipan. Cover the top of the cake first then the sides. Stick on an extra strip of marzipan to form the base.

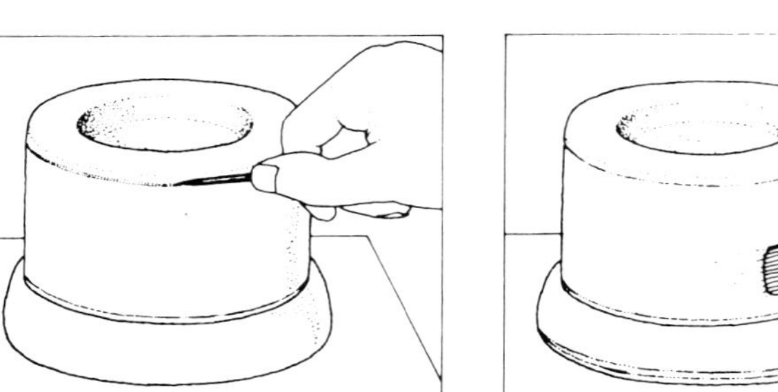

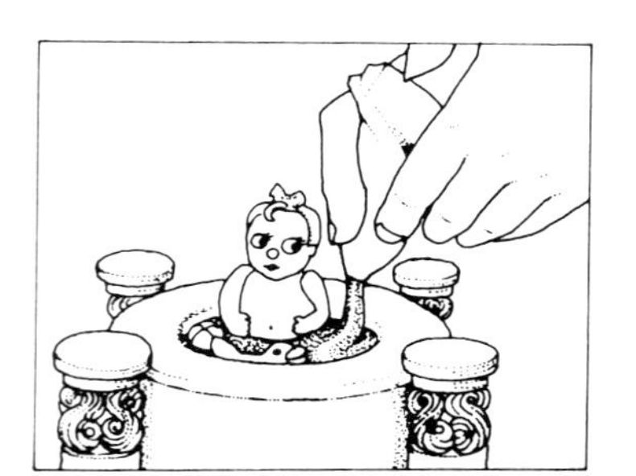

8 Roll out the remaining icing. Dampen and cover the cake all in one, pressing the icing down into the hole carefully. Put the cake on the turntable and with a modelling tool score 4 lines around the base, 2 round the join at the lower edge and 2 round the upper edge. Let it dry for about 30 minutes.

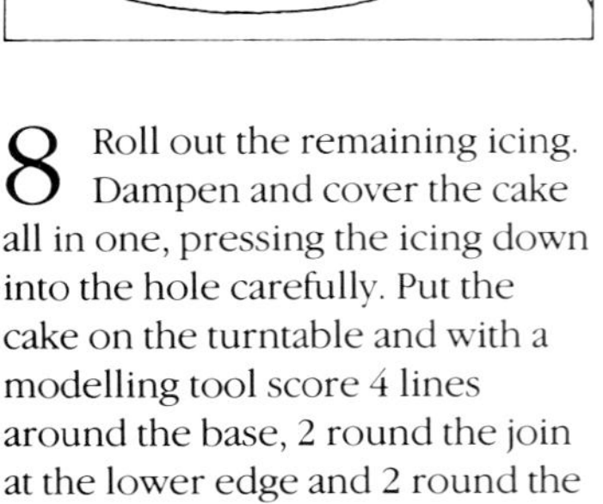

9 Using some cream colour mixed with water, paint the font with the brush, moving the turntable round as you go. Paint the pillars and discs.

10 Roll out the white trimmings and cover the remainder of the board. Assemble the pillars with a little royal icing and stick them to the cake. Pipe some patterns with a no. 44 nozzle. Cut some little strips of icing and stick them under the piping on the pillars. Let everything dry. Meanwhile put the baby, duck and ball in the font. Add a little water and blue colour to the remaining royal icing and flood it into the font. Paint over the pillar trimmings.

Bible

A cake in the shape of a book always looks effective. Use a large rectangular cake and shape the pages before you cover it. If you only want a small cake, a closed book can also look lovely – perhaps a white prayer book with a cross and the baby's initial on the front.

A Happy Baby

It's very simple to model a baby's head, and if you cover him or her with a little blanket it looks really sweet. Keep all the piping on Christening cakes such as this very light and delicate.

WEDDINGS

Perhaps the most wonderful reason of them all to make a cake. Wedding cakes are part of the great heritage of British feasting, and have assumed a huge significance in the bridal ceremony. It's important to discuss with the couple exactly what they would like – just because you think you're rather good at piping doesn't mean they should necessarily have a traditional three-tiered cake covered with scrolls and extension work. It's their day, and if they feel like a one-tiered green cake then their wishes must be carefully considered, although occasionally a little guidance doesn't come amiss. If they're stuck for ideas then there are the seasons to consider (see pages 89 to 91 and 95 to 97), or the flowers in the bride's bouquet, or the hobbies of the couple. Give yourself plenty of time and start well ahead, as if you're involved closely in the wedding there'll no doubt be plenty of other things to think about as the great day approaches.

BRIDAL TEDDIES

This delightful cake would be ideal for a couple with a sense of fun who want their cake to be pretty but not too formal. The bride and groom could be any animals you choose, but do make sure they have chunky legs like these two or you could have great difficulty in getting them to stand up. I expect this couple met at a picnic in the woods.

Serves 30

INGREDIENTS
30 cm (12 in) oval Fruit Cake (page 166)
1.1 kg (2½ lb) marzipan
2.5 kg (5½ lb) Roll-Out Icing (page 166)
675 g (1½lb) Royal Icing (page 166)
sieved jam
brown, black, green, pink and purple food colours

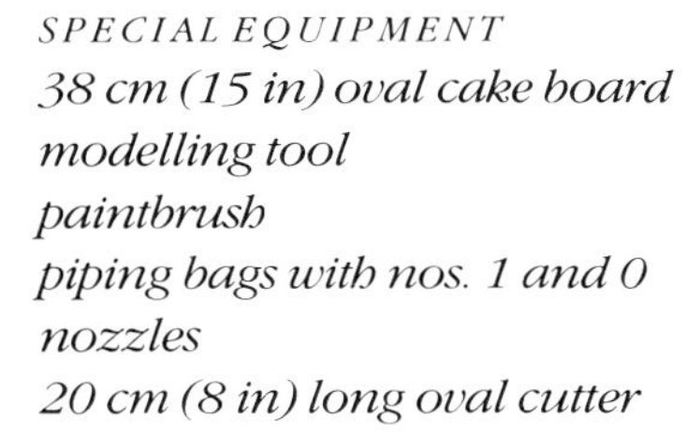

SPECIAL EQUIPMENT
38 cm (15 in) oval cake board
modelling tool
paintbrush
piping bags with nos. 1 and 0 nozzles
20 cm (8 in) long oval cutter

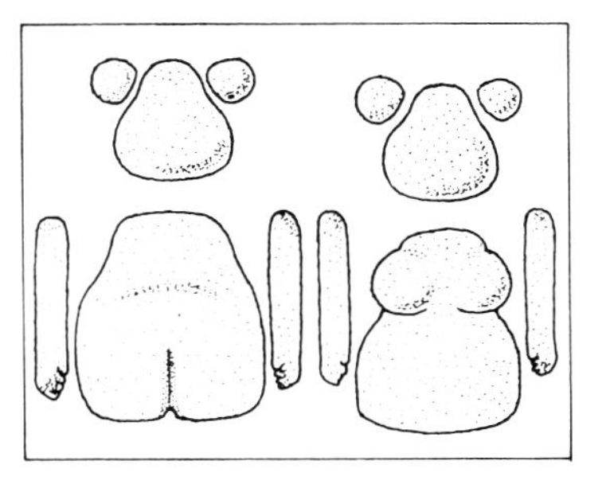

1 Colour 675 g (1½ lb) of the roll-out icing brown. Model 2 torsos, 2 heads, 4 ears and 4 arms.

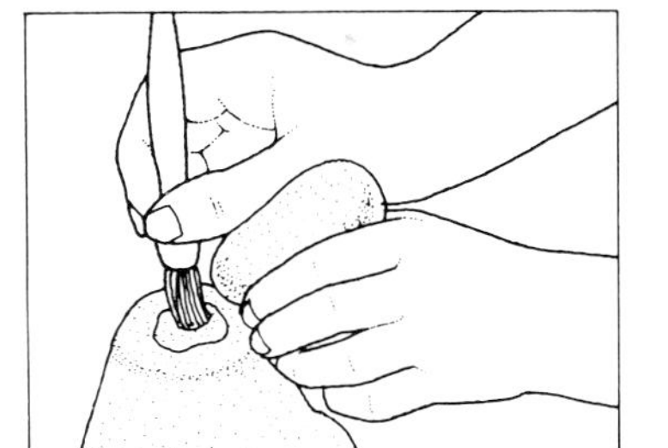

2 Stick the heads to the bodies with small dampened pieces of brown icing.

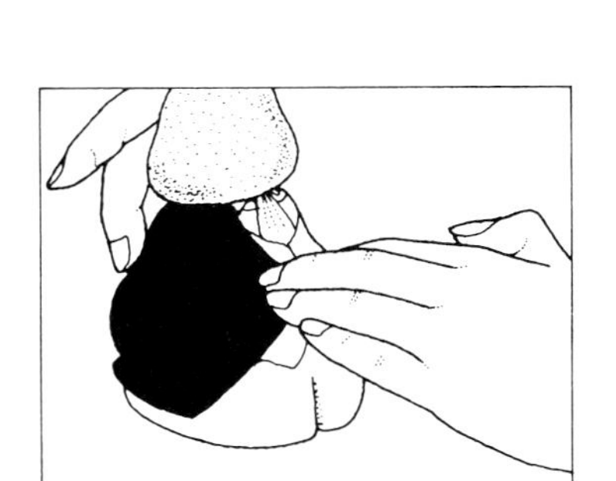

3 Using small pieces of icing, colour, roll out and cut some clothes piece by piece. Stick the clothes to the bodies and arms separately with a little water. Make a hat and let it dry a little.

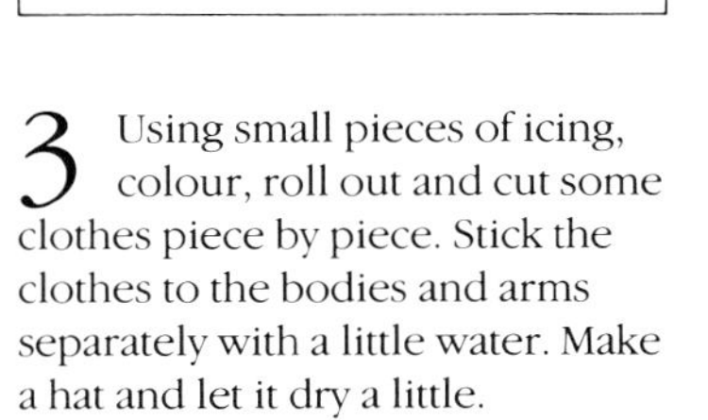

4 Stick the arms to the bodies and entwine the groom's arm into the bride's. Stick on the ears and hat. Add black feet for the groom.

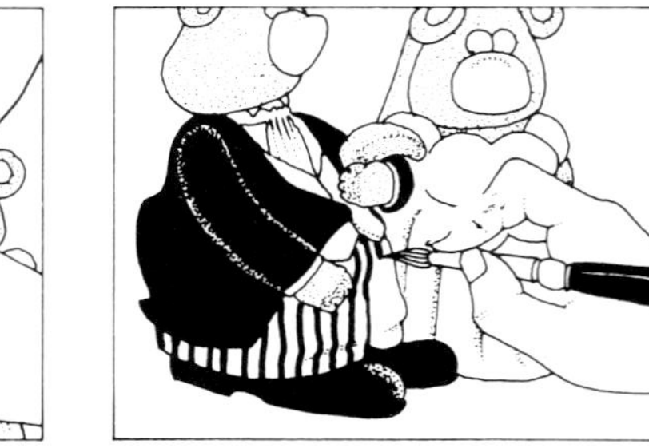
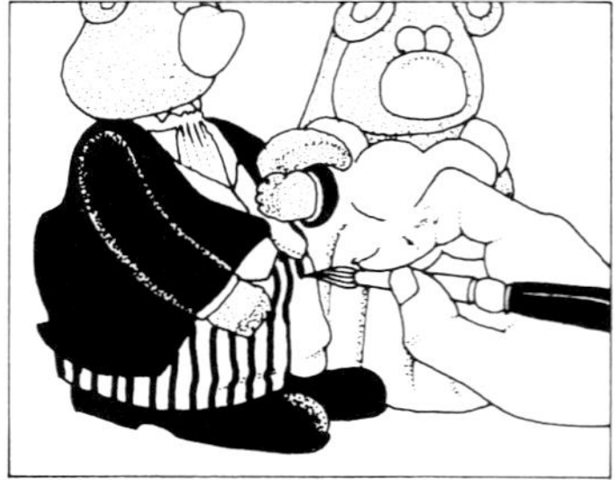

5 Colour a small piece of icing beige and add inner ears and muzzles.

6 Paint black stripes on to the trousers. Add small white icing eyes and brown icing eyelids. Paint on black facial features.

7 Colour tiny amounts of royal icing pastel colours and pipe squiggles for the bouquet and headdress using a no. 1 nozzle. Add some green leaves. Pipe pink dots on to the dress. Leave everything to dry.

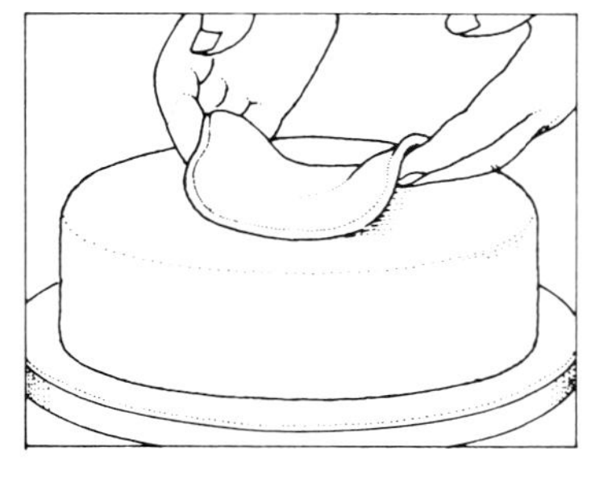
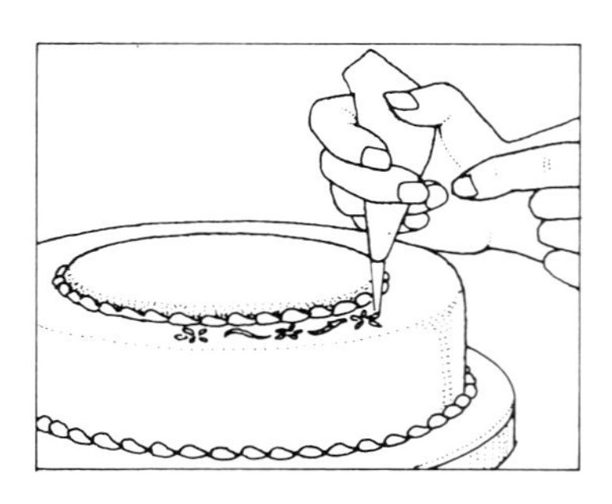

8 Spread the cake with jam. Roll out the marzipan and cover smoothly. Stick the cake to the board with a little royal icing. Colour all but 175 g (6 oz) of the remaining icing pale pink. Dampen the marzipan, roll out the pink icing and cover the cake smoothly. Roll a strip from the trimmings. Dampen the remainder of the board and cover it with the strip of icing. Roll and cut an oval out of white icing and stick it to the cake.

9 With a cut-off piping bag, pipe a small snail's trail round the plaque and the base of the cake in white royal icing. Using nos. 0 and 1 nozzles, pipe decorations round the side and top of the cake. Pipe darker pink edging on to the board. Stick the teddies on top of the cake with royal icing.

A Charming Wedding

Cinderella we usually think of in her rags, but a wedding cake is a lovely excuse to produce her looking beautiful and happy. For a bride who has found her Prince, what could be a more romantic wedding cake?

Start 2 days before

Serves 45

INGREDIENTS

23 cm (9 in) square Fruit Cake (page 166)
750 g ($1\frac{1}{2}$ lb) marzipan
1.75 kg (4 lb) Roll-Out Icing (page 166)
75 g (3 oz) gum tragacanth
750 g ($1\frac{1}{2}$ lb) Royal Icing (page 166)
100 g (4 oz) Petal Paste (page 167)
peach, paprika, yellow, purple, brown, gold, black, blue, green and red food colours
sieved jam
yellow sparkle petal powder
purple and pink petal powder

SPECIAL EQUIPMENT

23 cm (9 in) square cake board
13 cm (5 in) square cake card
Wilton moulds of man and woman
cocktail sticks
piping bags with nos. 1 and 0 nozzles
large blossom cutter
ball tool
kitchen foil
piece of foam
medium primrose cutter
small pointed flower cutter
straight frill cutter
paintbrush
perspex cake divider

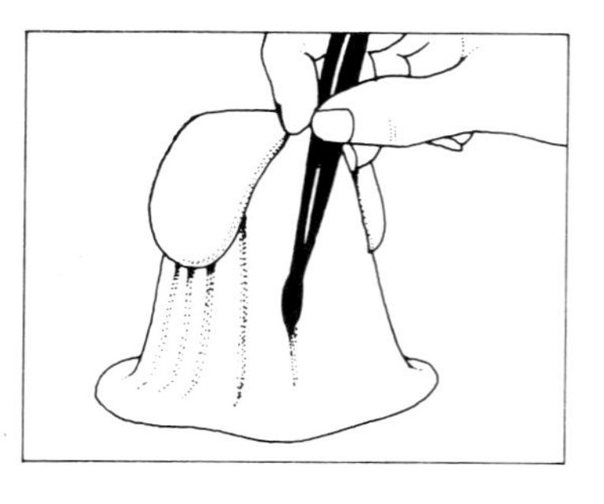

1 Colour about 1.25 kg ($2\frac{1}{2}$ lb) of roll-out icing peach. Using about 350 g (12 oz) of the peach icing, roll out and cut a block about 13 cm (5 in) square and 2 cm ($\frac{3}{4}$ in) deep. Dampen of the base of the block and stick it to the cake card. Let it dry for a few hours. Model the skirt and panniers from solid white icing.

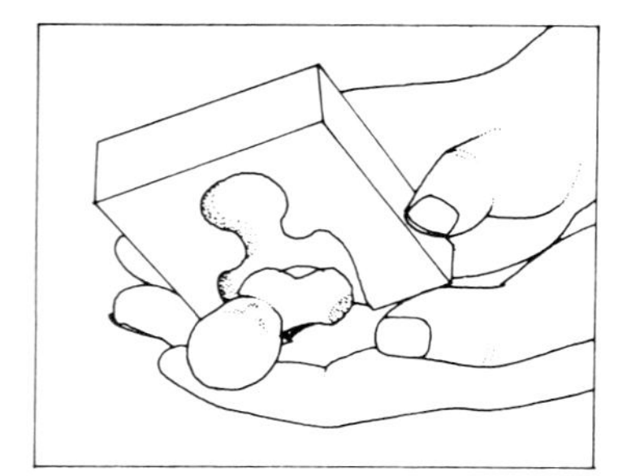

2 Stick the skirt to the block. Colour about 750 g ($1\frac{1}{2}$ lb) of roll-out icing flesh by using tiny amounts of paprika. Knead in the gum tragacanth. Following the directions, use the Wilton moulds to make a model of a man. Make a model of a woman's torso and head only, excluding the arms and legs.

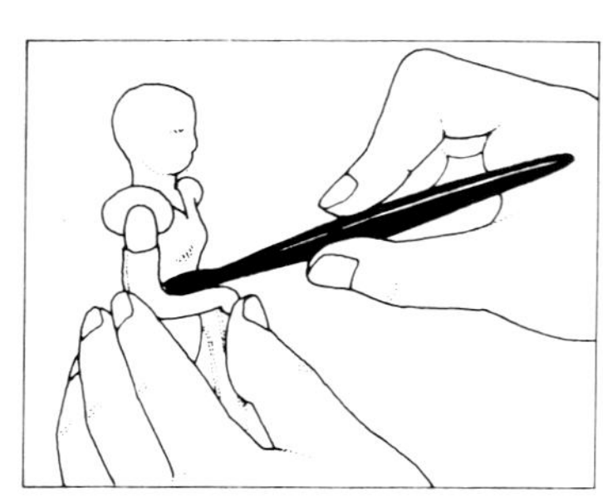

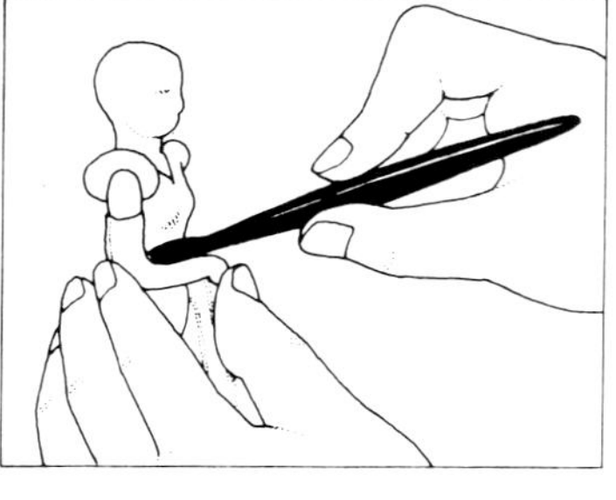

3 Stick the woman's torso to the skirt with a tiny amount of royal icing. Add pink upper arms and solid long white gloves. Bend the arms on to the skirt and stick them down.

4 Roll out some icing and cut out and stick a bodice and sleeves to Cinderella. Colour a little icing yellow and add some hair and a white hairband.

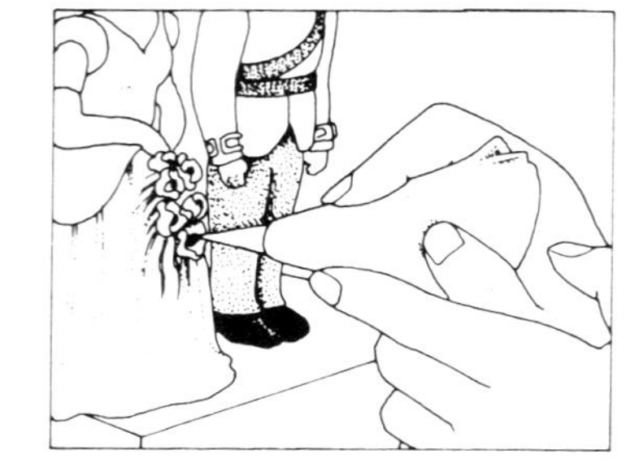

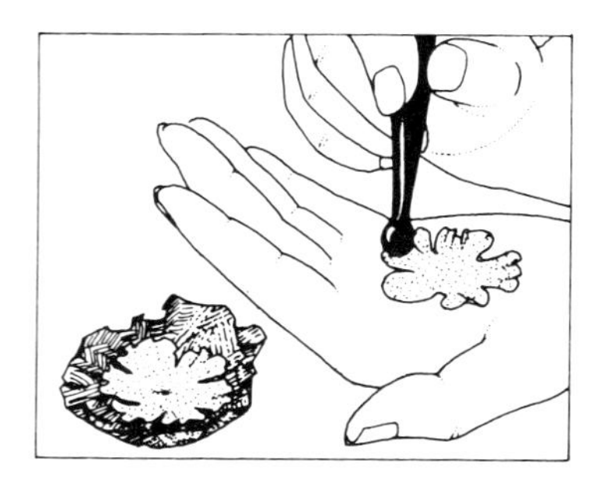

5 Colour some pieces of icing and roll, cut and stick some clothes on to Prince Charming. Push a cocktail stick up into each of his legs and stick them into the block of icing so that he stands up.

6 Using a no. 1 nozzle and coloured royal icing, pipe Cinderella's bouquet. Paint on green leaves to complete the bouquet.

7 Colour about half the petal paste purple. Roll it out very, very thinly and cut 4 large blossoms. With a ball tool, go over the edges to create ripples. Dry them in cupped kitchen foil.

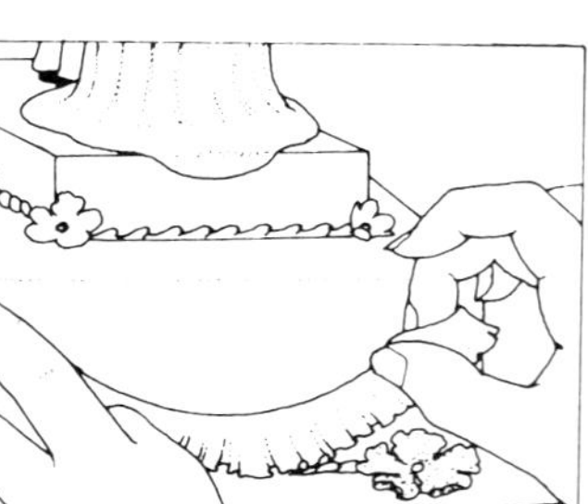

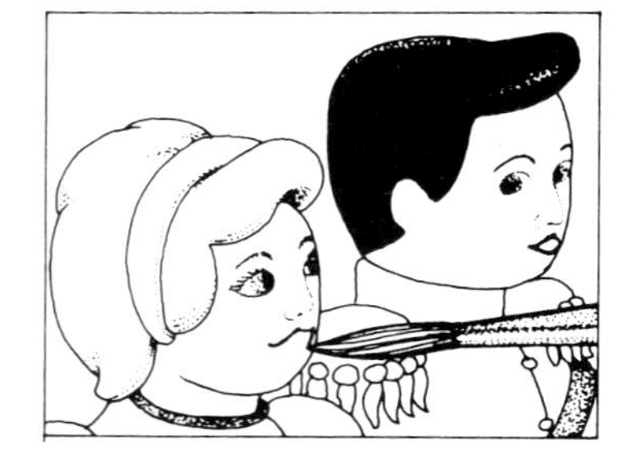

8 Colour about three-quarters of the remaining petal paste dark peach. Roll very thinly again and cut out 11 large primroses and 4 small flowers. Use the ball tool as before and dry them in cupped foil. Cut out 6 white stars, pushing them into a piece of foam to shape them.

9 Spread the cake with jam and cover with marzipan. Cover the cake and board with the remaining peach icing. Stick the flowers on to the top and the board. With the cut-off end of a piping bag, pipe a snail's tail round the base of the cake and the top of the block. With the remaining white icing make some frills round the sides (see page 104).

10 Using a no. 1 nozzle, pipe some trimming on to the tops of the frills. Using nos. 0 and 1 nozzles, pipe decorations above the frills. Pipe some edging on to the board. Paint the features on the models.

Winter Wedding

A wedding in winter should be like something out of 'White Christmas' – sparkling snow, red-cheeked children laughing in delight as the beautiful bride is swept off covered in soft (fake!) fur in a tinkling sleigh with her handsome groom. A little difficult to achieve in a drizzling grey London, but the cake can reflect such a fantasy to the full.

Serves 150, or 125 without the top tier

INGREDIENTS

15 cm (6 in), 23 cm (9 in) and 30 cm (12 in) Fruit Cakes (p. 166)
2.25 kg (5 lb) marzipan
225 g (8 oz) Petal Paste (p. 167)
3.2 kg (7 lb) Roll-Out Icing (page 166)
2 kg (4½ lb) Royal Icing (p. 166)
gooseberry green, brown, yellow and holly green food colours
sieved jam
castor sugar
green petal powder

SPECIAL EQUIPMENT

23 cm (9 in), 30 cm (12 in) and 38 cm (15 in) cake boards
small, medium and large blossom cutters
medium and large rose leaf cutters
small, medium and large ivy leaf cutters
kitchen foil
kitchen paper
cocktail sticks
piping bags with nos. 58 and 1 nozzles
piece of polystyrene, Oasis or plasticine
paintbrush
3 × 9 cm (3½ in) and 3 × 7.5 cm (3 in) pillars plus supports

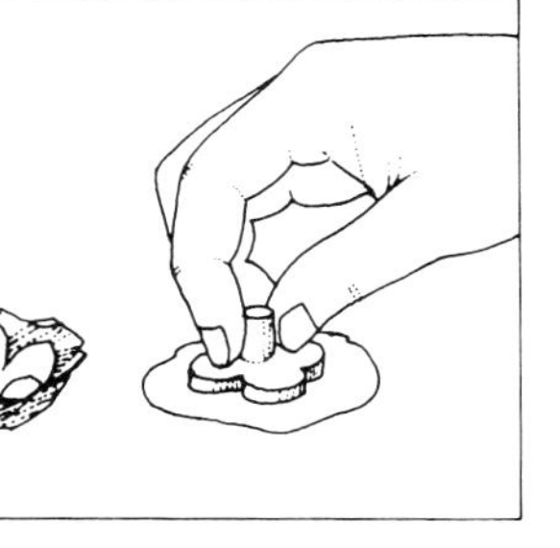
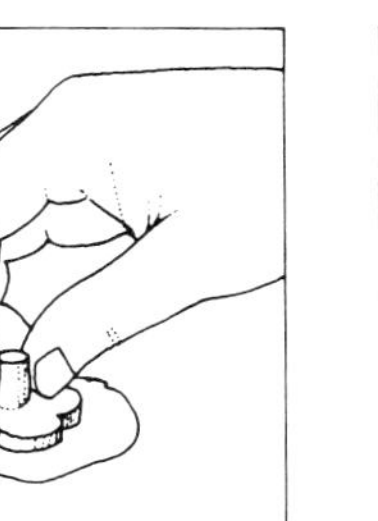

1 Taking tiny amounts at a time, roll out the petal paste very, very thinly. Cut out 6 large, 14 medium and 2 small roses using the blossom cutter. Make cup shapes from the kitchen foil and leave the roses in them to dry, to create curved flowers.

2 Colour the remaining petal paste with gooseberry green. Cut out about 40 assorted leaves, leaving them to dry on crumpled paper so they aren't flat.

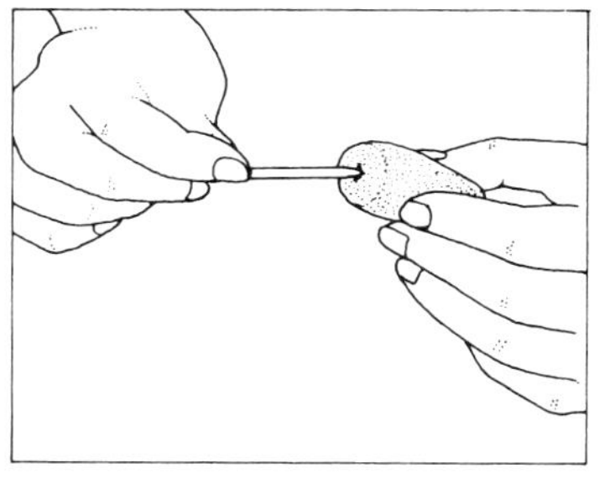

3 Colour about 350 g (12 oz) of roll-out icing brown. Make small cone shapes and insert a cocktail stick into the base of each one.

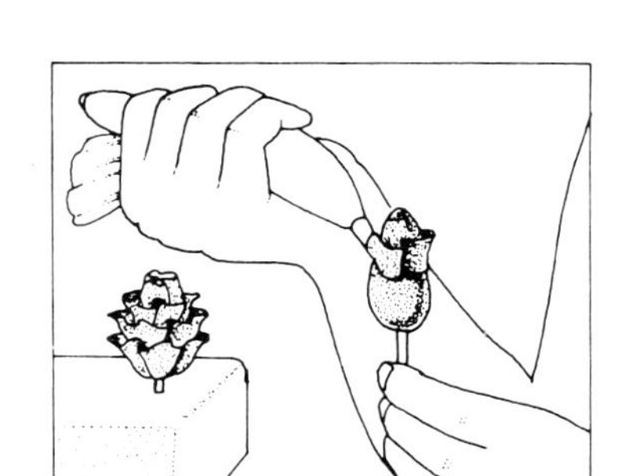

4 Colour about 350 g (12 oz) of royal icing brown. Using a no. 58 nozzle, pipe frills round and round the cones, turning the cocktail sticks as you go. Leave them to dry inserted in a piece of polystyrene, Oasis or plasticine.

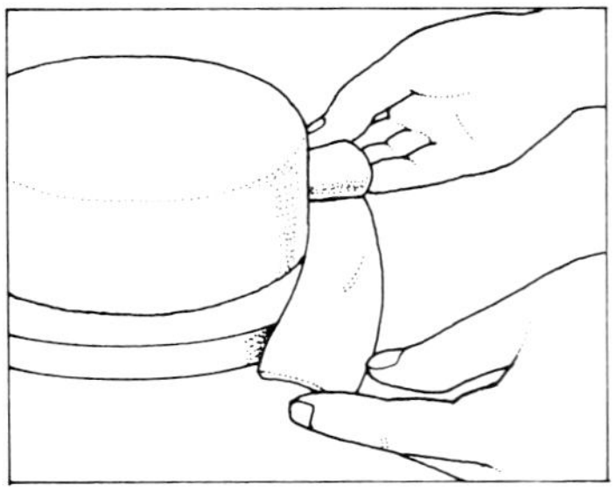

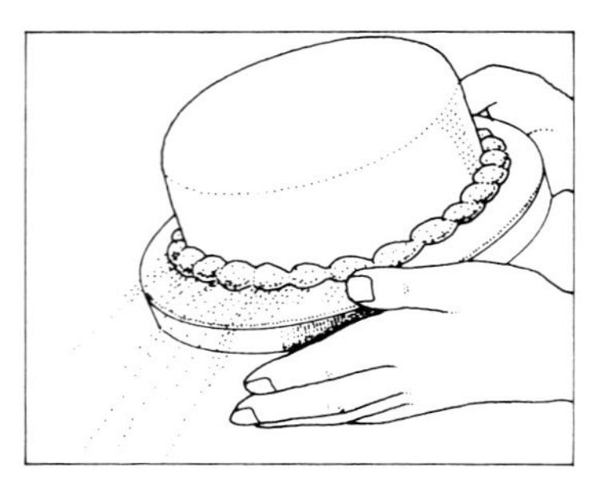

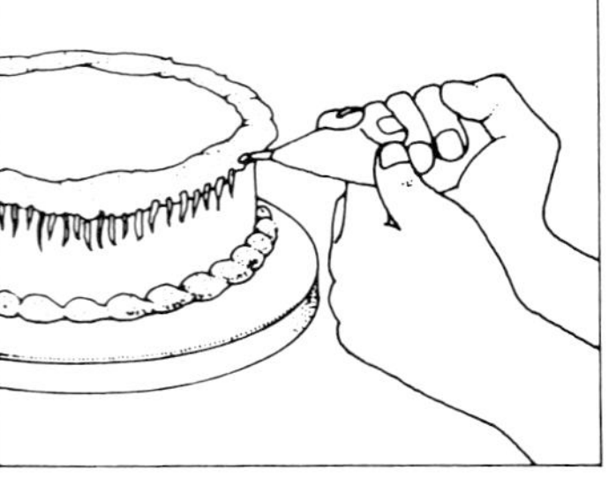

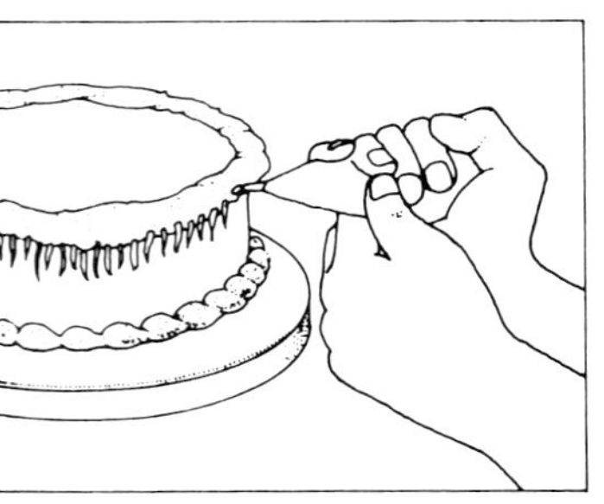

5 Spread the cakes with jam and cover with marzipan. Stick the cakes to their boards with a little royal icing. Cover with roll-out icing, dampening the marzipan a little with water to stick. Roll out strips of icing, dampen the remainder of the boards and cover with the strips of icing.

6 Pipe a large snail's trail with the cut-off end of a piping bag round the bottom edges of the cakes. Dust the piping immediately with castor sugar and gently shake off the excess.

7 Spread 'snow icing' along the top edges with a palette knife then pipe little icicles with the cut-off end of a piping bag. Dust with castor sugar as before.

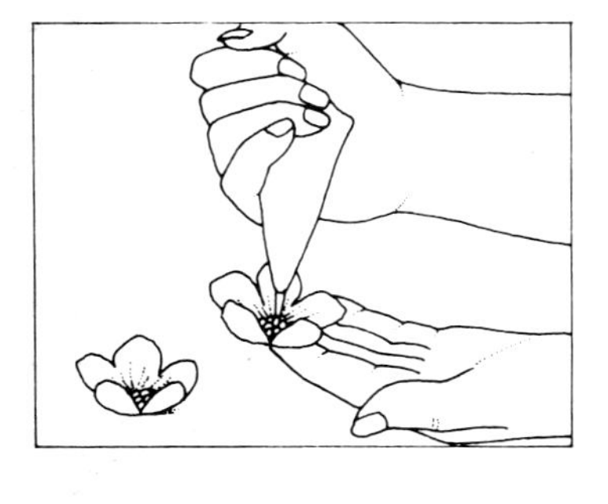

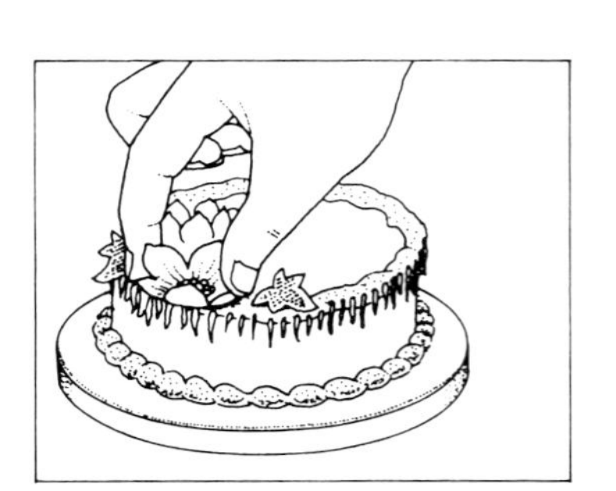

8 Dust the centres of the roses with green petal powder. Paint green details on to the roses and pipe yellow dots into the centres using a no. 1 nozzle.

9 Paint the leaves in differing greens. Stick the flowers, leaves and pine cones to the cakes with royal icing, including a cluster on to each board. Paint green twining stems round each bunch. Assemble the three tiers as desired using the pillars and supports.

Chocolate Wedding Cake

There's no need to stick rigidly to fruit cake for a wedding. If the happy couple are chocoholics a really rich, wicked cake is lovely on such a special day. If you find it difficult to make the roses out of chocolate then coloured icing would look just as good.

Serves 100

INGREDIENTS

15 cm (6 in), 20 cm (8 in) and 25 cm (10 in) round Chocolate Sponge Cakes (page 165)
900 g (2 lb) Buttercream (page 167)
1.4 kg (3 lb) good quality, dark chocolate
1 litre ($1^3/_4$ pints) double cream
225 g (8 oz) white chocolate (for piping)
50 ml (2 fl oz) double cream
450 g (1 lb) white chocolate
175 g (6 oz) liquid glucose
OR 675 g ($1^1/_2$ lb) Roll-Out Icing (page 166) instead of white chocolate and glucose
peach and moss green powder food colours

SPECIAL EQUIPMENT

33 cm (13 in) round cake board
15 cm (6 in) and 20 cm (8 in) round thin cake cards
cooling rack
greaseproof paper
piping bags with nos. 44, 5, 3 and 1 nozzles
cake dividers or paper
medium and small rose leaf cutters
veiner (optional)

1 Split each cake in half horizontally and sandwich together with the buttercream. Break the chocolate into small pieces into a heatproof bowl. Bring the double cream to the boil, stir it into the chocolate and allow to cool.

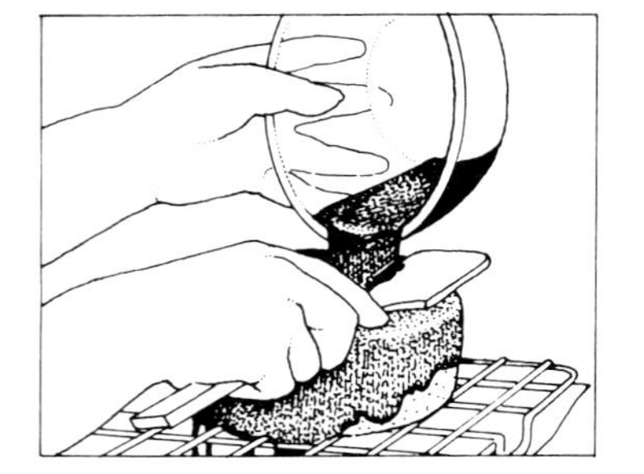

2 Stick the smallest cake on to the 15 cm (6 in) card with a tiny amount of melted chocolate and put it on a cooling rack over a large sheet of greaseproof paper. Pour the chocolate mixture over the cake, using a spatula to help to spread it, working quickly before the covering begins to set.

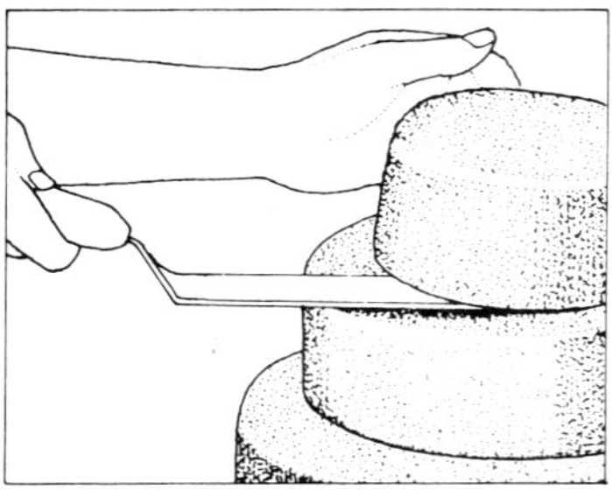

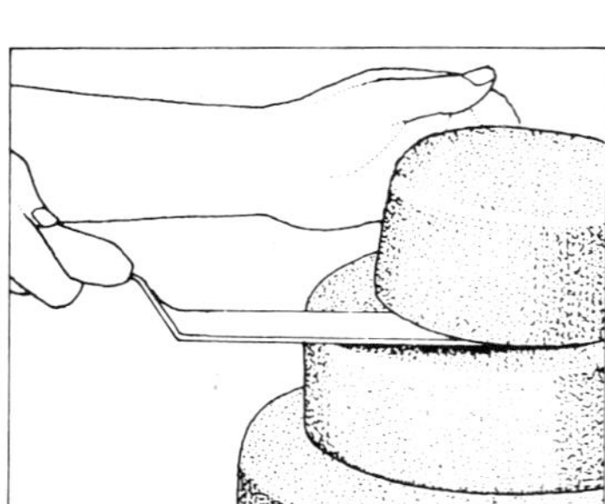

3 Repeat with the medium-sized cake. Put the large cake directly on to the cooling rack and coat it in the same way. Repeat the covering on all the cakes if the finish is not good enough. Stick the large cake on to the board and put the other 2 cakes on top, using a fish slice and trying not to touch the coating as it marks very easily.

4 Scoop all the excess chocolate from the paper and combine it with the remainder in the bowl. Leave it to cool until it is of piping consistency. Using the cooled chocolate and a no. 3 nozzle, pipe a snail's trail around the base of each cake.

5 Mark each cake in 12 sections. In the same way as for the dark chocolate, combine the white chocolate and double cream and leave to cool to a piping consistency. Using a no. 2 nozzle and dark chocolate, pipe a looped line from section to section. Using the no. 2 nozzle add white chocolate snail's trail immediately below loops. Pipe dark chocolate scrolls around the top edges. Start with a no. 44 nozzle then overpipe with a no. 5, then a no. 3 and finally a no. 1. Keep the remaining piping chocolate for later.

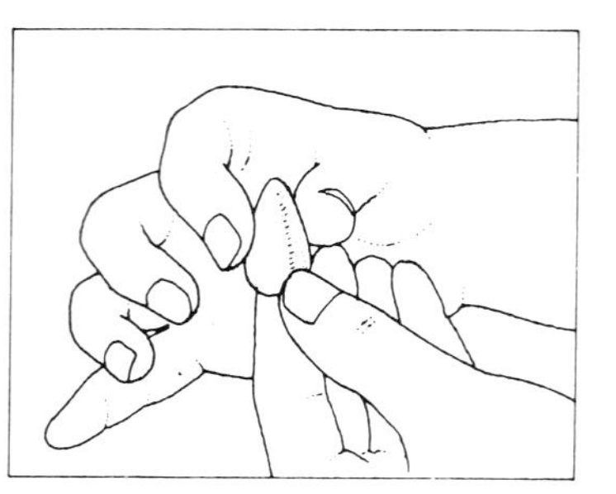

6 To make the roses and leaves, melt the white chocolate and mix it with the liquid glucose. Allow it to harden for a while in the fridge until it is of modelling consistency. Knead peach powder into about one-quarter of the chocolate to make pale peach, and more powder into another quarter to make a darker peach. Model a small cone shape from the pale peach chocolate.

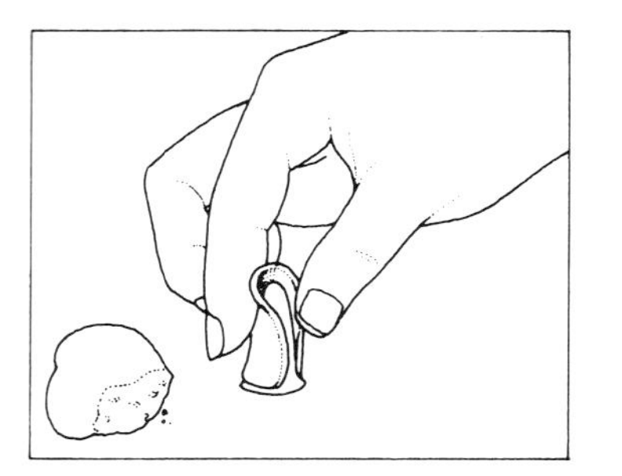

7 Take a further small piece and roll a ball, then press it out into a petal shape. Stick the base of the cone onto the work surface to free both hands to make the petals. Stick the petal to the cone to start the rose.

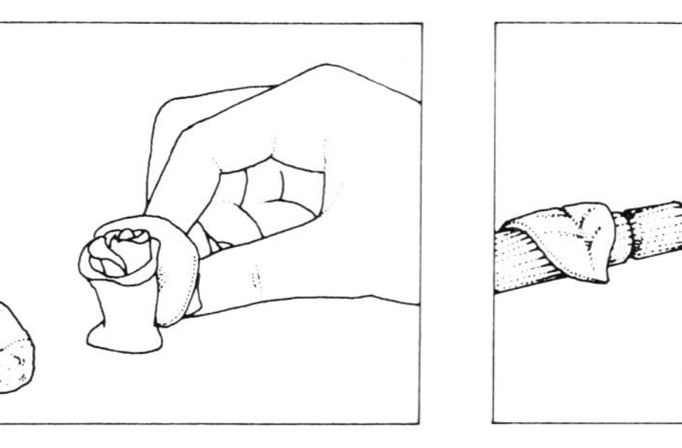

8 Build up the rose petal by petal, making each petal slightly larger than the last, and allowing between 5 to 7 petals for each rose. Repeat with the darker peach and half of the remaining white chocolate mixture.

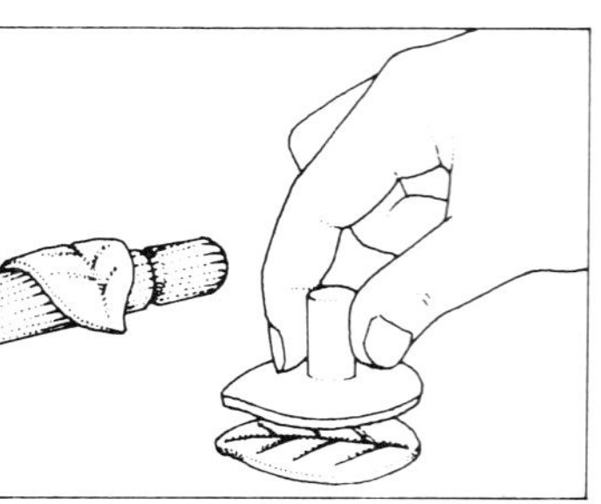

9 Colour the remaining white chocolate mixture green. Roll it out and cut out some medium and small leaf shapes, using the veiner if you have one. Let the leaves dry over a curved surface such as the handle of a wooden spoon.

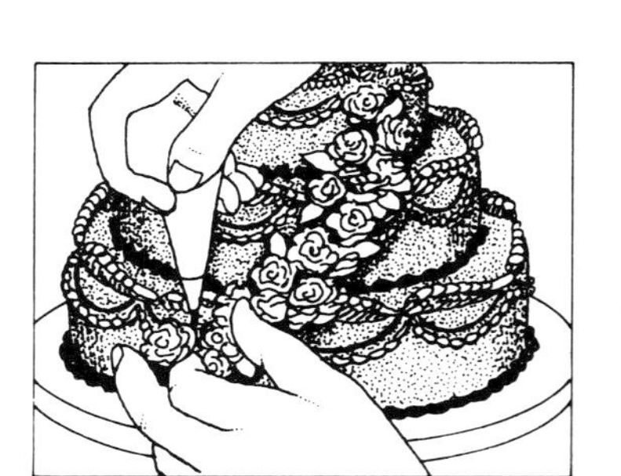

10 Using a little of the piping chocolate, stick the roses and leaves on to the cake, spiralling them downwards from the top. Keep your hands very cool when handling the flowers and leaves.

Spring Wedding

Use primrose cutters as for the large blossoms on the Winter Wedding (page 89) and roll out the edges of the petals with a cocktail stick. It can be a lovely idea to copy the flowers in the bride's bouquet, too, and you can buy cutters for almost every type of flower.

Summer Wedding

As you can see, I've used ivy in most of the floral wedding cakes. I originally did this because it looks so pretty climbing over the cakes, but when I checked its meaning to make sure I wasn't saying anything unsuitable, I found ivy stands for matrimony. Not, I hope, because it's clinging and destructive – I like to think it's because its tenacious and long lasting.

Autumn Wedding

The colours of this one work very well. It's based on a pale peach coloured cake. Use oak leaf cutters, and make the poppies with a large blossom cutter as for the Winter Wedding roses (page 89). Make the wheat out of long cone-shaped pieces of icing slit into kernels with a sharp knife.

Golden Cherubs

This shows how dramatic even a single tier cake can be. I originally made this for a lady who collected models of cherubs, and it looked so striking that I've now made it for several weddings. All the piping is very simple, and the gold and white give it a formality and grandeur, but remember to remove all gold trimmings before cutting the cake.

Pretty Primroses

The swags are made in the same way as the hedgehog's spikes (page 51) but using a no. 1 nozzle. It's a very easy and striking kind of piping and can be used in all sorts of different ways, but I like the simplicity of this version, with just the touch of colour in the flowers. It would look very sweet with pink roses, too.

Romantic Swans

This is just to show that you don't have to stick to a traditional shape for a wedding cake. Many couples are choosing to move away from the tiered cake to something more expressive, and I love these swans with their graceful necks making a heart shape between them. The necks are based on non-edible support covered in icing and the bodies are made from very large round cakes trimmed and built up to shape.

Anniversaries

Here your ideas are already given to you. There are many different ways of interpreting them, as you can see from the cakes I have shown you. The strange selection of materials designated to celebrate the passing years – chosen because that is the order in which the wedding presents would wear out and so need replacing – offers a large choice of wonderful subjects. Look on page 175 for a full list of the different anniversaries and base your design around them (you can always combine them – for example I made a cake for a forty-ninth wedding anniversary recently and put an icing pottery bowl full of sugar rubies on the top), unless you prefer to make something like the Bridal Teddies (page 83) which would work wonderfully for almost any number of years. A simple cake with the names or initials of the husband and wife entwined together would also look lovely, or one of the funnier cakes in the book could easily be adapted to suit the couple involved.

Ruby Wedding

Jewels are difficult to reproduce on a cake unless you use sweets, which seem a bit frivolous for an occasion as important as this. The combination of a lovely deep ruby red with some elegant flowers is the answer. It needn't necessarily be roses – you could model any beautiful red flower – but roses do symbolize love, and if the couple has stuck it out for 40 years they must at least *like* each other . . .

Serves 30

INGREDIENTS

23 cm (9 in) round Fruit Cake (page 166)
550 g (1¼ lb) marzipan
1 kg (2¼ lb) Roll-Out Icing (page 166)
225 g (8 oz) Royal Icing (page 166)
red and green food colours
sieved jam

SPECIAL EQUIPMENT

28 cm (11 in) round cake board
piping bag with nos. 1, 0 and 2 nozzles
Garrett frill cutter
cocktail sticks
clingfilm
scissors and card
small blossom plunger cutter
piece of foam
ivy leaf cutters
paintbrush

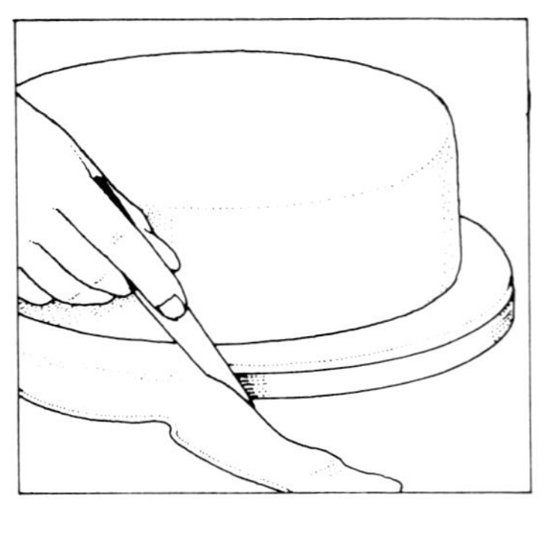

1 Spread the cake with jam and cover it with rolled out marzipan. Stick the cake to the board with a tiny piece of dampened roll-out icing or royal icing. Dampen the marzipan slightly and cover the cake with about 550 g (1¼ lb) of roll-out icing. Trim round the lower edge. Cover the remainder of the board with icing, sticking it with water and trimming round the edge.

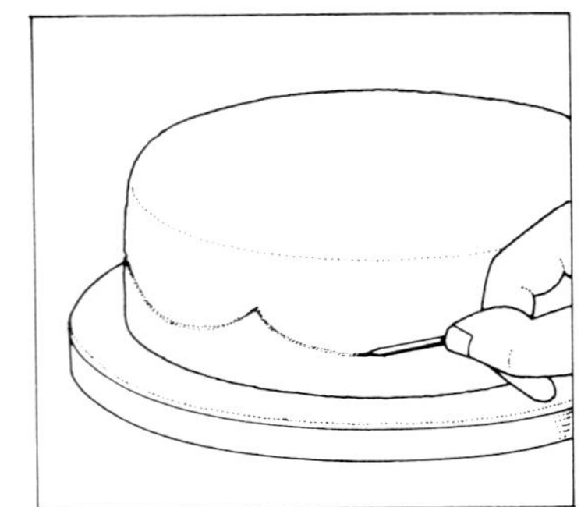

2 Mark the side of the cake with a knife or cocktail stick into 8 scalloped sections (see page 171). Using a no. 1 nozzle, pipe a snail's trail round the bottom of the cake and a fancy pattern round the edge of the board.

Congratulations
40 years

3 Colour about 225 g (8 oz) of roll-out icing red. Roll it out very thinly and cut out 8 circles with the frill cutter. Remove the centres and reserve the trimmings. Keep the circles covered with clingfilm while you work. One at a time, roll a cocktail stick over the scalloped edge of each circle to create a frilled effect.

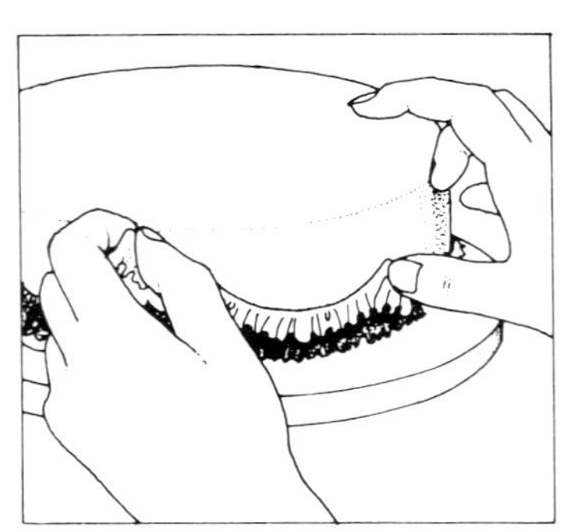

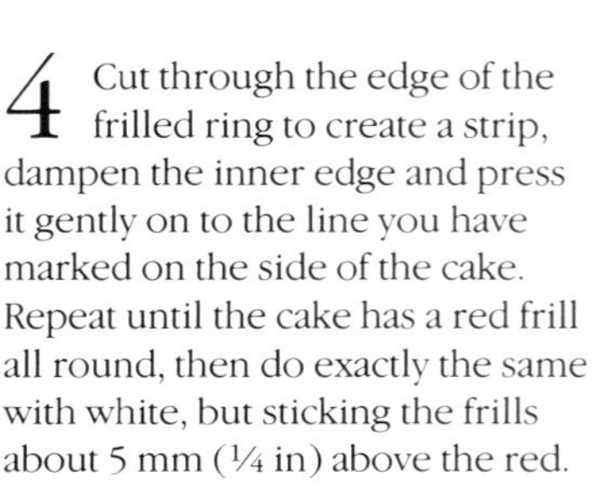

4 Cut through the edge of the frilled ring to create a strip, dampen the inner edge and press it gently on to the line you have marked on the side of the cake. Repeat until the cake has a red frill all round, then do exactly the same with white, but sticking the frills about 5 mm (¼ in) above the red.

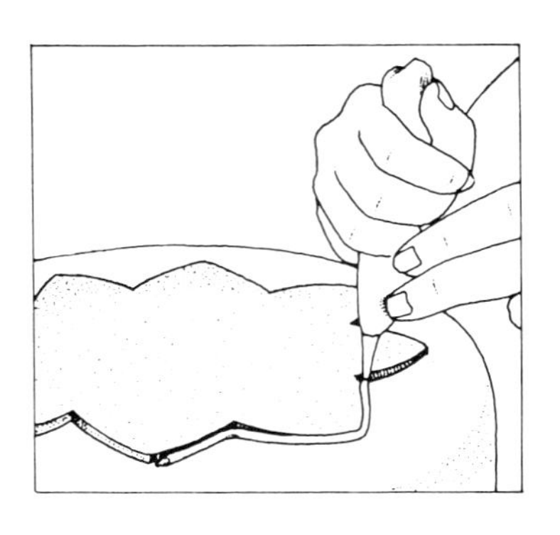

5 Using nos. 0 and 1 nozzles, pipe some decorative trimming on to the frill tops with white royal icing. Using the guide on page 182, cut a template from card. Place it on to the cake and pipe round the edge using a no. 2 nozzle and white icing. Remove the template then, using a no. 1 nozzle, pipe a further white line on top of the previous one, and another line just inside the shape. Change to a no. 0 nozzle and pipe a fancy line within the shape.

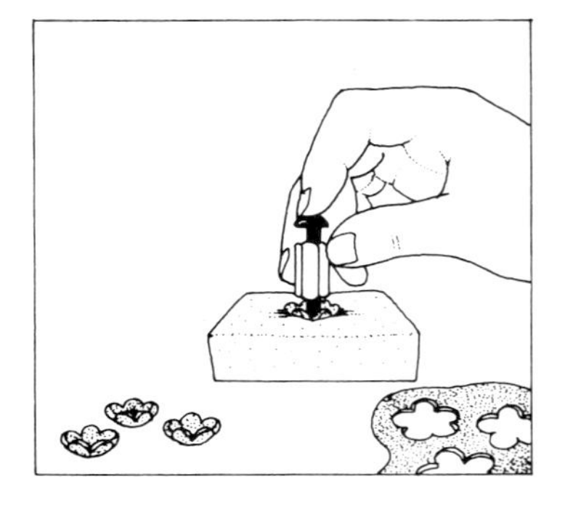

6 With a little red royal icing and no. 1 nozzle, pipe a red line on top of the 2 white lines to create a raised edge. Change to a no. 0 nozzle and pipe an embroidery pattern on the side. Roll out a small quantity of red icing thinly and cut out 16 small plunger flowers, pressing them into a soft surface (a piece of foam is ideal) to form cupped shapes.

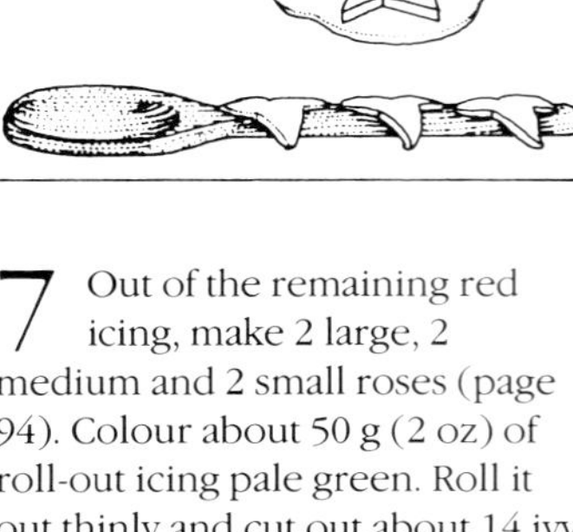

7 Out of the remaining red icing, make 2 large, 2 medium and 2 small roses (page 94). Colour about 50 g (2 oz) of roll-out icing pale green. Roll it out thinly and cut out about 14 ivy leaves in different sizes. Dry them over the handle of a wooden spoon to make them curve.

8 Paint the centres of the ivy leaves with dark green. With small amounts of royal icing, attach 8 plunger flowers round the sides of the cake and 8 on top. Add piped white centres and lines either side of the plunger flowers on the top. Stick the roses and leaves to the top of the cake and pipe a message using a no. 1 nozzle.

Golden Jewellery Box

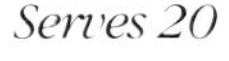

If real gold is too expensive, why not make this beautiful jewellery box full of gleaming gold for a Golden Wedding anniversary? Or fill it with silver if it's the twenty-fifth anniversary. It makes a wonderful centrepiece for any occasion, and you could add brightly coloured 'jewel' sweets if it's for somebody fond of extravagance. Remember if you use either the gold or silver food colour that you must pull it completely off the cake before you eat it. If you want the jewellery to be edible you must use gold leaf, which does look fabulous, but which is expensive and *very* fiddly.

Serves 20

INGREDIENTS

20 × 15 cm (8 × 6 in) Fruit Cake (page 166)
450 g (1 lb) marzipan
1.1 kg (2½ lb) Roll-Out Icing (page 166)
50 g (2 oz) gum tragacanth
225 g (8 oz) Royal Icing (page 166)
pink and gold food colours
sieved jam

SPECIAL EQUIPMENT

25 cm (10 in) and 20 cm (8 in) square cake boards
non-stick baking parchment
string
piping bag with no. 1 nozzle
paintbrush

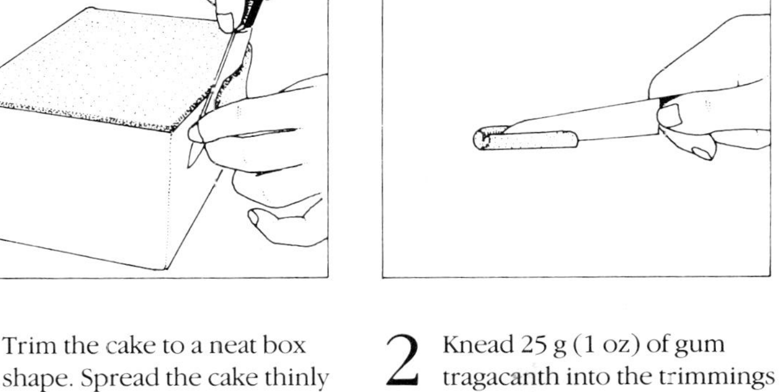

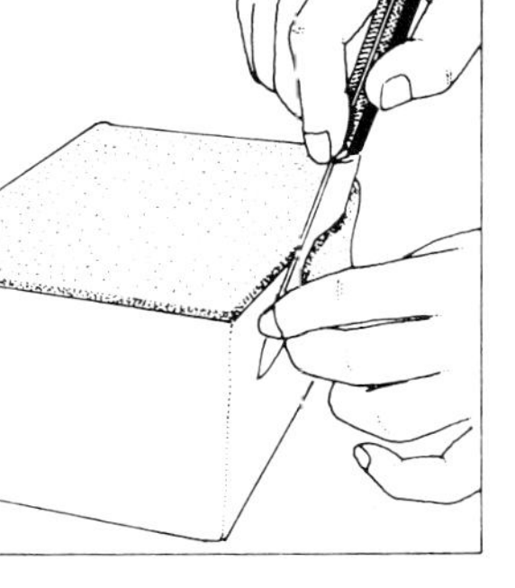

1 Trim the cake to a neat box shape. Spread the cake thinly with jam, roll out the marzipan and cover the top then the sides of cake, making sharp edges. Colour about 350 g (12 oz) of roll-out icing deep pink and use about half of it to cover the top of the cake, dampening the marzipan slightly with water.

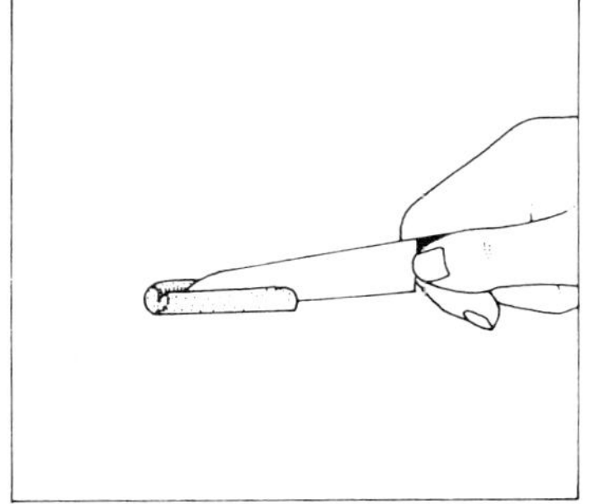

2 Knead 25 g (1 oz) of gum tragacanth into the trimmings of deep pink that you used for the top of the cake, still keeping the other 175 g (6 oz) ungummed. From the gummed icing, roll and cut 8 strips to make the sides and divisions of the tray, measuring the top of the cake for guidance, plus a sausage for the ring holder. Add a slit for the rings. Leave everything to dry for a short while on non-stick paper.

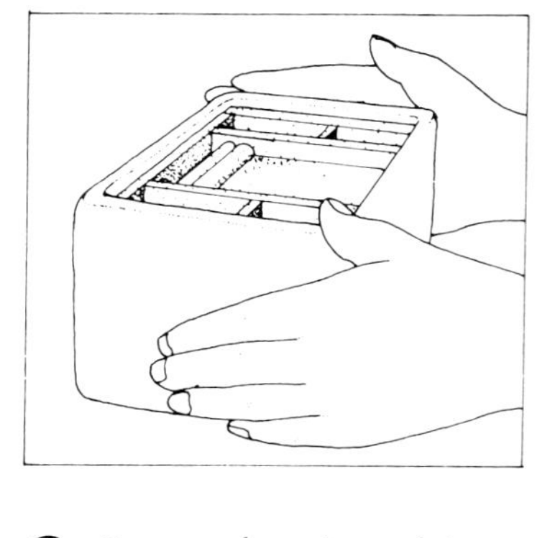

3 Dampen the strips and ring holder and stick them in position. Measure round the sides of the cake with string. Roll out about 450 g (1 lb) of icing and cut a strip the length of the string and the height of the cake plus 5 mm (¼ in) above the tray. Dampen the marzipan and stick the icing in position.

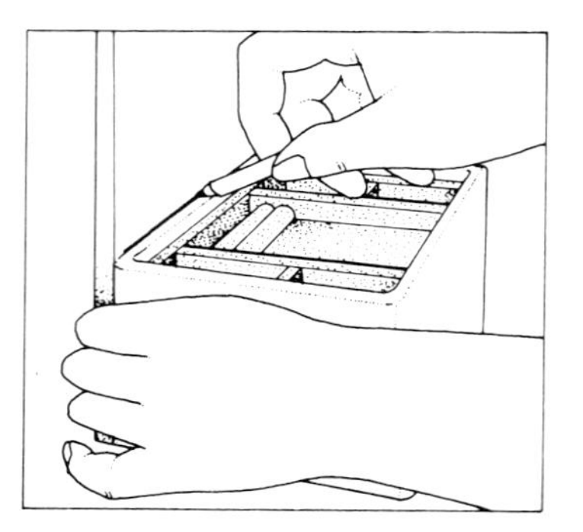

4 Stand the smaller cake board at the back of the cake and mark where the top of the box comes to on one side (it doesn't matter which).

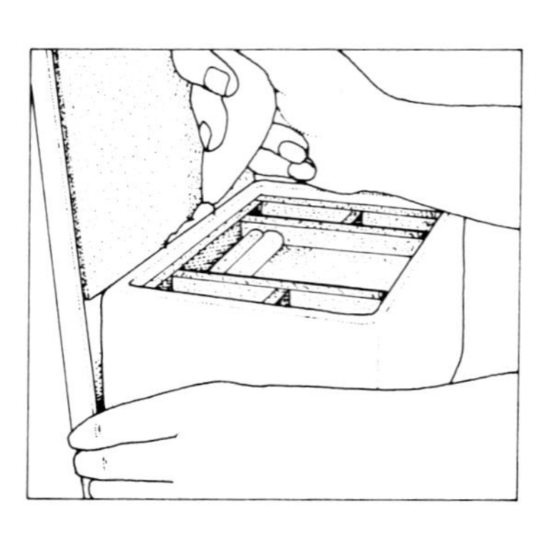

5 Roll out about 175 g (6 oz) of icing and stick it to the unmarked side of the extra cake board with water, including the edges. Turn the board over and with the remaining pink icing cover the other side as far down as the mark. Stick the covered board to the cake with royal icing.

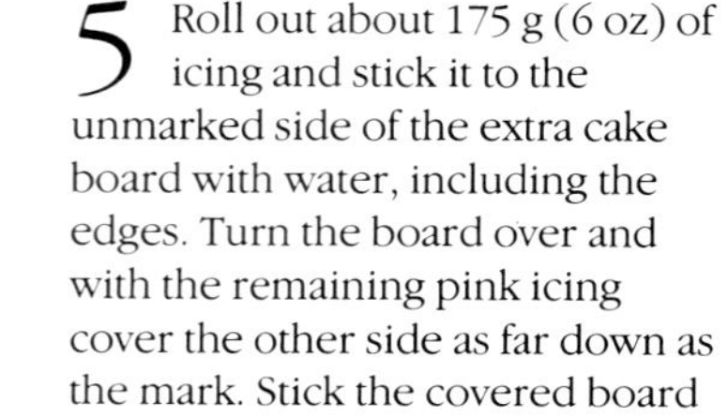

6 Knead the remaining gum tragacanth into the white trimmings. Roll them out and cut strips to fit round the edges of the 'lid'. Let them dry a little then stick them in position round the lid edges.

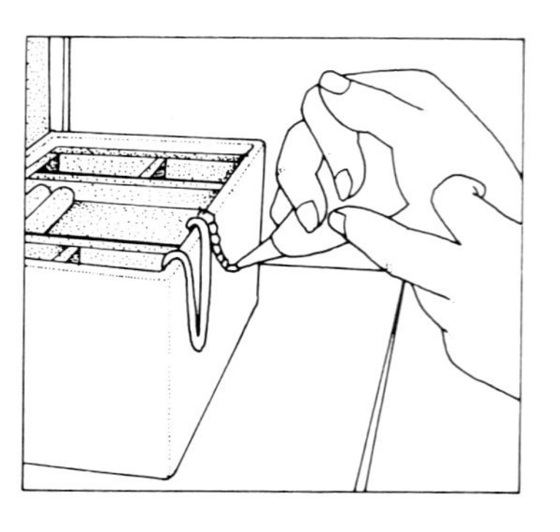

7 Model some bracelets, earrings etc. from white or pink trimmings. Using a no. 1 nozzle, pipe some rings, chains and decorations round the box. Cut out and stick the two parts of the lock to the lid and base.

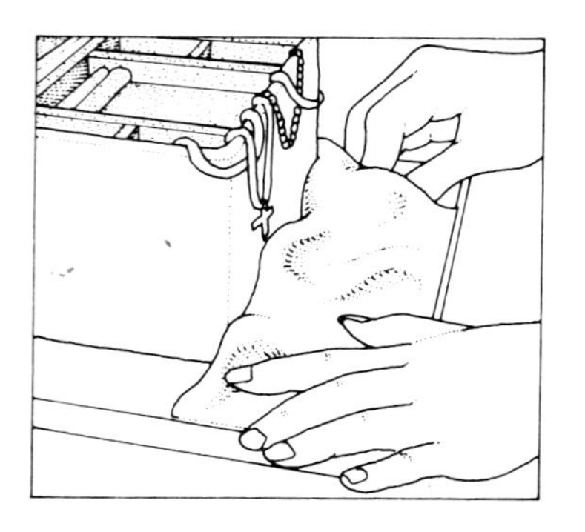

8 Colour the remaining roll-out icing pale pink. Roll it out and drape it in sections on to the dampened board. Place the jewellery in the box and paint decorations, lock and jewellery with gold food colour.

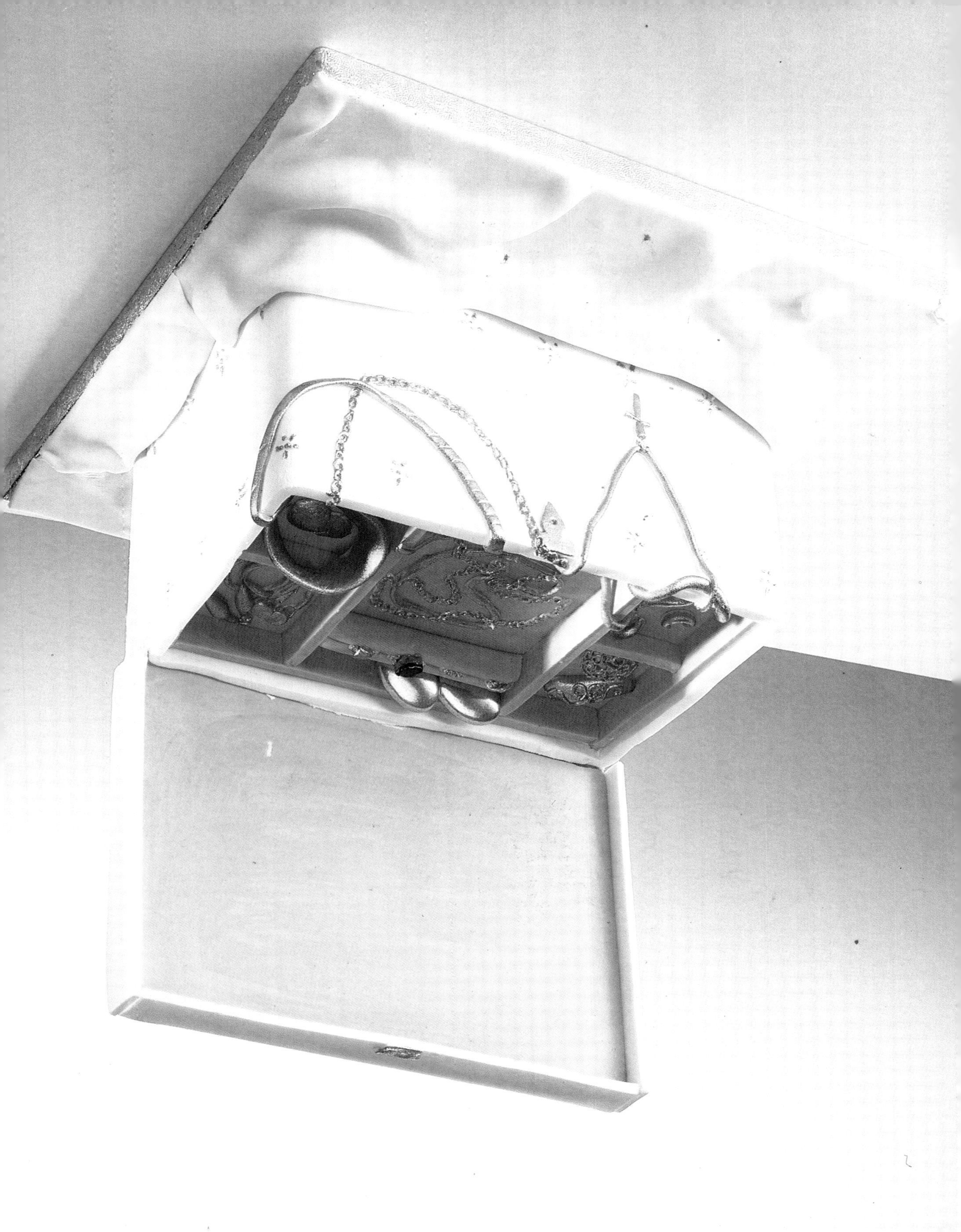

PAPER

The first anniversary is very special, and this block of paper and packet of envelopes looks charming. Use blocks of cake inside both, and achieve the wood effect for the board by mixing in the brown colour unevenly.

China

This has relatively little cake inside it but makes a wonderful centrepiece for a china wedding anniversary. You could always use it on top of a large cake if you need to. In this version the tea pot, jug and cup all contain cake, but if you made it entirely out of icing it could be kept almost indefinitely as a souvenir.

PEARL

Use the frills technique as shown on page 104, and dust the pearl with plenty of pink and white sparkle petal powder after it is made. The shell is modelled from icing, and a few plunger and cutter flowers have been added.

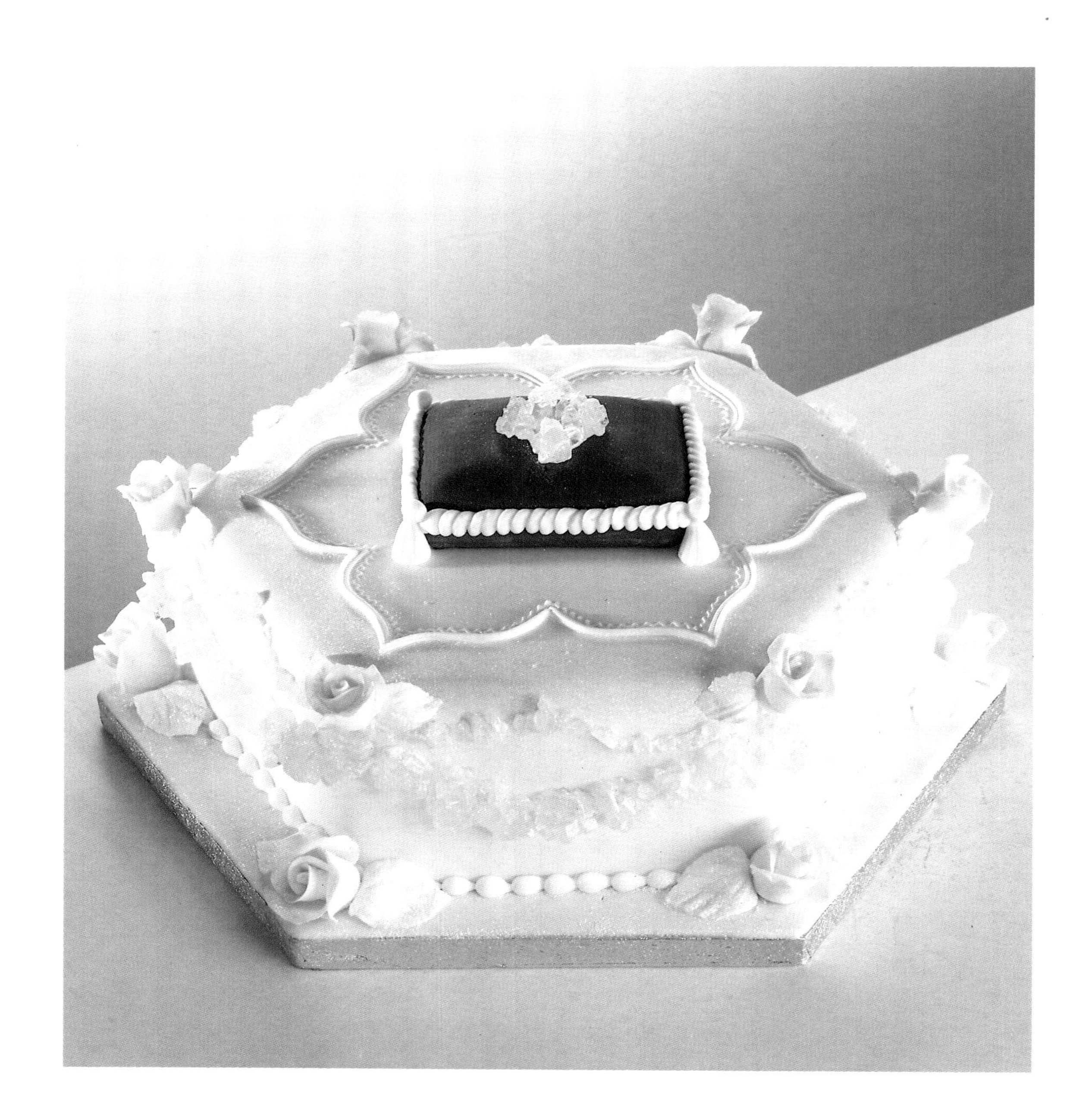

Diamond

The swags are made from sugar crystals which I broke off some swizzle sticks I found in a delicatessen. They sparkle beautifully and are the nearest thing to diamonds I could find.

CHRISTMAS

You'd think that Christmas would be one of the easiest times to make a wonderful cake for, but to come up with new ideas when the same theme is used every year can be quite difficult. There's nothing wrong with the good old yule log or holly, but it's fun to try something different.

Last year I made a bible open at the nativity story. Make this exactly as for the Christening cake (page 80) and write out some of the words from the gospels in black food colouring. Try to make the first letter 'illustrated' as in the days of monks, and copy a nativity scene (perhaps from a Christmas card) on to the opposite page.

The winter wedding cake (page 89) also adapts very well to Christmas. Make one tier only and add some icing mistletoe and holly and a few pretty presents. The American candy canes look very Christmassy and bring a bit more colour – simply twist rolled out strips of pink and white icing together, trim and bend the tops into curved cane shapes.

Don't make your cake too complicated. There will be plenty of other decorations around and you'll be far too busy to land yourself with a time-consuming cake.

Pile of Presents

It isn't always easy to think of a good design for a Christmas cake, especially as it isn't a time of year when you have hours to spare to spend piping intricate patterns or modelling Alpine scenes. The parcel cake is an extremely simple idea that I have used in several variations since I first made one many years ago, and this way of piling them on top of each other looks particularly attractive. There is a great deal of cake in this version, but the advantage is that if you put each individual parcel on its own tiny board before you pile them up, then you can keep any that don't get eaten for several weeks. Also, if some of the family prefer sponge cake, you can vary the type of cake used from parcel to parcel. You could even make little individual parcels and add an icing name tag to each (good for a birthday too) – or one large label with 'Happy Christmas'; the permutations are endless.

Serves 50

INGREDIENTS

1 × 25 cm (10 in) and
2 × 15 cm (6 in) square Fruit Cakes (page 166)
1.8 kg (4 lb) marzipan
2.5 kg (5½ lb) Roll-Out Icing (page 166)
100 g (4 oz) Royal Icing (page 166)
various food colours
sieved jam

SPECIAL EQUIPMENT

35 cm (14 in) square cake board
little thin cake boards (optional)
paintbrush
piping bag with no. 1 nozzle

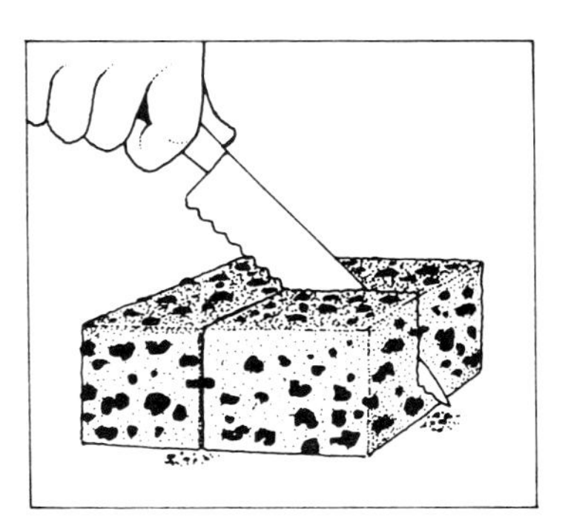

1 Cut one of the 15 cm (6 in) cakes into 4 differently-sized small rectangles.

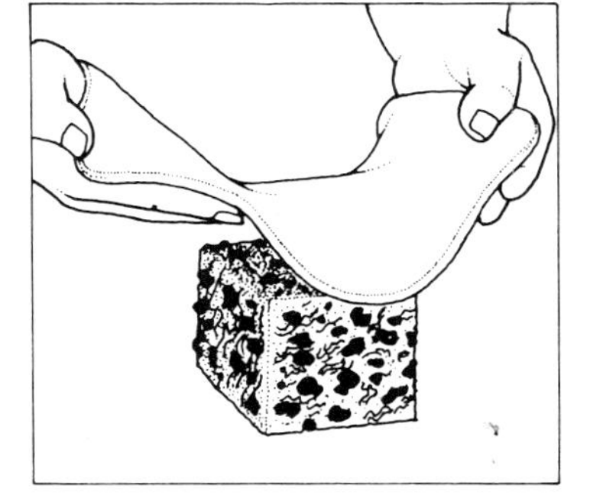

2 Divide about 800 g (1¾ lb) of marzipan into 4. Spread the 4 small shapes with jam. Roll out the marzipan and cover the cakes. Jam and cover the 25 cm (10 in) cake with about 675 g (1½ lb) of marzipan and the 15 cm (6 in) cake with the remainder.

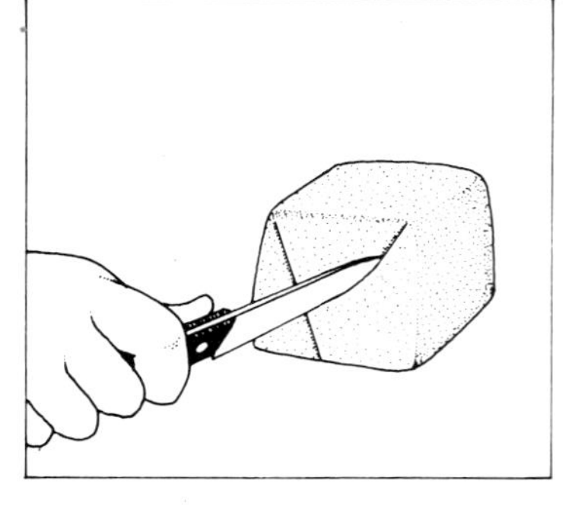

3 Divide about 750 g (1½ lb) of roll-out icing into 3 and knead different colours into each piece. Dampen the marzipan slightly and cover 3 of the small cakes. Colour about 1 kg (2 lb) of roll-out icing red. Using about half of it, cover the 15 cm (6 in) cake. Cover the 2 remaining cakes with white. Mark lines for the folded paper ends on 2 sides of each cake with a knife.

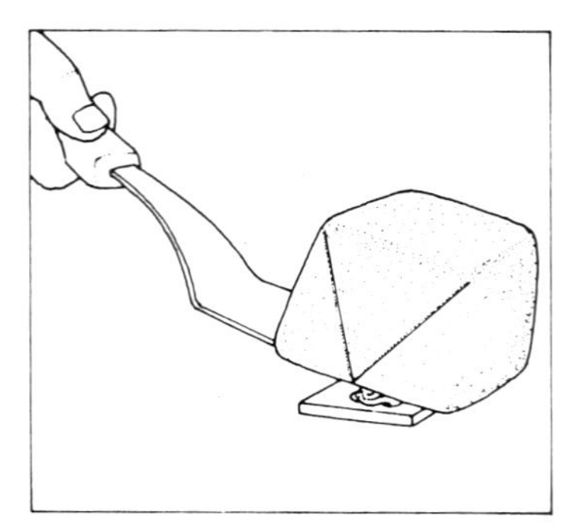

4 Stick each cake except the largest to a tiny board with royal icing if you want to be able to keep them individually.

5 Paint holly, snowmen etc. on to the white parcels. Using a no. 1 nozzle, pipe a bell design in white royal icing on to one coloured parcel and dots on to another.

6 Using about three-quarters of the remaining red icing, cover the large cake board, dampening with a little water to stick and trimming the edges.

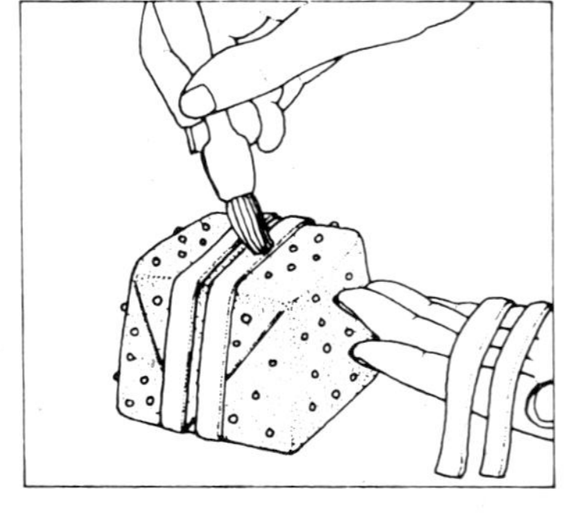

7 With the trimmings and remaining red icing, roll and cut some ribbons for 3 of the cakes. Stick them to the parcels with water. With scraps of differently-coloured icing make some more ribbons and stick them to the other parcels.

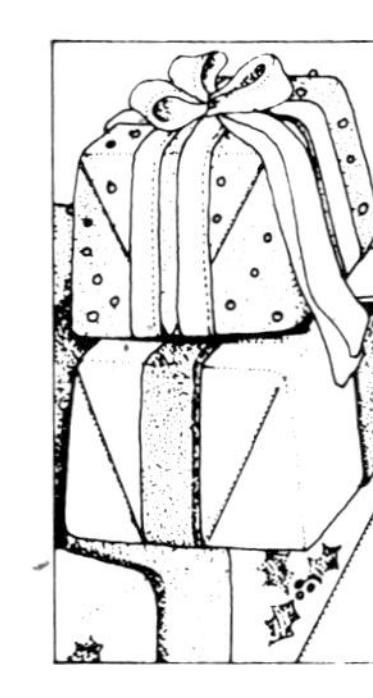

8 Stick the large cake to the centre of the board with a little royal icing. Pile up the others, sticking them with royal icing as necessary. Add some icing bows to the top parcels. Roll and cut out a tag from some white icing and pipe a suitable message if desired.

CHRISTMAS TREE

A beautiful, dramatic cake. If you're feeling really brave you could make it three dimensional and stand it up, but this version is much simpler to do. Start from a rectangular cake and use the cut off pieces to build up height in the middle.

OFFICE PARTIES

An opportunity to be funny, rude (use something like Politically Incorrect, page 146) or tasteful, depending on whether it's a retirement party, a Christmas do where everyone lets their hair down, or the managing director's birthday. Bring in as many personal touches as you can – people are very flattered by being included. All of the examples I have given could be added to or adapted to include references to company employees or management.

AN UNTIDY DESK

My desk is usually in a very similar state to that of my handbag – descriptions could vary from a kind 'characterful' to an honest 'chaotic', but I do occasionally have a blitz and sort it all out. It's amazing what I come across hidden under layers of interesting and diverse objects. This desk is relatively tidy, but you could really go to town and pile it up with all sorts of stuff relevant to the particular person. I like this one being obviously that of a female, and I like to think that the user has achieved a good mixture of power and frivolity in her life – I'm sure that's an extremely important document she's working on between doing her nails.

If you use the gold colour on the handles do remember to remove them completely before cutting the cake. If you want them to be edible you could use a golden yellow instead.

Serves 25

INGREDIENTS

2 × 20 × 15 cm (8 × 6 in) Sponge Cakes (page 165)
350 g (12 oz) Buttercream (page 166)
1.1 kg (2½ lb) Roll-Out Icing (page 166)
100 g (4 oz) Royal Icing (page 166)
various food colours, including brown, black and gold

SPECIAL EQUIPMENT

25 cm (10 in) square cake board
paintbrush
piping bag with no. 1 nozzle
photograph

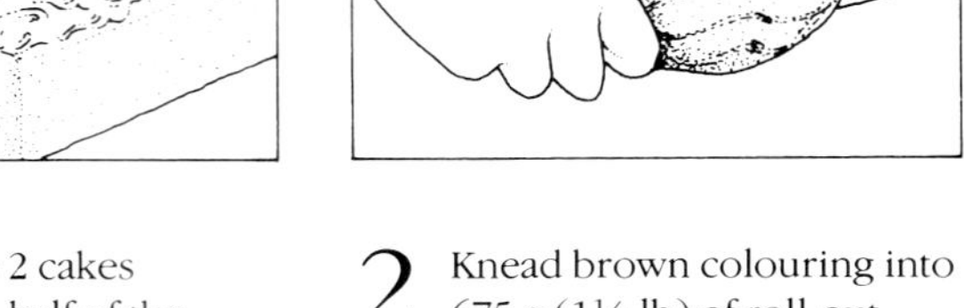

1 Sandwich the 2 cakes together with half of the buttercream.

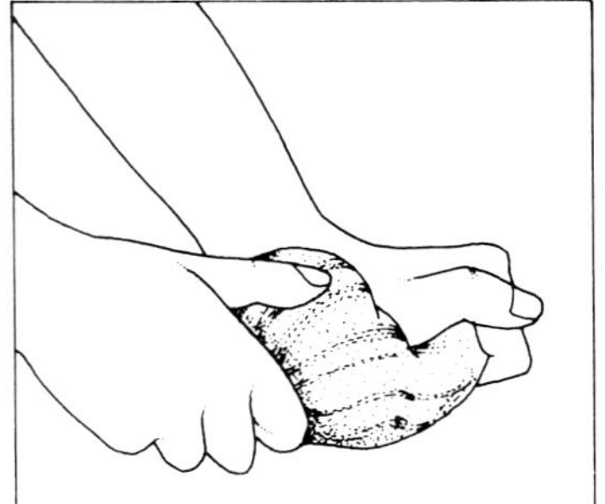

2 Knead brown colouring into 675 g (1½ lb) of roll-out icing to create a mottled wooden effect. Stick the cake towards the back of the board with a tiny amount of dampened icing. Roll out the brown icing and cover the entire cake, smoothing the sides well and making sharp corners.

ELLE
VOGUE

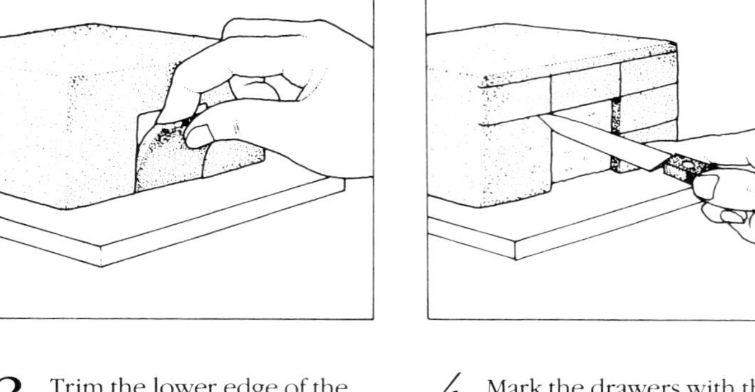

3 Trim the lower edge of the cake and cut out a kneehole shape from the icing on one long side.

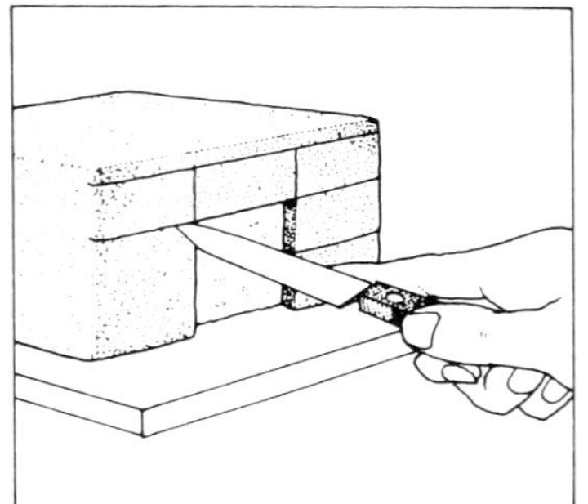

4 Mark the drawers with the back of a knife.

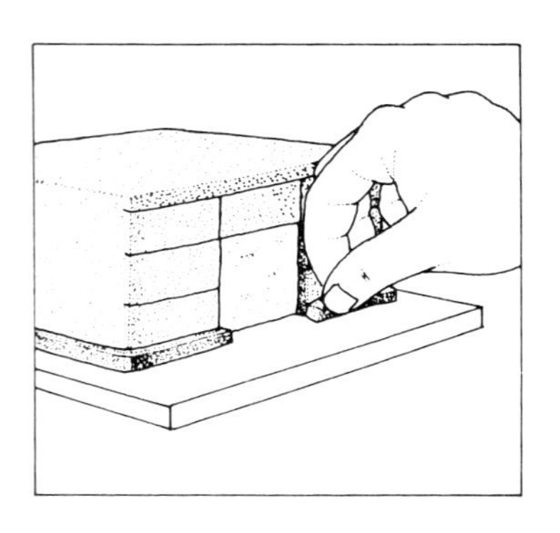

5 From the brown trimmings, roll out and cut some strips to go round the bottom edge, leaving out the kneehole shape.

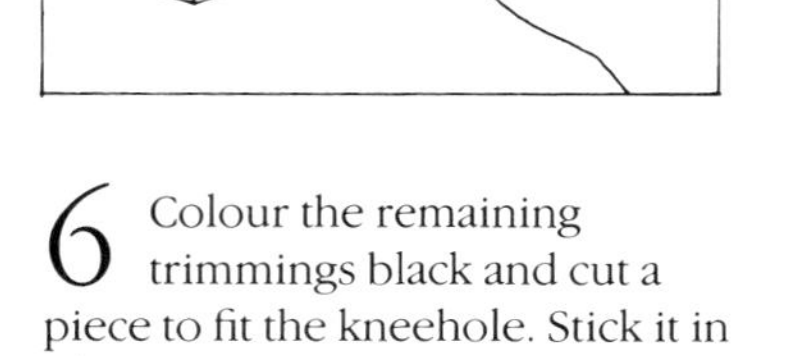

6 Colour the remaining trimmings black and cut a piece to fit the kneehole. Stick it in place with scraps of buttercream.

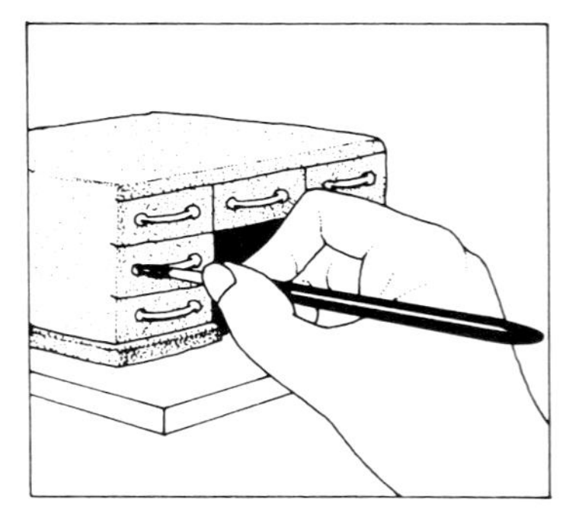

7 Using the no. 1 nozzle, pipe handles on to the drawers and let them dry. Paint them gold or yellow.

8 Use the remaining roll-out icing to model some suitable objects for the desk. Cut out a little icing 'frame' and stick it over the photograph. Add a back and a strut. Let everything dry then paint, damp and stick them to the desk, and the waste paper bin to the board.

Telephone

Modern telephones can do such an extraordinary range of things – from sending faxes to telling you the cost of your calls – that I'm sure it won't be long before they make the lunch at the same time. This one looks relatively simple, but is just as effective at sending happy birthday wishes down the line.

Serves 15

INGREDIENTS

20 cm (8 in) square Fruit Cake (page 166)
450 g (1 lb) marzipan
900 g (2 lb) Roll-Out Icing (page 166)
sieved jam
blue, cream and black food colours

SPECIAL EQUIPMENT

25 × 20 cm (10 × 8 in) cake board
crimpers (optional)
modelling tool
paintbrush

1 Colour about 350 g (12 oz) of roll-out icing blue. Dampen the board. Roll out the icing and cover the board. Trim and crimp the edges.

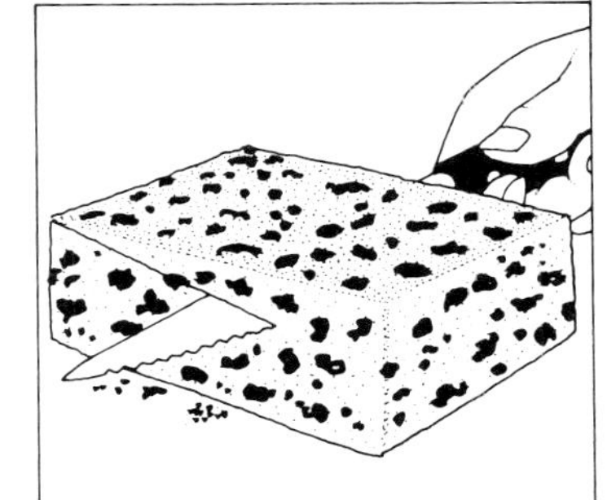

2 Cut 5 cm (2 in) strip off one side of the cake. Trim the larger piece to a slant.

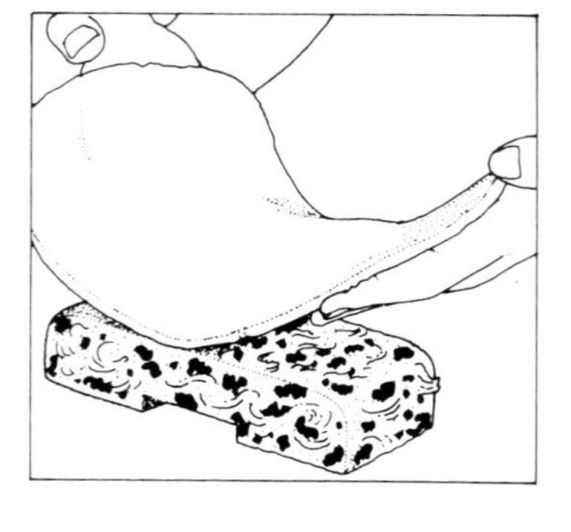

3 Trim the smaller piece down to a receiver shape. Spread both shapes with jam and cover with the marzipan.

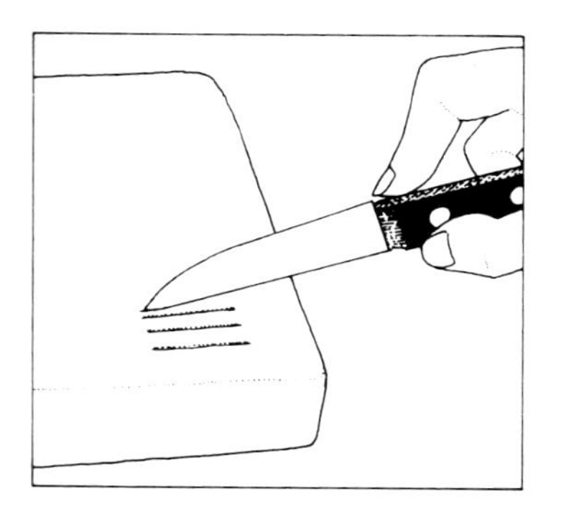

4 Keeping back about 50 g (2 oz), colour the remaining roll-out icing cream. Dampen and cover the telephone and receiver separately. Mark some sound slots with a modelling tool or the back of a knife.

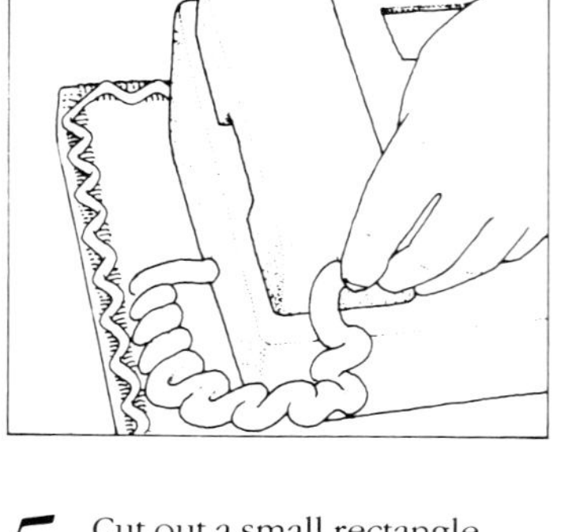

5 Cut out a small rectangle from the top right corner of the icing on the telephone cake. Stick the cake to the board with a small piece of dampened icing. Dampen and stick the receiver in position. Roll a long sausage from the icing trimmings and twist it into a spiral. Stick it in position.

6 Roll out the remaining white icing and cut out a small rectangle. Stick it into the hole. Add a small frame from cream trimmings. Cut out 12 little squares and stick them in position. Let them dry a little then paint on the details with black colour.

123 4567890
POLICE
AMBULANCE
FIRE
999
operator-100
1 2 3
4 5 6
7 8 9
* 0 #

Cash Box

Make this in the same way as the Golden Jewellery Box (page 105). I've used silver and gold colouring on icing coins which must be removed before cutting the cake, but if you are short of time the chocolate, foil-covered coins would work just as well.

Company Logo

You can see how very effective a run-out can be. The principle is exactly the same as for the car (page 129) but you have to be very careful not to flood the letters too much or the icing will spill over. I've used white food colouring in the centre of the plaque – it's worth buying some as it can be used in many ways, including covering up mistakes.

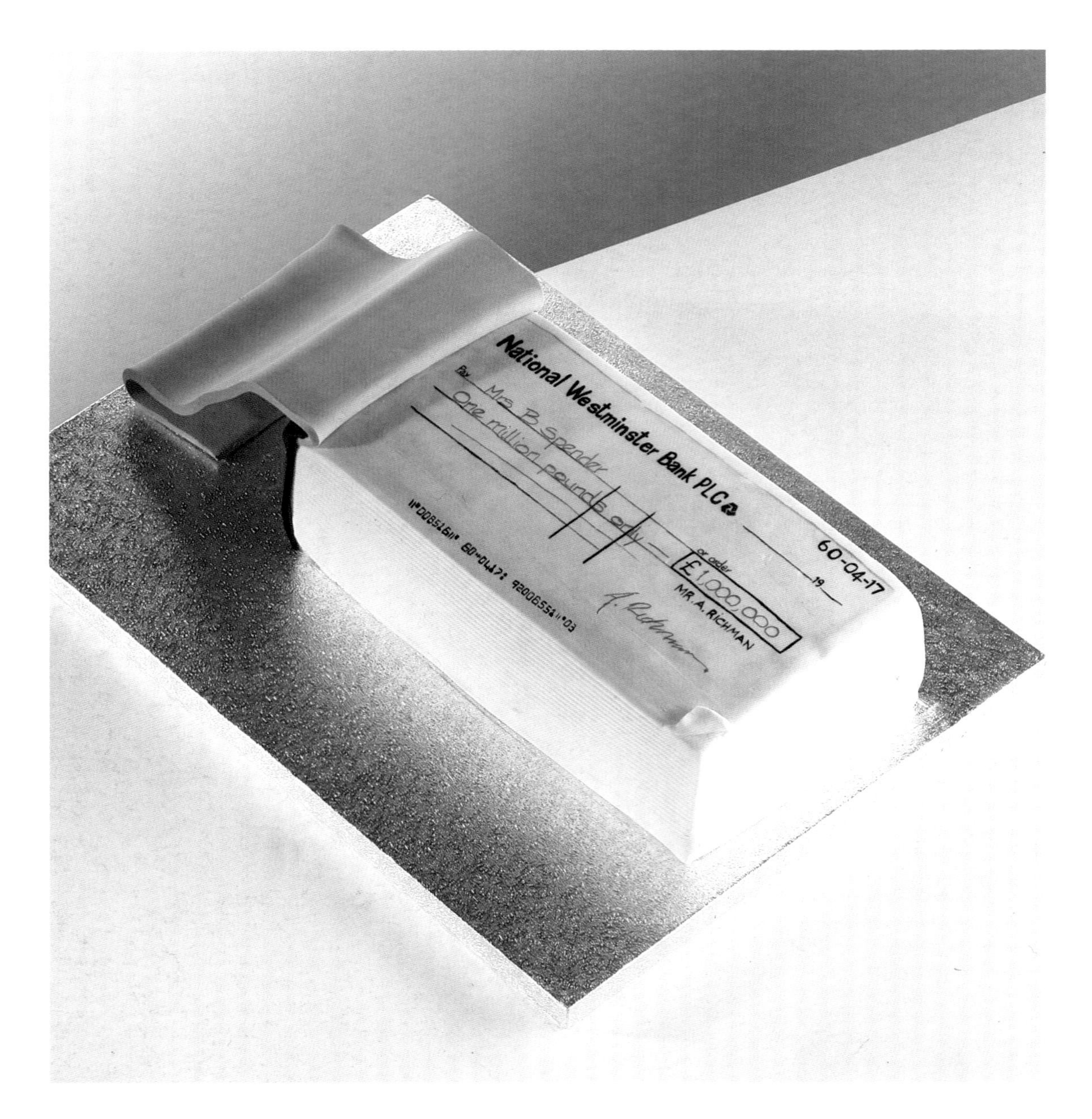

Cheque Book

A good way of giving somebody a million pound birthday present! When you have covered the cake with icing, mark narrow lines on the sides with a ruler or the edge of a side smoother and make sure you copy the details off a real cheque to give it authenticity. Be careful if you sign your own name – they say you can write a cheque on anything . . .

Word Processor

Not the most beautiful of machines – certainly the old typewriters had more character – but for anyone that writes it can become a very close companion. When I started using one the little flashing cursor made me feel uncomfortable, as if it were impatiently waiting for me to start, but now that I'm used to it I wouldn't want to work on anything else. Use the screen to write whatever message you like.

Cars and Bikes

If someone is fond of their car it can make a very satisfying subject for a cake – or make someone a miniaturized version of the one they've always wanted. There are several different techniques given in this section which you can almost certainly adapt to produce the vehicle in question.

You don't have to stick to modern means of transport, of course. The painting or run-out method would work very well for reproducing all sorts of ideas, from a stage coach to a sledge pulled by huskies. And don't forget trains and aeroplanes – both are extremely popular and make magnificent subjects.

As usual, if you find the idea you want to reproduce rather daunting then take a small, representative piece of it instead. A bicycle bell, a steering wheel, a well-known car insignia, a driving glove, a tyre – there's always something that can easily be made.

Racing Car

This way of making a picture on top of a cake – called a 'run-out' – is a technique well worth mastering as it is easier than it looks and very effective. It's worth using a picture of exactly the right size so you can copy it directly on to the cake; use a photocopier at a local stationer to scale it up or down if necessary. When you have learnt how to do it straight on to a cake, you can start experimenting with doing run-outs on to non-stick baking parchment. Left long enough to dry, they can be lifted off carefully and stuck on to the cake later – very useful for last-minute decorations such as on to ice-cream cakes.

Serves 12

INGREDIENTS

20 cm (8 in) square Sponge Cake (page 165)
225 g (8 oz) Buttercream (page 166)
450 g (1 lb) Roll-Out Icing (page 166)
450 g (1 lb) Royal Icing (page 166)
blue, brown, red and black food colours

SPECIAL EQUIPMENT

25 cm (10 in) square cake board
crimping tool
tracing paper or greaseproof paper
picture to copy
paintbrush
knitting needle
sewing needle
piping bags with nos. 1, 2 and 6 nozzles

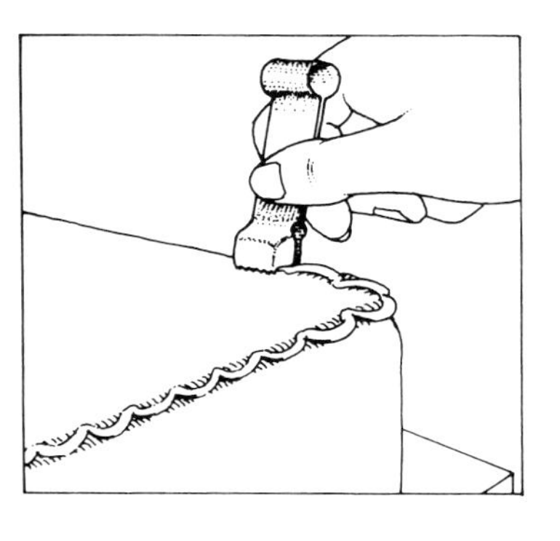

1 Split the cake in half horizontally and sandwich it together with some buttercream. Stick the cake to the board with a little buttercream then spread the remainder all over the cake. Roll out the roll-out icing and cover the cake. Crimp round the top edge.

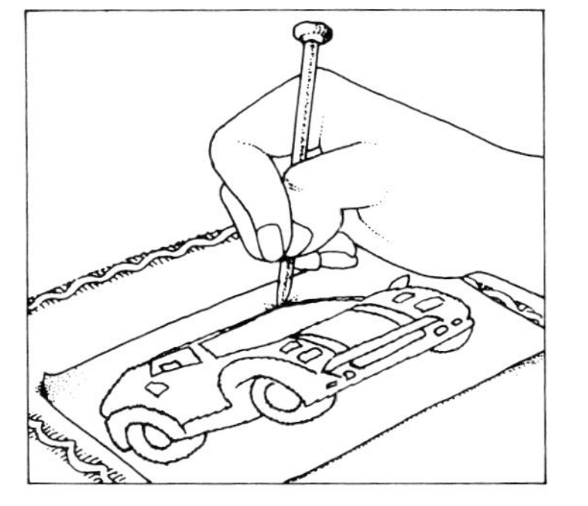

2 Trace the picture on to greaseproof paper. Place the picture over the cake and use the end of a paintbrush or a knitting needle to mark over the lines, indenting them slightly into the icing. Use the sewing needle to mark through the lines at key points as well if necessary.

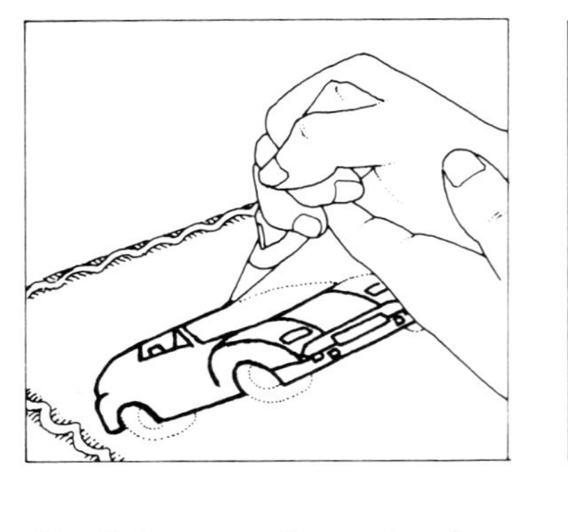

3 Colour a small quantity of royal icing red and pipe over the lines, excluding the wheels, using a no.1 nozzle.

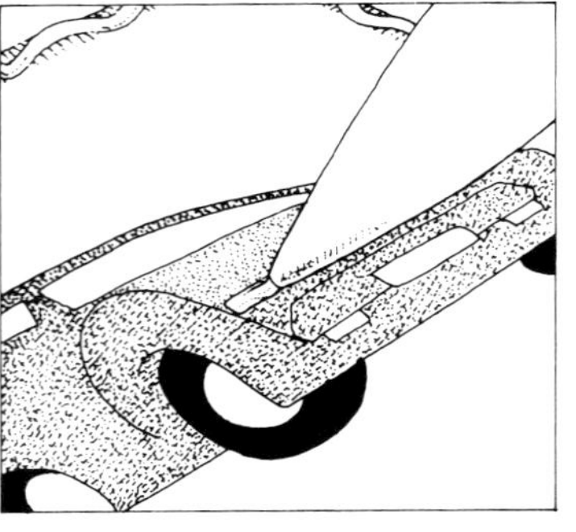

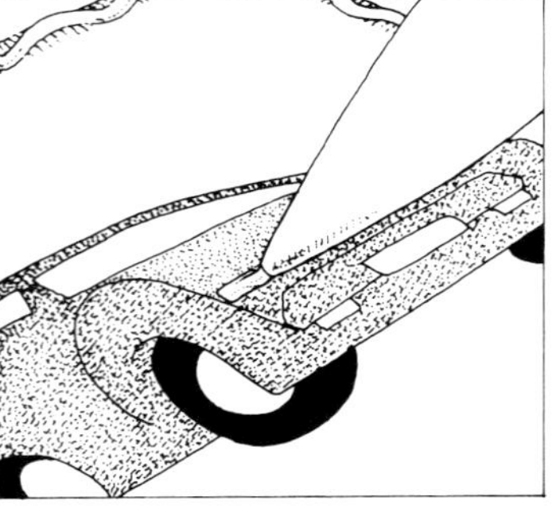

4 Colour a small quantity of royal icing black and pipe round the wheels. Add a little water to the red icing until it is of flooding consistency. Using no. 2 nozzle or a piping bag with the end snipped off, flood each red section of the car, letting adjacent sections dry before adding the next.

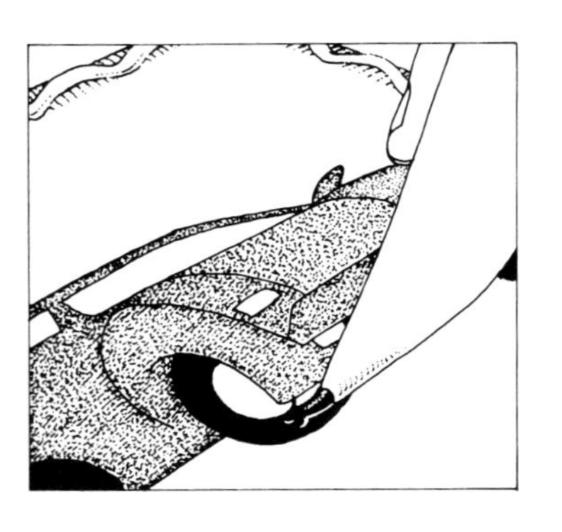

5 Flood the wheels in black.

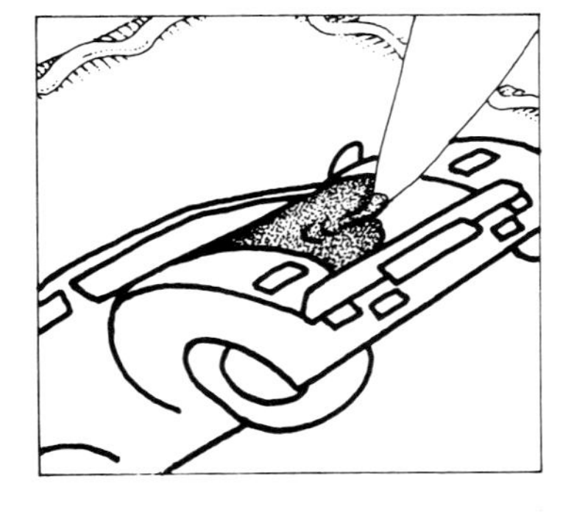

6 Flood the windscreen, number plate and headlights in white icing. Let it all dry.

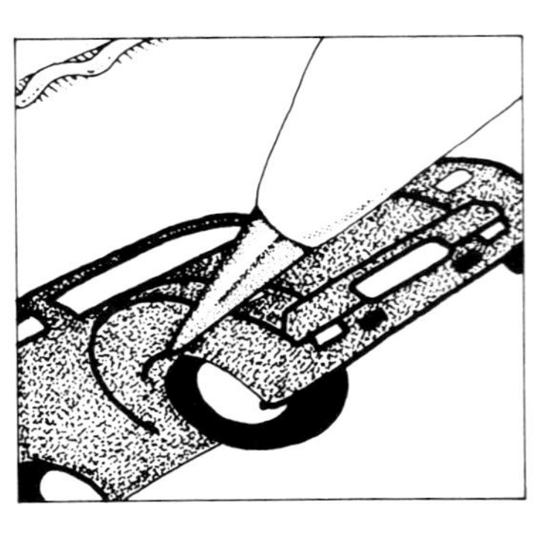

7 Using a no. 1 nozzle, pipe over the lines in black to define them.

8 Pipe the windscreen wipers and details on to the car, including the number plate. Paint the centres of the wheels and a blue sheen on the windscreen. Paint the ground mottled brown. Using a no. 6 nozzle, pipe a shell pattern round the lower edge of the cake with the remaining royal icing.

UR 18
Happy Birthday

PORSCHE

If you can't afford to give him the real thing – and which man *hasn't* wanted a Porsche at some stage of his life? – then why not make him this magnificent substitute. It uses no petrol, gives off no fumes and is wonderfully silent. If you press me, though, I have to admit it doesn't go very fast.

Serves 20

INGREDIENTS

25 × 25 cm (10 × 10 in) Fruit Cake (page 166)
900 g (2 lb) marzipan
1.1 kg (2½ lb) Roll-Out Icing (page 166)
25 g (1 oz) gum tragacanth
black, red, tangerine and silver (page 164) food colours
sieved jam
edible glaze

SPECIAL EQUIPMENT

30 cm (12 in) long oval cake board
6 cm (2½ in) round cutter
non-stick baking parchment
plastic bags
paintbrush
modelling tool

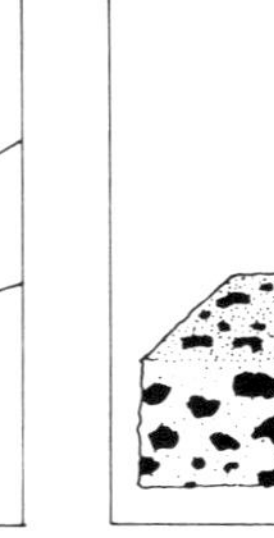

1 Cut from the cake a rectangle 25 × 11.5 cm (10 × 4½ in) and 5.5 cm (2¼ in) high. Cut another piece 15 × 11.5 cm (6 × 4½ in) and 4 cm (1½ in) high.

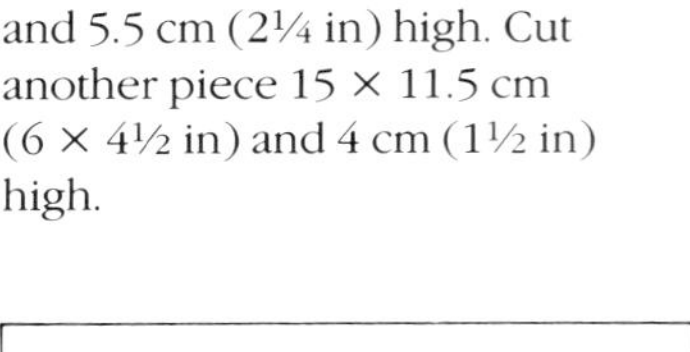

2 Stick the smaller piece on top of the larger one towards the back with jam.

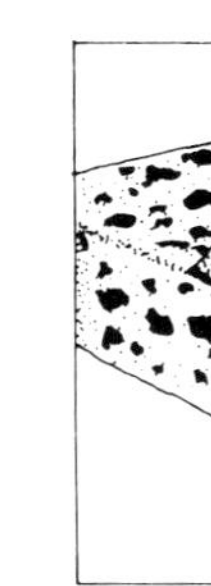

3 Cut slanting pieces off the top cake to shape the windows and windscreen, until the top of the roof measures about 6 cm (2½ in) square.

4 Trim the back of the car at a sloping angle.

UR A 1

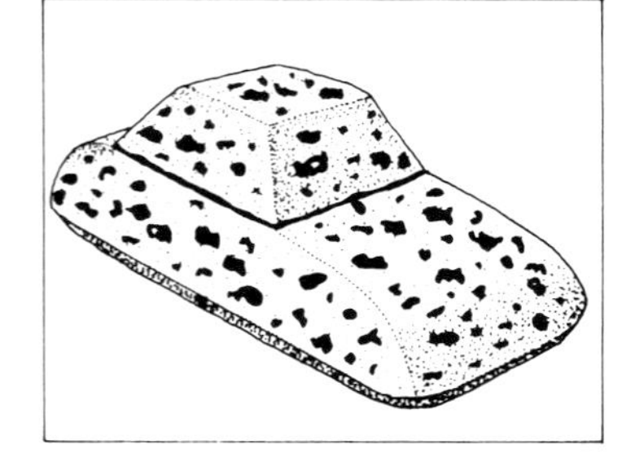

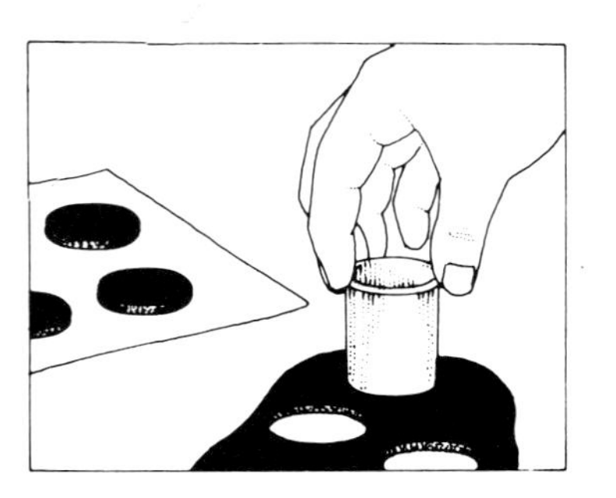

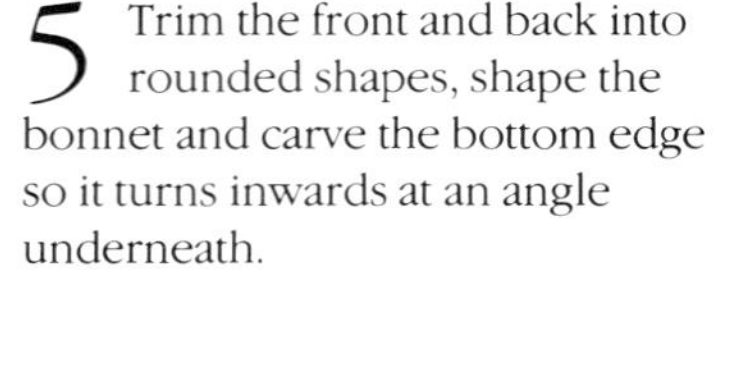

5 Trim the front and back into rounded shapes, shape the bonnet and carve the bottom edge so it turns inwards at an angle underneath.

6 Fill any holes or gaps with pieces of marzipan. Roll out 2 sausages of marzipan and stick them to the bonnet with a little jam to make the headlight shapes. Spread the cake with jam and cover it with the remaining marzipan.

7 Colour about 175 g (6 oz) of roll-out icing black. Knead the gum tragacanth into about one-third of the black icing, keeping the rest in a plastic bag. Roll out and cut 4 wheels with a round cutter. Leave them to dry on non-stick paper. Colour 675 g (1½ lb) of roll-out icing red. Dampen the car, excluding all the windows, wheels and a strip about 1 cm (½ in) round the bottom edge. Roll out the red icing and smooth it over the car.

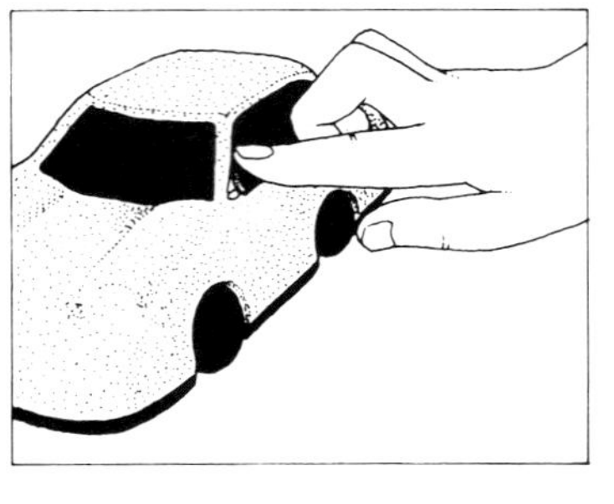

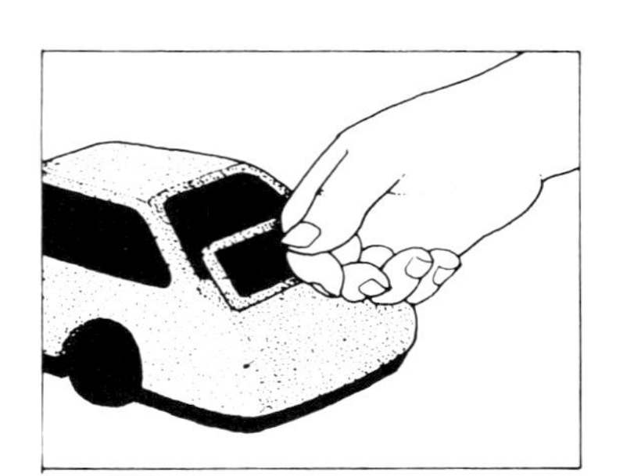

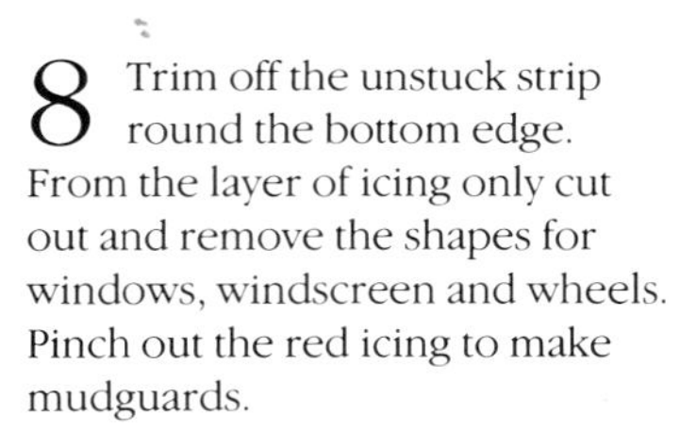

8 Trim off the unstuck strip round the bottom edge. From the layer of icing only cut out and remove the shapes for windows, windscreen and wheels. Pinch out the red icing to make mudguards.

9 Mark the doors, bumpers, bonnet line and lights with the modelling tool. Stick the wheels in position, roll out the remaining black icing and cut pieces to fit into the windows, windscreen and along the lower edge. Stick them in position with a little water. Add some little red wing mirrors.

10 Cut a rectangular shape from the red trimmings for the back and stick it in position. Cut out the middle and fill with black. Cut and stick some reflectors and paint them orange. Cut 2 white circles for the headlights. Paint silver on the wheels and cut, stick and paint the registration plates. Add a spoiler to back. Colour the remaining roll-out icing grey and cover the board. Lift the car on to the board. Paint it with edible glaze.

Suzuki Jeep

Simply cut two shapes in a similar way to the Porsche (page 132) and pile one on top of the other to create this jeep. It also shows how you can create a scene on the board – here a road and grass verges – using two different types of icing.

Classic Citroën 2 CV

If you don't feel up to creating a car entirely out of cake – like the Porsche (page 132) – then you can make a little model and put it on top of a simple cake. It has the advantage that the car can be kept indefinitely as a souvenir.

HARLEY-DAVIDSON®

Half way between a model and a run-out this 'bas relief' technique can be useful for all kinds of cakes. Sketch the shape roughly on to the icing with food colour then fill it in with pieces of icing moulded to shape. Let it dry a little before painting – and remember to remove all the silver before eating.

Mountain Bike

This shows how effective simply painting a picture on to a cake with food colours can be. Try to find a picture to copy, and if necessary trace it on to the cake (as for the run-out car page 129) before filling in the colour.

His and Hers

Yes, I'm being sexist, I know, by admitting there could be a difference in the types of cakes suitable for the two genders. But remember they can often be swapped to great effect; don't be bound by the stereotypes! A basket of dirty washing for a man can make a wonderful hint (unless you have one of the endangered species that actually does it already?). Subjects that a few years ago we would have thought of as essentially masculine like cars, boats, carpentry tools or football boots could nowadays equally well apply to women.

BASKET OF WASHING

I made a cake like a sink full of washing up a few years ago for Mother's Day and it was a great success. This one is along similar lines, and it's fun to make it as personal as possible, adding John's football shirt or Dad's dirty socks as applicable. I promise it smells a lot sweeter than the real thing.

Serves 30

INGREDIENTS
2 × 20 cm (8 in) round Fruit Cakes (page 166)
675 g (1½ lb) white marzipan
900 g (2 lb) Roll-Out Icing (page 166)
various food colours
sieved jam

SPECIAL EQUIPMENT
25 cm (10 in) long oval cake board
paintbrush

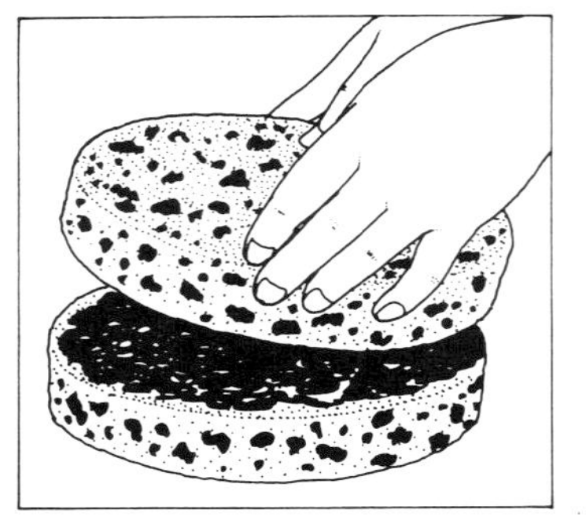

1 Trim the tops of the cakes and stick one on top of the other with jam and a thin layer of marzipan.

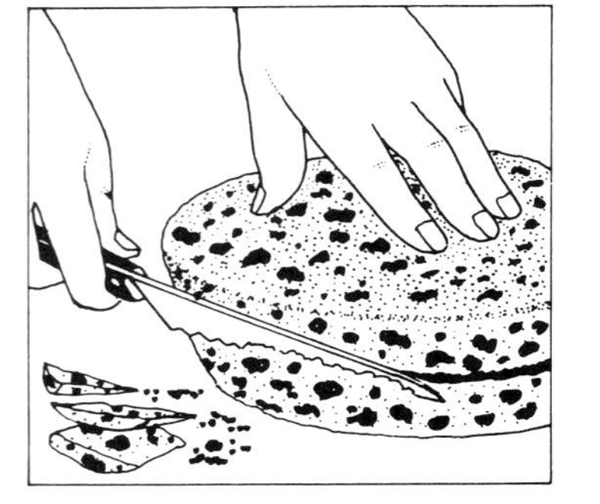

2 With a sharp serrated knife, trim the cake to an oval, then shape slanted sides and top. Using the trimmings, make a domed top.

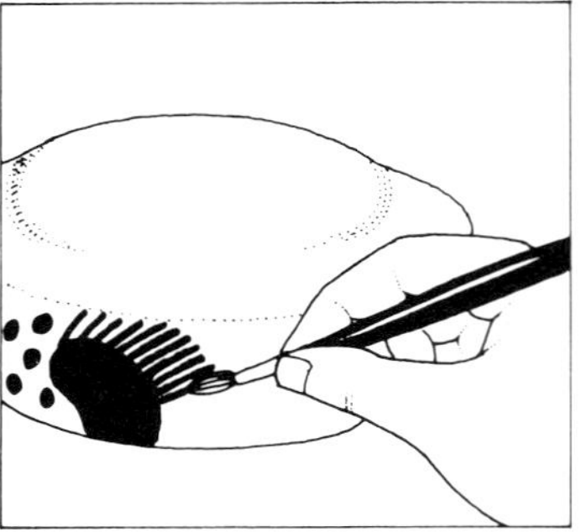

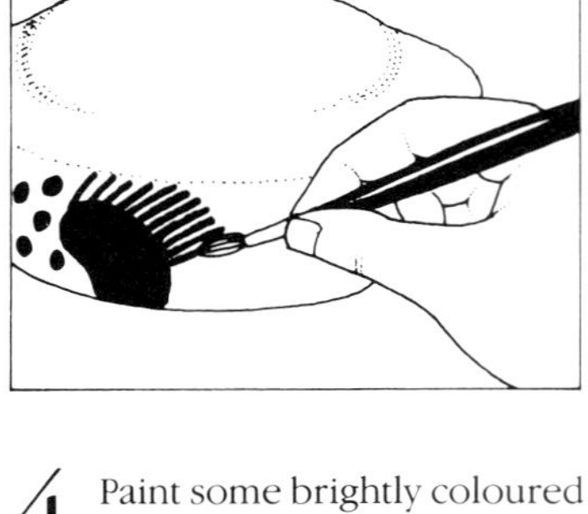

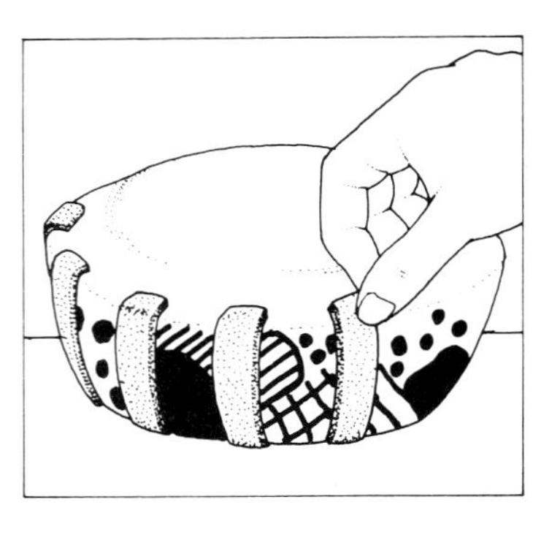

3 Stick the cake to the board with a tiny bit of dampened icing. Spread the cake all over with jam. Roll out the remaining marzipan and cover the cake. Let it dry for a few hours.

4 Paint some brightly coloured 'washing' on the side of the cake.

5 Colour 450 g (1 lb) of roll-out icing red. Roll out and cut some strips about 2 cm (¾ in) wide and the height of the cake. Stick them to the sides of the cake with water.

6 Roll and cut out 2 long red strips to go round the side and stick them on with water. Roll, cut and stick a thicker strip for the top edge. Model 2 handles from the trimmings and stick them on.

7 Model 'washing' from differently coloured pieces of the remains of the icing. Roll and cut out small 'shirts', 'socks' etc. Paint on some brown food colour 'dirt'.

8 Drape and stick the washing on to the basket. Paint some patterns on to pieces that show with the paintbrush and food colours.

Saucy Boat

I first decorated a cake with undressed ladies about twenty years ago, and it created a very satisfying sensation. They remain extremely popular, and however much we may like to think the world has moved on, I suspect a beautiful yacht with gorgeous women draped alluringly over it will still be a fantasy for many men. As few of them will achieve this in reality – either the boat or the women willing to strip off and lie around being decorative – why not produce one for him in sugar? Or model some naked men for a girl friend? Do remember to remove the cocktail sticks and the silver ladder rails before cutting the cake.

Serves 18

INGREDIENTS

20 cm (8 in) square Fruit Cake (page 166)
675 g (1½ lb) marzipan
1.1 kg (2½ lb) Roll-Out Icing (page 166)
900 g (2 lb) Royal Icing (page 166)
blue, brown, black, red, paprika, yellow and silver food colours
sieved jam

SPECIAL EQUIPMENT

25 cm (10 in) square cake board
paintbrush
1 packet cocktail sticks
piping bag with no. 1 nozzle
palette knife.

1 Trim the cake to a boat shape, using the template on page 177 as a guide.

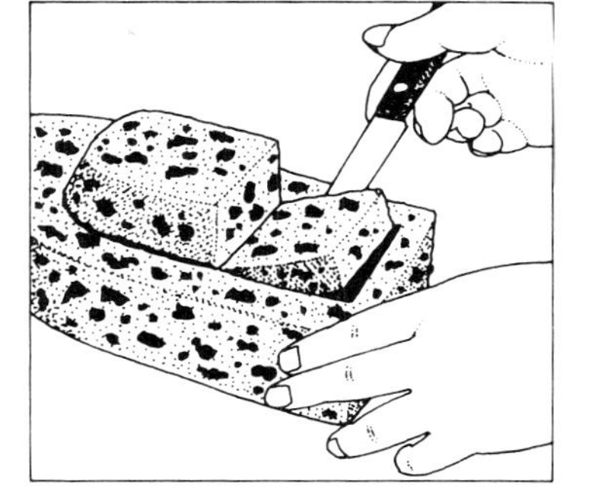

2 With the trimmings, build up a raised section in the centre of the boat, about 5–7.5 cm (2–3 in) high. Stick it in place with jam, and use little pieces of marzipan to fill any gaps as necessary. Hollow out a square section about 1 cm (½ in) deep behind the raised piece to form the sunbathing lower deck.

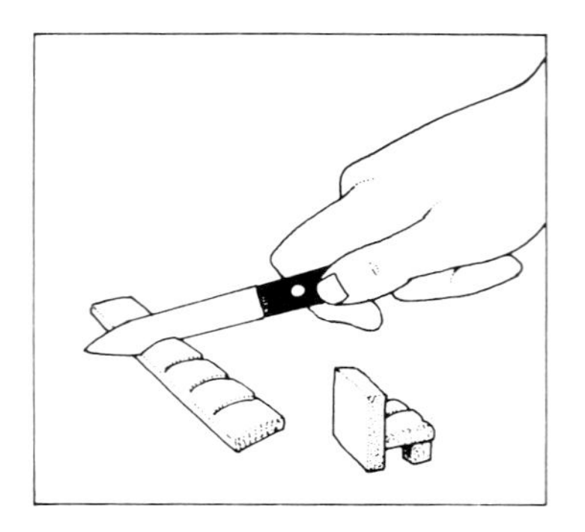

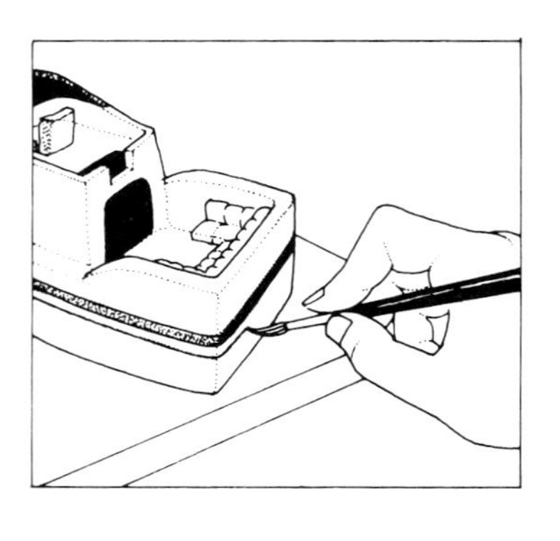

3 Spread the cake with jam. Roll out the marzipan and drape it over the entire shape, smoothing it into corners etc. Stick the cake to the board with a little royal icing. Roll out about 675 g (1½ lb) of icing and cover the entire cake, smoothing and pressing into the hollow section. From the trimmings, roll and cut 3 strips to go around the back of the deck. Roll and cut a windscreen and stick it to the front of the raised section.

4 Colour about 100 g (4 oz) of roll-out icing pale blue. Cut out a little seat for the upper deck and a strip for the sunbathing area. Mark the strip into seats with a knife. Stick it in place with a little water.

5 Cut out and stick 2 little hold covers on to the front deck. Model and stick a wheel. Paint the windscreen and hold covers black. Paint brown doors and a brown strip on the upper deck. Paint blue and red lines round the side and a name.

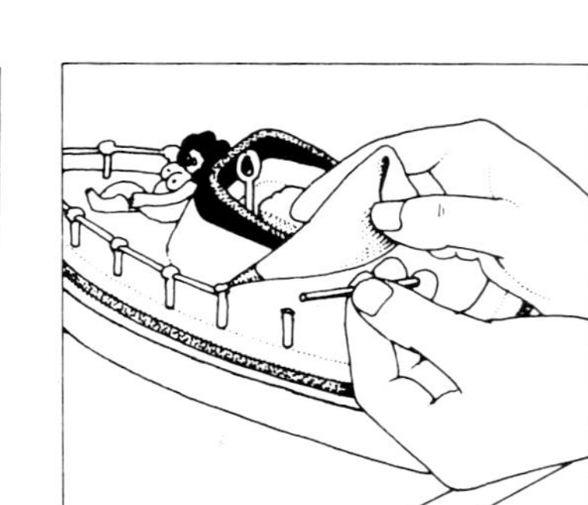

6 Model 2 ladder rails and stick them in position. Colour the remaining icing with a tiny amount of paprika to make flesh colour and model 3 ladies. Pipe hair on with coloured royal icing and paint on the features. Stick the ladies to the boat in interesting positions.

7 Trim about 42 cocktail sticks with scissors to equal lengths. Push some into the cake and stick the others across the top with piped royal icing. Let them dry.

8 Paint cocktail sticks and ladder rails with silver colour, making sure the paint does not touch the icing on the cake itself. Keeping back a small amount of white, colour the royal icing blue. Spread it on to the board and the sides of the boat with a palette knife to look like waves. Pipe some sea spray with the white icing, using a piping bag with the end snipped off.

J.A.P.C. 1

Politically Incorrect

Well it's not to my taste but it's quite a funny cake for the right person, and after all if you can't have the cake you want in the privacy of your own home . . . Use one large and one small square cake, slice pieces off the smaller one to lower the height and add the cut-off pieces to the larger one to increase the difference. Shape sensually . . .

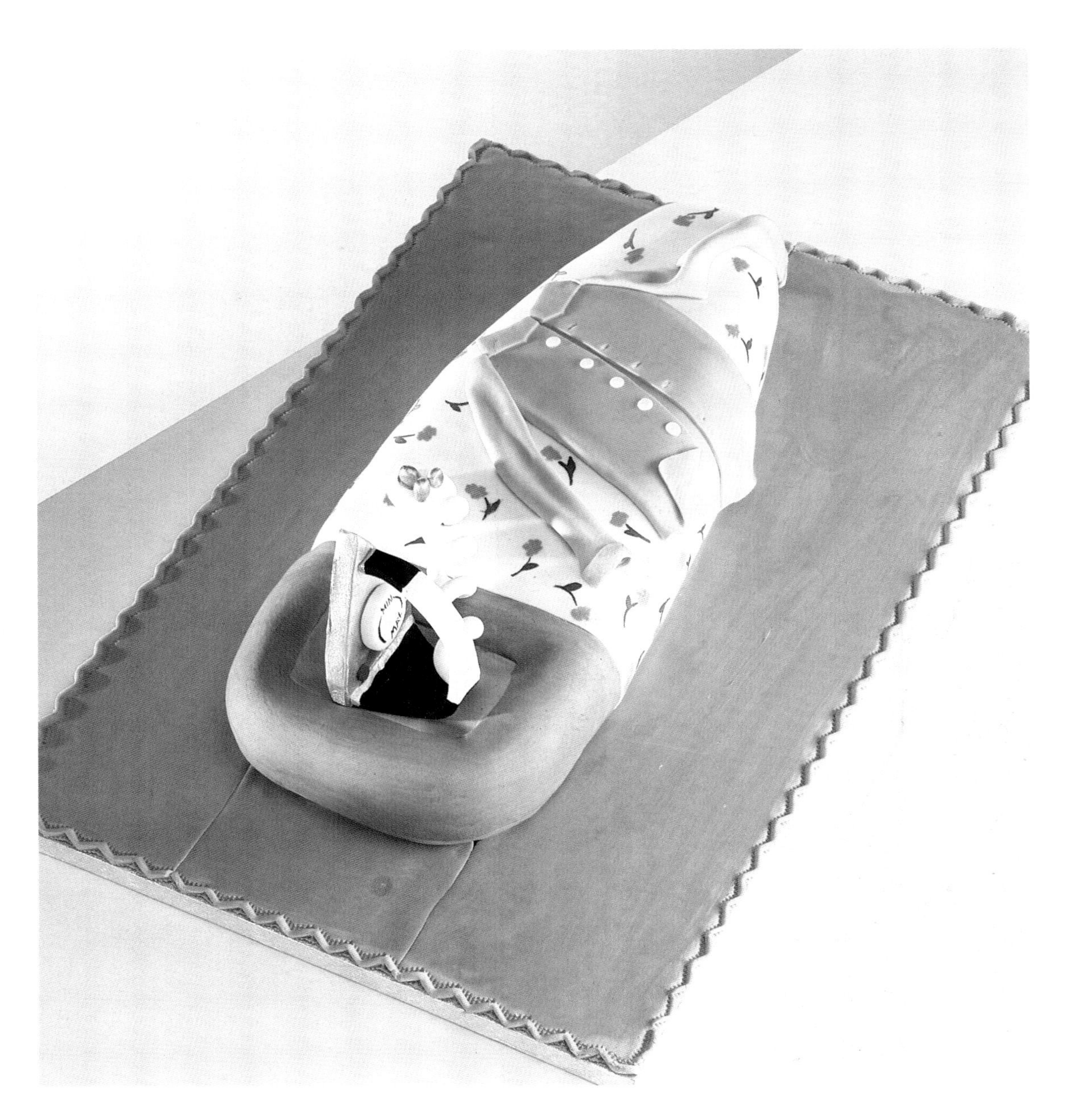

Iron and Ironing Board

A variation on the washing basket theme. As with the washing, it might be a good idea to make it for the man in your life, especially as an antidote to the previous cake – we don't want them to think life's *all* going to be fun, do we?

Briefcase

A very easy cake to make, and if you add the newspaper you can write all sorts of relevant headlines. I've sometimes made this for Father's Day with a little sugar baby on the top. It would also be a lovely cake for a businesswoman, perhaps in pink with a magazine on the top – oh dear, here I go being sexist again.

Chanel Handbag

I was originally asked to make this for a man (well, *chacun à son goût*, as they say) and I thought it made a very elegant cake. For a woman who likes to dress well a little Chanel accessory like this will make her day.

FAVOURITE CHARACTERS

An almost limitless area for good ideas – think of cartoons, for instance. When I was young they were mostly those in comics (I loved Keyhole Kate and Beryl the Peril) but with the advent of television a whole new range of them has developed. It's largely a question of finding out which one is currently popular, and certainly don't assume that because your niece Jenny liked Princess Toadstool last time you talked to her that she will still like her now. An up-to-date check is essential – last year's craze is usually this year's has-been. Look at Ninja Turtles . . . who?

Sooty's Castle

Of course, you can put whichever characters you like on to this beautiful castle, but I thought it was about time Sooty, Sweep and Soo had somewhere really grand to live. I have loved them ever since I was very small – from the days of black-and-white television – and I'm delighted to see a whole new generation of children appreciating their charms. I once performed in a play at the Mayfair Theatre in the evenings when Sooty was appearing in a matinée every afternoon, and I was very honoured to be sharing a dressing room with him. I kept hoping to be introduced, but every time I asked his friend, Matthew Corbett, he said Sooty was resting . . .

Start the day before

Serves 30

INGREDIENTS
675 g (1½ lb) Pastillage (page 167)
cornflour
2 × 20 cm (8 in) square Sponge Cakes (page 164)
450 g (1 lb) Buttercream (page 167)
1.1 kg (2½ lb) Roll-Out Icing (page 166)
225 g (8 oz) Royal Icing (page 166)
100 g (4 oz) castor sugar
various food colours

SPECIAL EQUIPMENT
5 30 cm (12 in) cardboard tubes, about 7 cm (2¾ in) diameter
clingfilm
cocktail sticks
non-stick baking parchment
card, scissors and sticky tape
basketweave rolling pin (optional)
13 cm (5 in) saucer or plate
paintbrush
5 cm (2 in) oval cutter
piping bags with nos. 2 and 1 nozzles

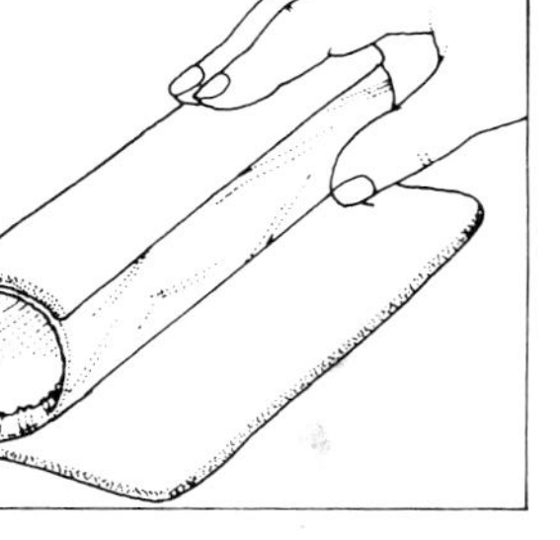

1 Cover one of the cardboard tubes with clingfilm and dust it with cornflour. Roll out about 100 g (4 oz) of pastillage and cover the tube, trimming as necessary and sticking the join with a little water. Leave it to dry for 8 to 10 hours on non-stick paper with the join underneath. Cover the three remaining tubes in same way making sure that all the icing tubes are of the same height and have straight ends.

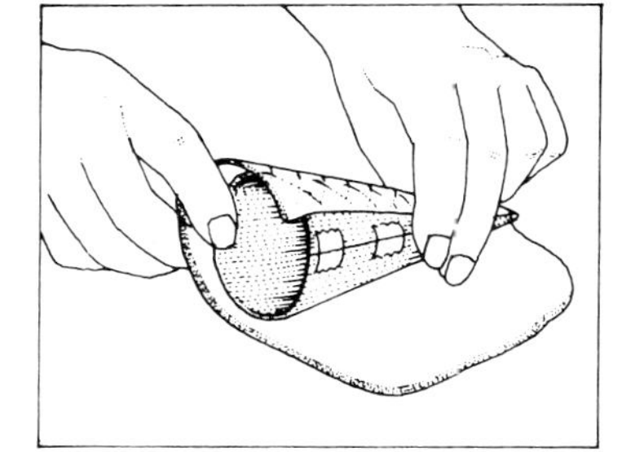

2 With the pastillage trimmings, cut 4 little flags and stick one side of each round a cocktail stick with a little water. Leave them to dry. Make 4 cones from triangular pieces of card measuring 5½ inches deep and 8½ inches wide as shown on page 163, and stick them with tape. Cover the cones with clingfilm and dust with cornflour. Colour the remaining pastillage blue. Take about one-quarter of the blue pastillage. Roll it out then mark it with a basketweave rolling pin if you have one. Cover one of the cones with the pastillage, trimming it as necessary and leaving a tiny hole at the top for the flag. Repeat for the other 3 cones. With the blue trimmings cut a door out. Leave everything to dry on non-stick paper.

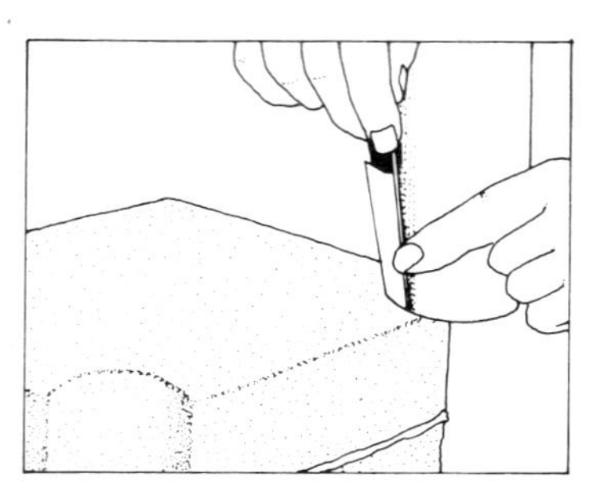

3 Model Sooty, Sweep and Soo – or whatever characters you like – by colouring pieces of icing and making bodies, limbs and heads separately and adding clothes before sticking them together with royal icing.

4 Sandwich the cakes together with half the buttercream. Using the 5th tube as a guide, cut 4 concave corners off both layers of the cake. Stick the cake to the board with a little buttercream. Spread the sides of the cake with about two-thirds of the remaining buttercream. Roll out about 450 g (1 lb) of roll-out icing and cover the sides of the cake.

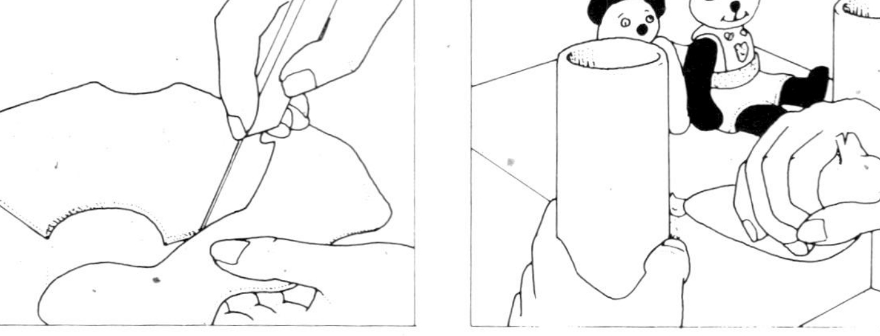

5 Spread the top of the cake with the remaining buttercream. Roll out enough icing to cover the top of the cake entirely. Place the icing on top of the cake. Trim the edges.

6 Stick Sooty and Soo into position with a little royal icing. Leave them to dry. Carefully pull the cardboard tubes out of the dry pastillage and stick the towers to the 4 corners with royal icing. Stick the cones to the top of the towers then insert the flags into the tops, using royal icing to stick them as necessary.

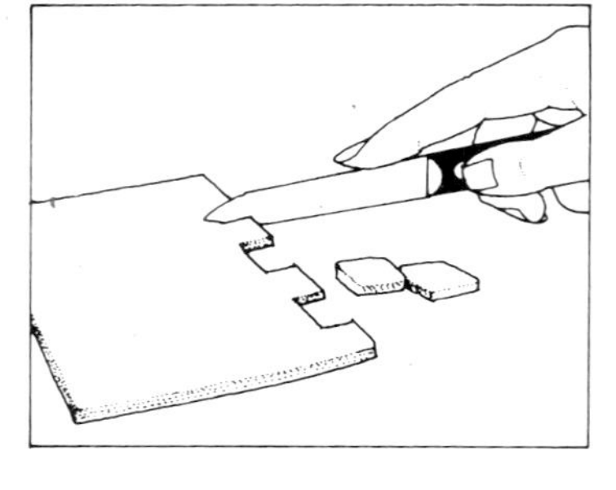

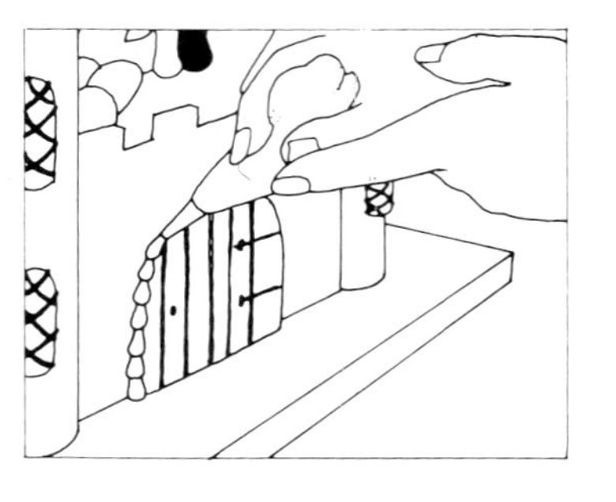

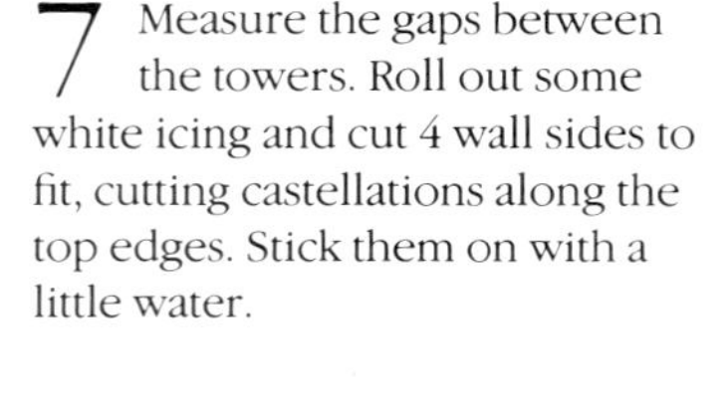

7 Measure the gaps between the towers. Roll out some white icing and cut 4 wall sides to fit, cutting castellations along the top edges. Stick them on with a little water.

8 Roll and cut 6 oval shapes. Cut off the bottoms to make straight edges and stick 4 to the front towers and 2 to the back. Stick the door in position. Paint some lattice work on to the windows and stripes etc to the door. Using a no. 2 nozzle pipe a snail's trail round the door and base of the turret roofs, and using a no. 1 nozzle, pipe round the windows.

9 With green royal icing and a piping bag with the end cut off, pipe some leaves climbing up the castle. Colour some castor sugar green. Cover the remainder of the board with any left-over buttercream or royal icing and press the coloured sugar into the icing. Stick Sweep against the door.

Pop-up Noddy

I first made a cake with a figure bursting out of it when my five-year-old demanded *Superman* for his birthday. The thought of the whole body – particularly flying – was very daunting, so I hit on the idea of Superman punching his way up out of the cake, partly inspired by the model of him in Madame Tussauds. Now I use this technique for all sorts of other ideas and it not only saves making the lower halves of bodies (and legs are always tricky) but it gives the cakes the illusion of movement, which, not being Geppeto or Professor Frankenstein, is the only way I can bring them to life.

Start the day before

Serves 12

INGREDIENTS

20 cm (8 in) round Sponge Cake (page 164)
900 g (2 lb) Roll-Out Icing (page 166)
50 g (2 oz) gum tragacanth
150 g (5 oz) Royal Icing (page 166)
225 g (8 oz) Buttercream (page 167)
red, paprika, yellow, blue, black, brown food colours

SPECIAL EQUIPMENT

25 cm (10 in) round cake board
piping bag with nos. 6 and 1 nozzles
paintbrush
non-stick baking parchment
plastic bags
cocktail sticks
crimper

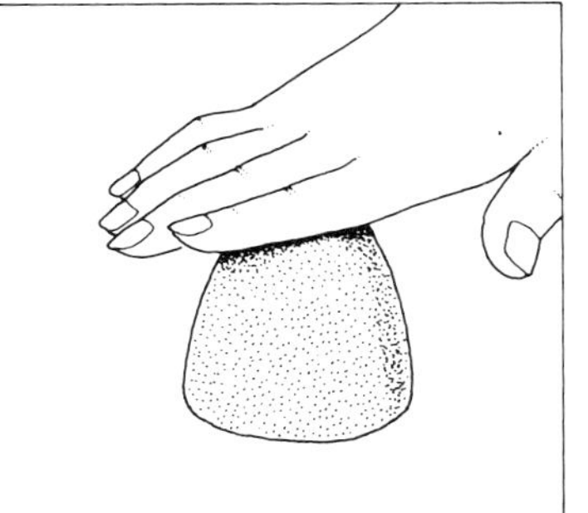

1 Colour about 175 g (6 oz) of roll-out icing red. Using two-thirds of it, form a cone shape then slightly flatten the top, front and back.

2 Colour 100 g (4 oz) of icing flesh colour with a tiny amount of paprika. Use a little piece to form a flattened circle and stick it to the body to make the neck. Colour about 75 g (3 oz) of icing yellow and cut out a scarf. Roll and stick on to chest three little buttons. Stick it to the body and add a little icing 'knot'. Paint red dots on scarf. Model a head from flesh colour icing and stick it to the body, adding a tiny ball for the nose. Make 2 ears and press them onto the sides of the head with a cocktail stick to make ear holes.

3 Roll 2 small balls of white icing in your fingers and press into oval shapes. Stick them on to the head for eyes. Paint blue irises and black pupils, eyelashes and brows and mouth. Colour 25 g (3 oz) of icing blue and model a cone shape. Indent the underneath with your fingers so that it will fit snugly over the head. Stick in place. Bend the top of the cone over and add a little yellow bell. Colour a tiny amount of royal icing brown and pipe spiky hair using the no. 1 nozzle.

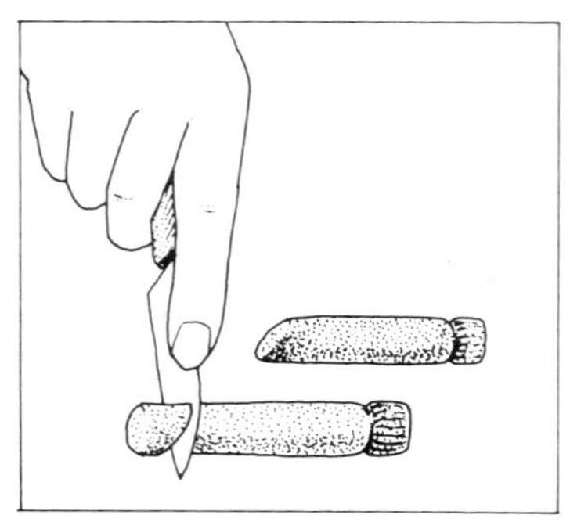

4 Add a little gum tragacanth to the rest of the red icing and roll out two sausage shapes. Mark the ends to look like ribbing and cut the other ends diagonally. Leave them to dry on non-stick paper, then stick them to the body with a little royal icing. Add two flesh coloured hands.

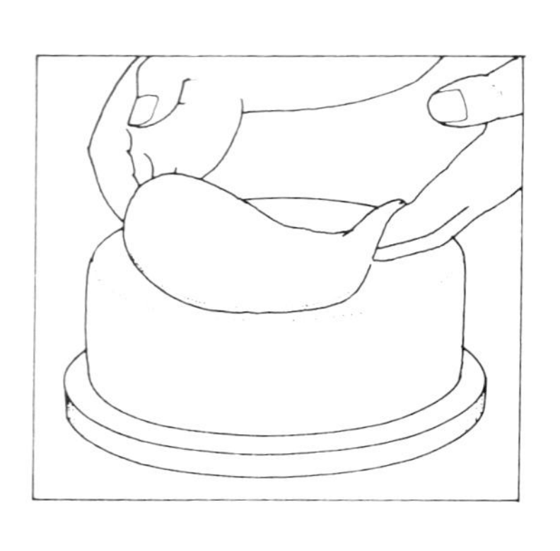

5 Cut the cake in half horizontally and sandwich it together with half of the buttercream. Stick the cake to the board with a little buttercream then spread it all over with the remainder. Roll out about 100 g (4 oz) of roll-out icing. Using a small plate as a guide, cut out a 15 cm (6 in) disc. Place it on the cake.

6 Roll out the remaining icing. Dampen round the edge of the cake top with a little water – do not dampen in the centre. Drape the icing over the cake, smoothing the sides and trimming the lower edge. With the trimmings, cover the board and crimp the edges.

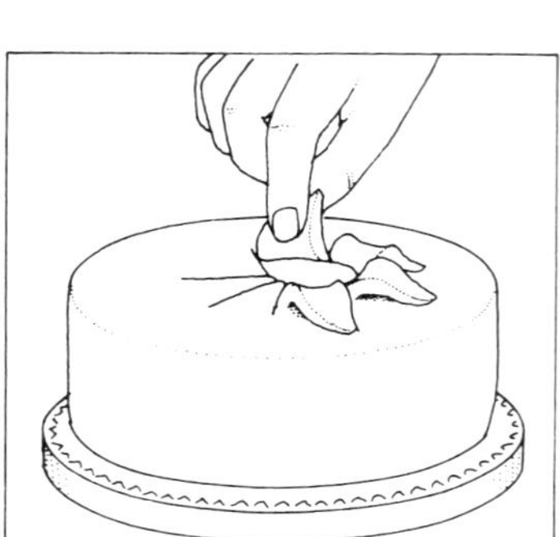
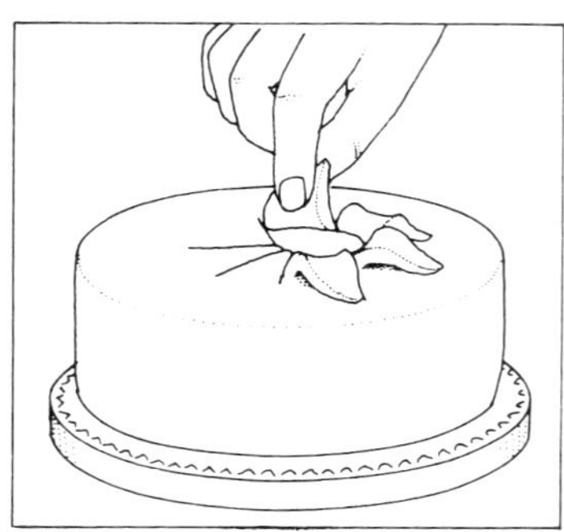

7 Using a saucer or plate as a guide, mark a circle about 10 cm (4 in) diameter in the centre of the cake with the back of the paintbrush. Slash some triangular shapes through the top layer of icing *only* and pull them back. Let them dry for 30 minutes.

8 Paint the pulled back flaps yellow. Stick Noddy into the hole with some royal icing. Pipe a snail's trail round the bottom edge of the cake using about 100 g (4 oz) of royal icing and a no. 6 nozzle. Colour the remaining royal icing red and pipe an inscription with a no. 1 nozzle.

Happy Birthday

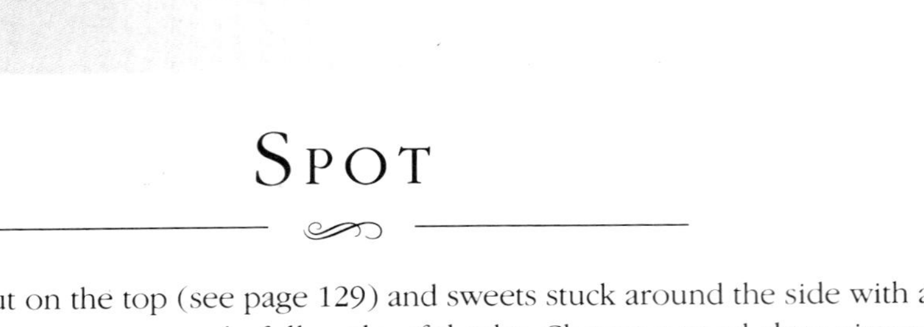

Spot

A simple run-out on the top (see page 129) and sweets stuck around the side with a little royal icing create a wonderfully colourful cake. Choose a good clear picture of the character to trace on to the cake.

Dinosaurs

Dinosaurs seem to be as popular as ever with young children, and if you model them entirely out of icing then they can be kept as little gifts – you may need to make one for each child at the party though!

Pingu and Family

If making a large three-dimensional figure seems a bit daunting this sweet cake shows how delightful small icing models on top can look. Putting them on a sofa has the great advantage of not having to worry about whether they will safely stand up, so this is a good idea for any character with spindly legs. If you include the television don't forget to paint on a programme. Here they're watching *Scott of the Antarctic*.

SPIDER-MAN

Most heads and faces are extremely difficult to reproduce in icing so are best done either small or caricatured. Spider-man's simple but dramatic costume makes him an ideal subject for this treatment. Any mask-like face could be done in the same way.

Basic Equipment, Recipes and Techniques

Over the years, I have assembled a very varied and interesting collection of useful gadgets and tins that help with my cake-making, but there is very little that is essential when you first start. The following brief list will give you an idea of what will be useful, but you can often substitute in an emergency. For instance, baked bean tins are excellent for baking tiny individual cakes.

Basic Equipment

CAKE TINS
You will not need any strangely shaped cake tins to produce the cakes in the book. Round, square, rectangular, pudding basin and occasionally oval are the only ones used. If you don't have rectangular you can always use a square cake and cut off the extra part. The oval is not essential and the designs given can just as easily be produced on a round or square cake.

KNIVES
A good, sharp, serrated knife is essential for cutting cakes to shape. A small sharp plain knife will also be useful. A palette knife is well worth having, too.

SIDE SMOOTHERS
These are very much worth buying to achieve a 'professional' finish.

CUTTERS
I find a good range of cutters very useful, particularly the set of round ones of varying sizes. If you don't have any, however, you can usually find an object of suitable size, such as a glass tumbler or egg cup which will help.

NOZZLES
The only nozzles you will need in this book are nos. 0, 1, 2, 3, 4, 6, 23, 44 and 58. The numbers referred to are those made by Bekenal.

TURNTABLES
A turntable is not essential but you will find it helpful if you are a keen cake decorator. It is particularly useful for marking straight lines round cakes.

PIPING BAGS
Until the last couple of years I have always used nylon piping bags, but I now find it better to make my own from greaseproof paper.

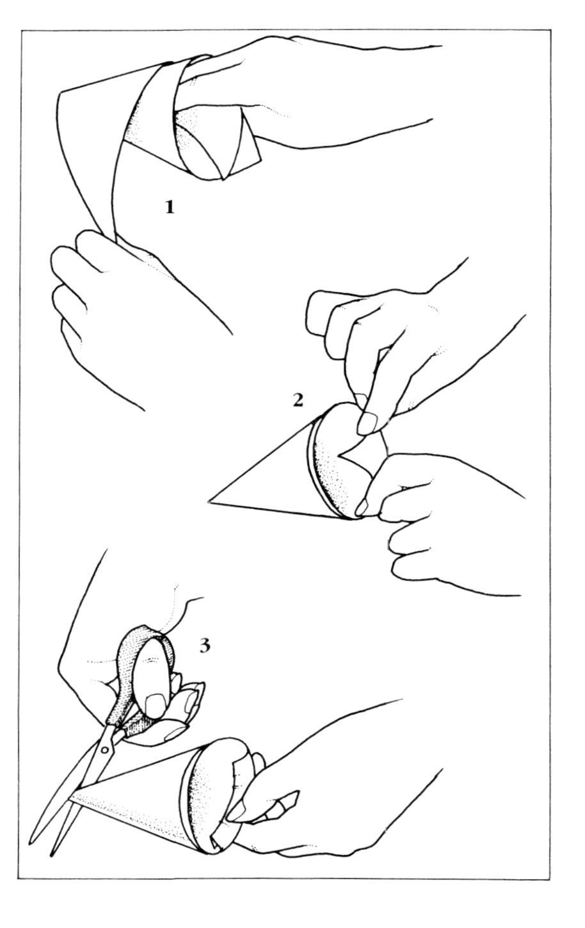

Cut a 25 cm (10 in) square out of greaseproof paper. Fold it in half diagonally.
1 Roll up the triangle into a cone shape, holding the inner edge of the greaseproof paper firmly with your thumb and fingers.
2 Fold back the corners and secure firmly with a paper clip or staple.
3 Snip off the end of the bag and drop in your nozzle.

Edible Equipment

ROLL-OUT ICING
This can be bought from supermarkets in packets, or you may have a local cake shop which will sell you larger quantities.

MARZIPAN
Use a good quality white marzipan, as this is less likely to stain the covering of icing.

FOOD COLOURS
A good selection of food colours is essential. If you are worried about using artificial colours there is now a range of natural colours which is almost as good. For anything that you may want to keep for some time, however, such as the Bridal Teddies or Cinderella, it's better to use the artificial ones which don't fade as quickly as the natural ones tend to do. You may find some icing can be bought ready-coloured – the icing used in this book is made by Renshaw. This saves a lot of time, particularly when using something like black, which takes a lot of colouring.

The silver and gold colours referred to in the book are categorized as non-toxic food colours but are now ruled as being unsuitable to eat. This means that they should not directly touch any part of the cake that is to be eaten. Either make sure that the icing painted with them is peeled off before cutting the cake or use a yellow or grey colour instead.

Basic Recipes

SPONGE CAKE (1 quantity = 1½ pints)

4 eggs
100 g (4 oz) castor sugar
100 g (4 oz) plain flour
75 g (3 oz) butter (optional)

Pre-heat the oven to gas mark 4, 180°C (350°F). Grease and flour the 6 inch round cake tin.

Whisk the eggs and sugar in a warm bowl for 5 to 10 minutes until the mixture is thick and creamy and a pale yellow colour. An electric mixer will do this more quickly if you have one. If you are using butter, melt it and allow it to cool. Sieve the flour little by little into the mixture, alternating with the butter. Fold in lightly with a large spoon. Turn the mixture into the prepared tin and bake in the oven (see below). The cake is done when the top is springy and the sides are shrinking from the sides of the tin.

CHOCOLATE SPONGE CAKE (1 quantity = 1½ pints)

150 g (5 oz) butter
175 g (6 oz) castor sugar
6 eggs, separated
100 g (4 oz) dark plain chocolate
150 g (5 oz) plain flour
1 teaspoon baking powder

Pre-heat the oven to gas mark 4, 180°C (350°F). Grease and flour the cake tin.

Cream the butter with 100 g (4 oz) of the sugar and beat in the egg yolks one by one. Break up the chocolate and place in a microwave bowl. Cover and cook on full power for 1 to 2 minutes until the chocolate is melted. Alternatively melt the chocolate in a bowl over hot water. Add the chocolate to the egg and sugar mixture. Whisk the egg whites until light and fluffy and fold in the remaining sugar. Sieve the flour and baking powder together. Fold in alternate spoonfuls of flour and egg white into the chocolate mix. Pour the cake mix into the tin and cook (see below). Allow the cake to cool before removing from the tin.

TIN	QUANTITIES OF SPONGE MIXTURE	BAKING TIMES
10 cm (4 in) round	½	15–20 mins
15 cm (6 in) round	1	20–25 mins
20 cm (8 in) round	1¾	25–30 mins
30 cm (12 in) round	5	50–55 mins
20 cm (8 in) square	1¾	25–30 mins
25 cm (10 in) square	3	45–50 mins
2.25 litre (4 pt) pudding basin	2½	45–50 mins

For rectangular shapes bake a square i.e. 20 cm × 15 cm (8 in × 6 in), cook 8 in cake and trim to size.

For chocolate sponge add 10–15 minutes to the baking times.

LIGHT FRUIT CAKE (1 quantity = 2 pints)

250 g (9 oz) butter
250 g (9 oz) castor sugar
6 eggs
250 g (9 oz) plain flour
100 g (4 oz) raisins
100 g (4 oz) currants
100 g (4 oz) sultanas
50 g (2 oz) candied peel

Pre-heat the oven to gas mark 4, 180°C (350°F). Grease and line the 6 inch round cake tin.

Cream together the butter and sugar. Beat in the eggs one at a time. Sift the flour into the mixture in 2 or 3 stages and mix in gently. Finally add the raisins, currants, sultanas and candied peel. Turn the mixture into the prepared cake tin and bake in the oven (see below). A skewer inserted into the middle of the cake will come out clean when the cake is ready. Cool on a wire rack.

TIN	QUANTITIES OF FRUIT MIXTURE	BAKING TIMES
15 cm (6 in) round	1	1½ hours
20 cm (8 in) round	1½	2 hours
23 cm (9 in) round	2	2 hours
30 cm (12 in) round	4	2¾–3 hours
15 cm (6 in) square	1½	1½ hours
20 cm (8 in) square	2	2 hours
23 cm (9 in) square	2½	2 hours
25 cm (10 in) square	3	2½ hours
30 cm (12 in) oval	3¼	2¾–3 hours

ROYAL ICING

2 egg whites
2 teaspoons lemon juice
450 g (1 lb) icing sugar, sieved

Break the egg whites with a fork then mix with the lemon juice. Add the mixture a little at a time to the icing sugar in a bowl, beating well until you achieve the desired consistency.

ROLL-OUT ICING

1 egg white
450 g (1 lb) icing sugar, sieved
1 tablespoon glucose liquid or syrup

Mix all the ingredients together with a wooden spoon, form into a ball and on a surface dusted with icing sugar, knead until pliable, adding a little water if necessary. Store in an air-tight polythene bag in a cool place for up to 3 months. When needed, roll out on to a surface dusted with icing sugar and use at once; put the rest back in the bag immediately or it will dry out.

BUTTERCREAM

100 g (4 oz) butter
225 g (8 oz) icing sugar, sieved
2 teaspoons lemon juice

Beat the butter in a bowl with a wooden spoon until light and fluffy then beat in the icing sugar and lemon juice.

WATER ICING

Just add water to some sieved icing sugar until the desired consistency is reached.

PASTILLAGE

450 g (1 lb) icing sugar
100 g (4 oz) cornflour
2 teaspoons gum tragacanth
2 leaves gelatine
5 tablespoons water
1 teaspoon liquid glucose

Sift the icing sugar, cornflour and gum tragacanth together. Dissolve the gelatine in the water. Add the glucose, then add this to the sugar and cornflour. Beat the mixture until it forms a paste, then knead it until it is smooth. Keep it in a plastic bag while you are working on the cake.

PETAL PASTE

450 g (1 lb) icing sugar
1 teaspoon gum tragacanth
2 teaspoons powdered gelatine
5 teaspoons cold water
5 teaspoons white fat
2 teaspoons liquid glucose
1 egg white

Sift the icing sugar and gum tragacanth into a bowl and stand it over hot water to warm it a little. Dissolve the gelatine in the cold water and place in a saucepan. Add the white fat and glucose and beat gently until it is dissolved. Pour the mixture over the egg white then add to the icing sugar. Ideally the mixture should now be beaten in a mixer with a strong attachment on medium speed for 2 to 3 minutes or until it becomes elastic. Hand beating will need 5 to 10 minutes. Leave the paste in a plastic bag in the refrigerator for 30 minutes or so before using.

Basic Techniques

CUTTING A CAKE TO SHAPE

Always use a sharp serrated knife. Remember that if you want height in your shape you will need to build it up from layers of cake stuck together with jam or buttercream. Always start by carving off less than you think – you can always take off more but it's very difficult to put little pieces back. If gaps appear – very likely when using fruit cake – fill them up with marzipan before covering the cake.

COVERING A CAKE WITH MARZIPAN

Once you are happy with your basic shape, spread the cake with sieved jam (1) (apricot is traditional but it could be any flavour you like). Dust the work surface with a little icing sugar then roll out the marzipan to about 5 mm (¼ in) thick.

For round cakes: Measure round the cake with a piece of string (2). Measure the height. Cut a

strip of marzipan to the length and height of the cake, allowing slightly extra for safety. Roll up the strip carefully (3) and place it against the side of the cake. Unroll it round the cake, smoothing it on with your hands (4). Trim the top edge level with the top of the cake (5). Cut a circle of marzipan slightly larger than the top of the cake. Drape over the cake and smooth carefully. Trim around the top edge (6). (If you find it easier you can tip the cake upside-down on to the circle of marzipan and trim round it before turning it over.)

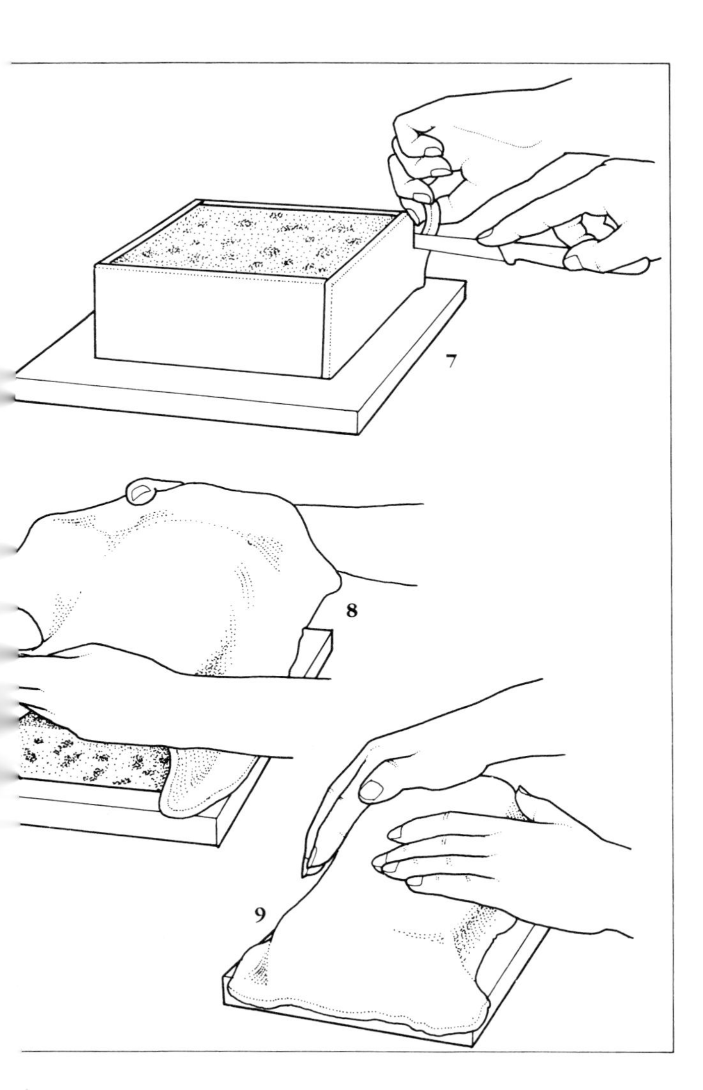

For square cakes: Either cut one long strip to go round all 4 sides or, if you want sharp corners, cover all 4 sides separately before covering the top as before (7).

For oddly shaped cakes: It is almost always easiest to cover the cake all in one by draping the sheet of marzipan over it (8) and then smoothing and coaxing the marzipan into the shape with your hands (9).

COVERING A CAKE WITH ROLL-OUT ICING

Proceed exactly as for marzipanning, but dampen the marzipan underneath with a little water to stick. If icing a sponge cake, spread with a little buttercream before icing.

Side smoothers are very useful. Use them after marzipanning or icing to create smooth even surfaces.

COVERING A CAKE BOARD

To cover an entire board: Roll out a sufficiently large quantity of icing on a work surface dusted with icing sugar. Dampen the board with water then stick the icing to the board. Trim the edges.

To cover the edges of a board: For a round board, cut and roll up a strip of icing long enough to go round the board. Dampen the board edge and unroll the strip on to it (1). Trim the edge (2).

For a square board, cut pieces of icing to fit sides and damp and stick separately (you may be able to do two at once with practice). Smooth the joins with a little water (3).

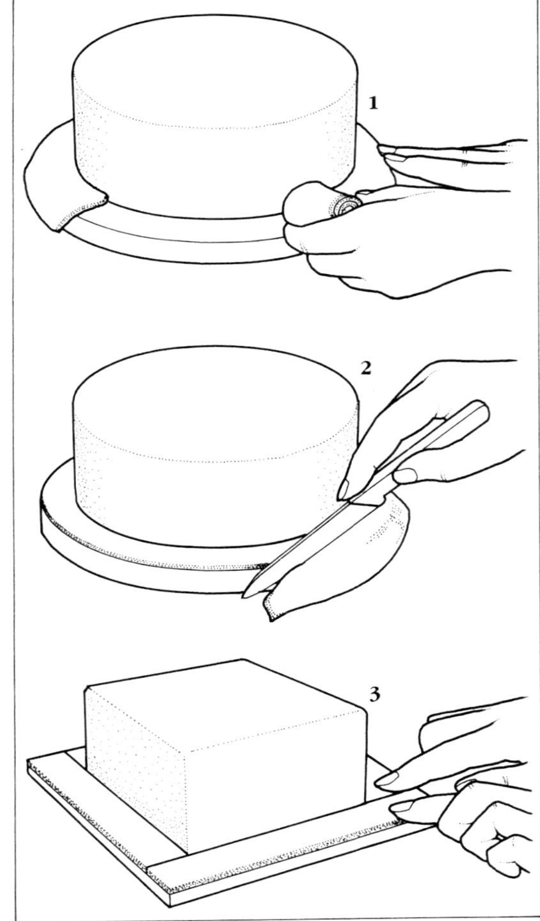

CRIMPING EDGES

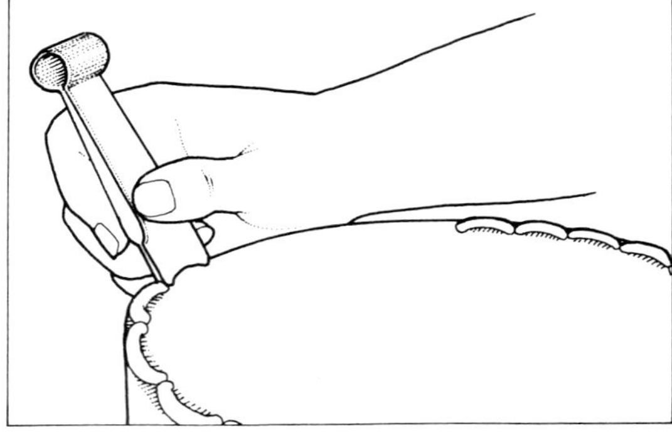

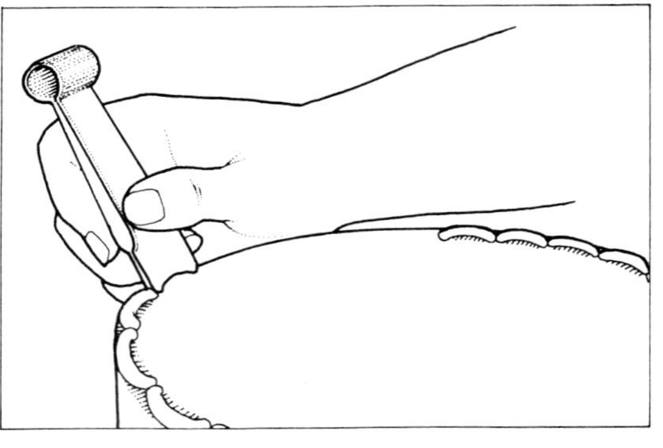

While the icing is still soft, using a desired crimper, pinch the edges together at the top edge of the cake and of the board.

COLOURING ROLL-OUT ICING

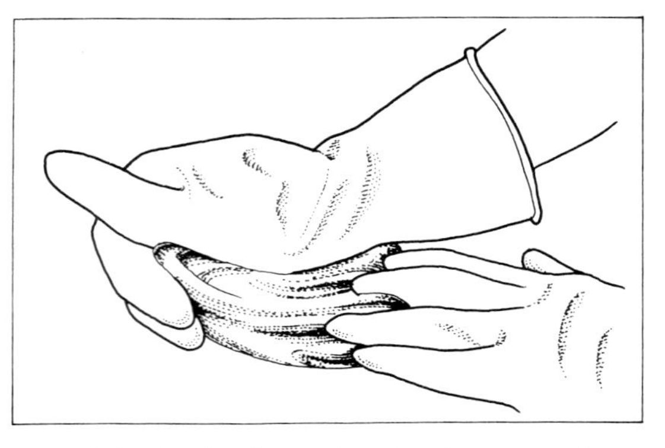

Knead the food colour, drop by drop, into the icing until the desired depth of colour is reached. If using a dark colour it is worth wearing rubber gloves. A mixer with strong attachment can be used for large quantities.

DIVIDING A CAKE INTO SECTIONS

Cake dividers are very useful for this (1), but if you don't have any you can use paper.

To divide the side of a round cake: Cut a strip of paper long enough to go round cake and trim it to fit exactly (2). Remove from the cake and fold into as many sections as desired (3). Replace round the cake and mark where the folds come on the cake with a pin or a dot of food colouring (4).

To divide the top of the cake: Cut a piece of paper to the size of the cake top, fold it into the number of desired sections (5) then unfold and place on top of the cake (6). This is also good for marking a pattern on top of the cake, by cutting the folded paper (7) before unfolding it again (8).

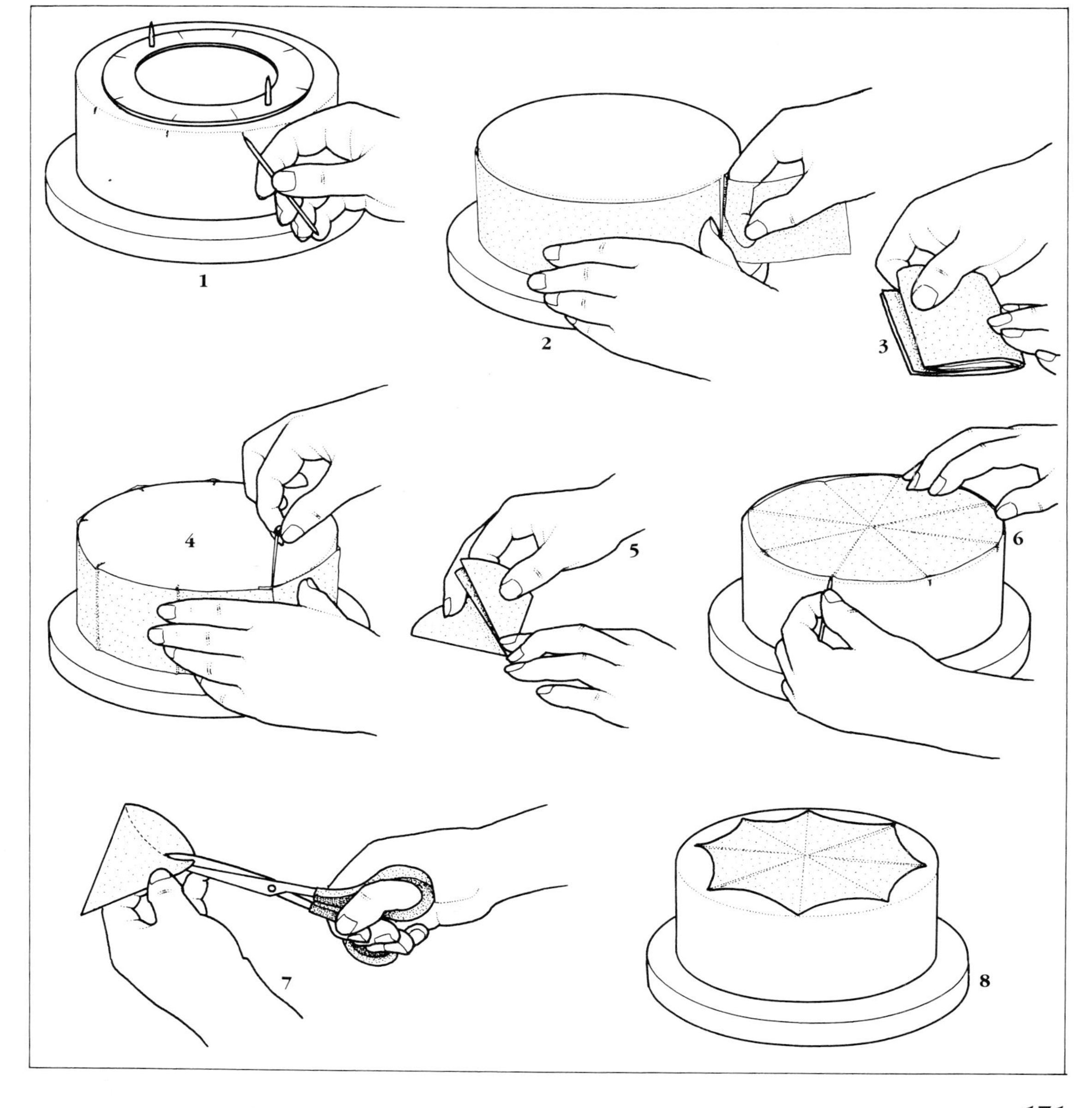

ADDING CANDLES TO A CAKE
It often spoils the design of a cake to have to add candles to it. They look less intrusive if stuck on to the board instead. Simply pipe blobs of royal icing using a no. 6 nozzle (1) and stick candles into them (2). If you're not using royal icing you can stick the candles into cut-out round or fancy pieces of roll-out icing (3) stuck to the board with a little water (4).

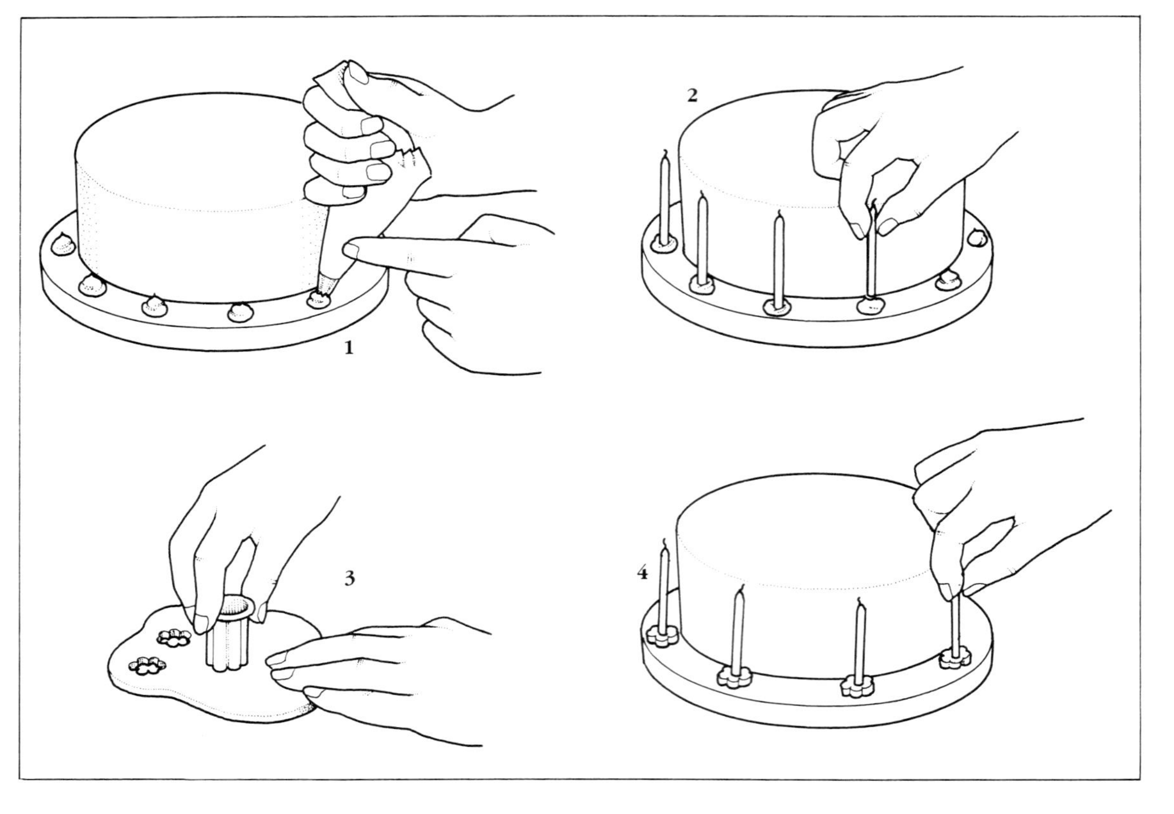

PIPING
I have used relatively limited and simple piping throughout the book, but obviously you can add far more fancy work on to many of the cakes if you like. I have used the following designs:

Shell: Using a no. 6 nozzle, push forward to create a wave effect (1) then pull backwards to make a 'tail' (2). Repeat as many times as necessary.

Snail's Trail: This can be done with a piping bag with the end cut off or with a plain nozzle. The movement is the same as for shell, and it's a very useful quick way of finishing off the lower edge of a cake neatly (4 and 5).

Scrolls: Using a no. 6 nozzle, twist the lines as you go to create texture and movement (3).

Inscriptions: Using a no. 1 nozzle (or larger if preferred), keep the lettering simple, squaring off letters that would normally be rounded (6).

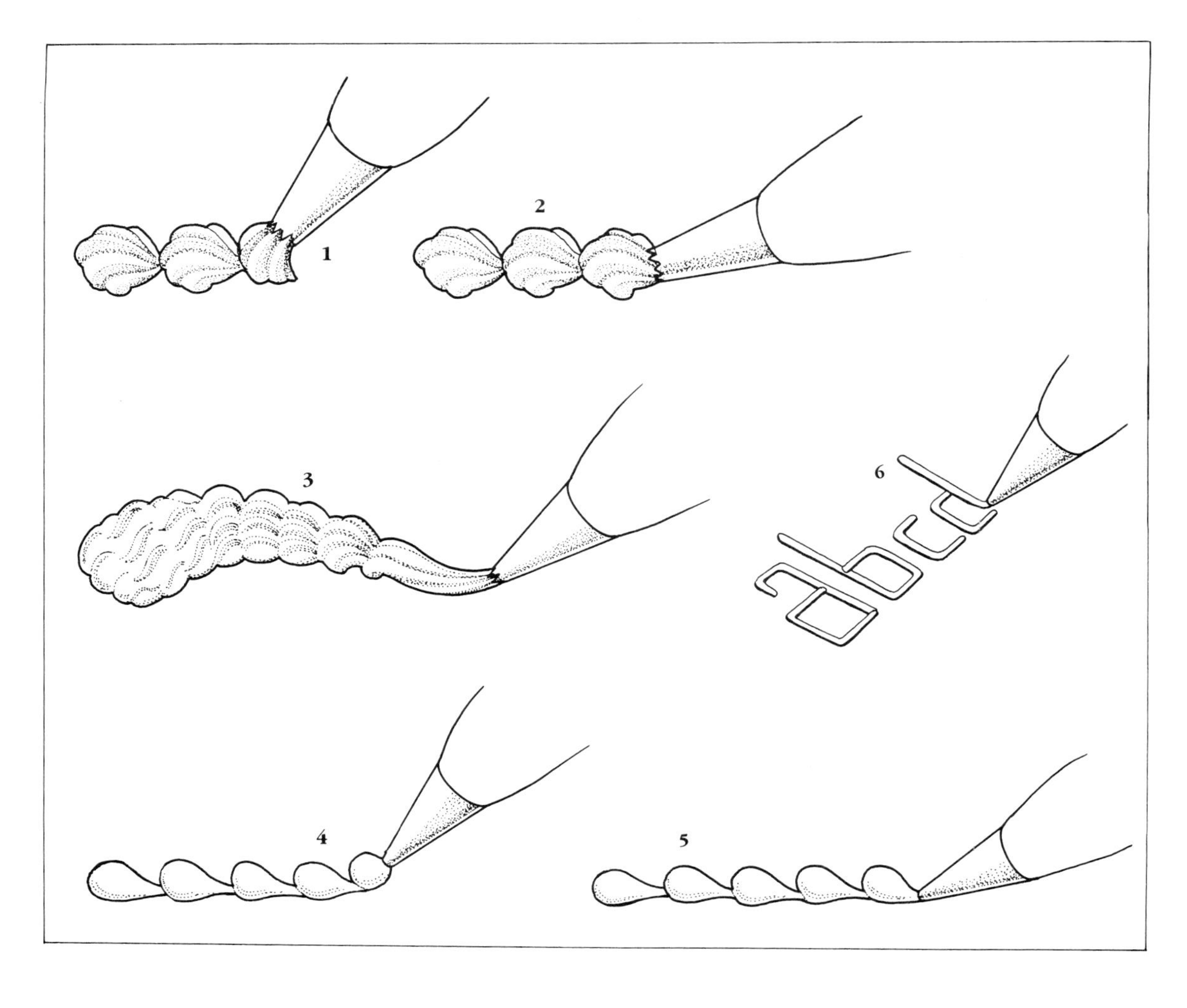

Flower Language

If you are looking for a symbolic meaning for your decorations, what better language is there than the language of flowers?

Acacia	Chaste love	Jonquil	Desire
Almond	Stupidity, thoughtlessness	Laburnum	Forsaken
Amaryllis	Pride	Laurel	Glory
Anemones	Forsaken	Lavender	Distrust
Apple	Temptation	Lily	Majesty
Apple Blossom	Preference	Lily of the Valley	Return of happiness
Balm	Sympathy	Marigold	Grief; pain
Basil	Hatred	Mistletoe	I surmount all obstacles
Beech Tree	Prosperity	Moss	Maternal love
Bluebell	Kindness	Mushroom	Suspicion
Bouquet	Gallantry	Oak Tree	Hospitality
Bramble	Remorse	Parsley	Feasting
Buttercup	Cheerfulness	Passion Flower	Religion
Carnation	Woman's Love	Peony	Shame
Cowslip	Pensiveness	Periwinkle	Pleasant memories
Daffodil	Regard	Pineapple	You are perfect
Daisy	Innocence	Plum Tree	Keep your promise
Fern	Sincerity	Pomegranate	Foolishness
Foxglove	Insincerity; a wish	Primrose	Early youth
Geranium	Comfort	Rose	Love
Hawthorn	Hope	Rosemary	Your presence revives me
Hazel	Reconciliation; peace	Snowdrop	Consolation
Holly	Am I forgotten?	Strawberry	Perfect example
Hollyhock	Fecundity	Thyme	Activity
Hyacinth	Sport; play	Tulip	Fame
Hydrangea	A boaster; you are cold	Vine	Drunkenness
Iris	Compliments; I have a message	Wallflower	Fidelity in misfortune
Ivy	Friendship; fidelity; marriage	Willow	Forsaken

Wedding Anniversaries

1 year	Paper	14 years	Ivory
2 years	Cotton	15 years	Crystal
3 years	Leather	20 years	China
4 years	Silk	25 years	Silver
5 years	Wood	30 years	Pearl
6 years	Iron	35 years	Coral
7 years	Wool	40 years	Ruby
8 years	Bronze	45 years	Sapphire
9 years	Pottery	50 years	Gold
10 years	Tin	55 years	Emerald
11 years	Steel	60 years	Diamond
12 years	Linen	65 years	White Sapphire
13 years	Lace	70 years	Platinum

Suppliers

All of the icing equipment, food colours (except gold and silver) and a good deal more besides can be obtained from my good friends:

Squire's Kitchen,
3 Waverley Lane,
Farnham,
Surrey,
GU9 8BB.
Tel: 0252 711 749.

The gold and silver food colours I obtain from:

Mary Ford Cake Artistry Centre,
28 Southbourne Grove,
Bournemouth,
Hampshire,
BH6 3RA
Tel: 0202 422653

For candles (including lovely sparkling ones) and a wonderful range of decorations, many of them edible, I recommend those made by Culpitts, which can be obtained from any good kitchen shop or department store.

And don't forget, if you're feeling lazy or uninspired, you can always have the cake of your dreams made for you at my shop in London (or just drop in for tea and a sandwich):

Jane Asher Party Cakes Ltd,
22–24 Cale Street,
London, SW3 3QU.
Tel: 071 584 6177.

Templates

You may find the templates on the following pages useful for certain cakes. Trace round the outlines and then cut the shape out of thick paper or card. Place each template on top of some rolled out icing and cut round it with a sharp knife. Use this technique to copy all sorts of designs from books, magazines and so on.

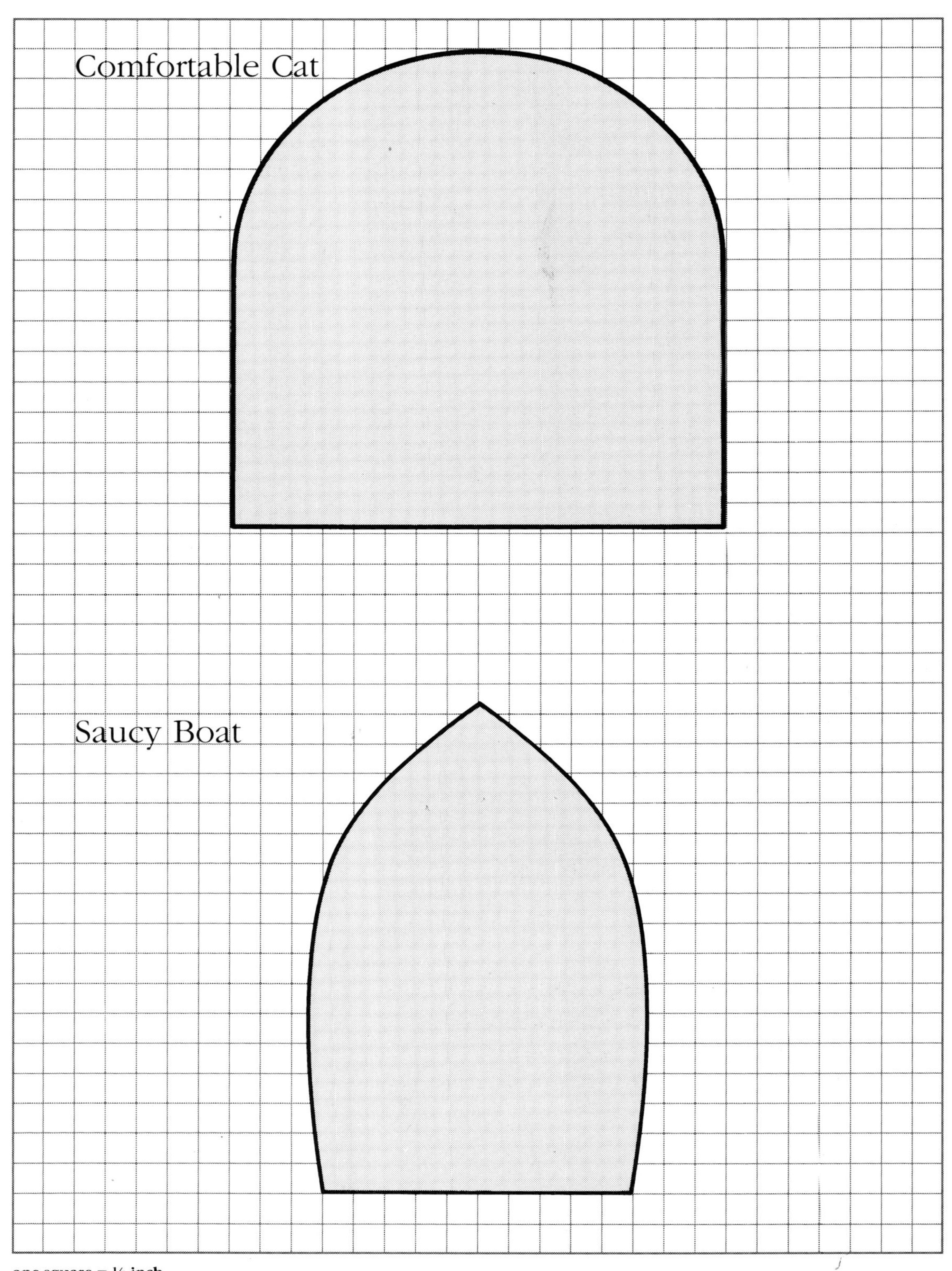

one square = ½ inch

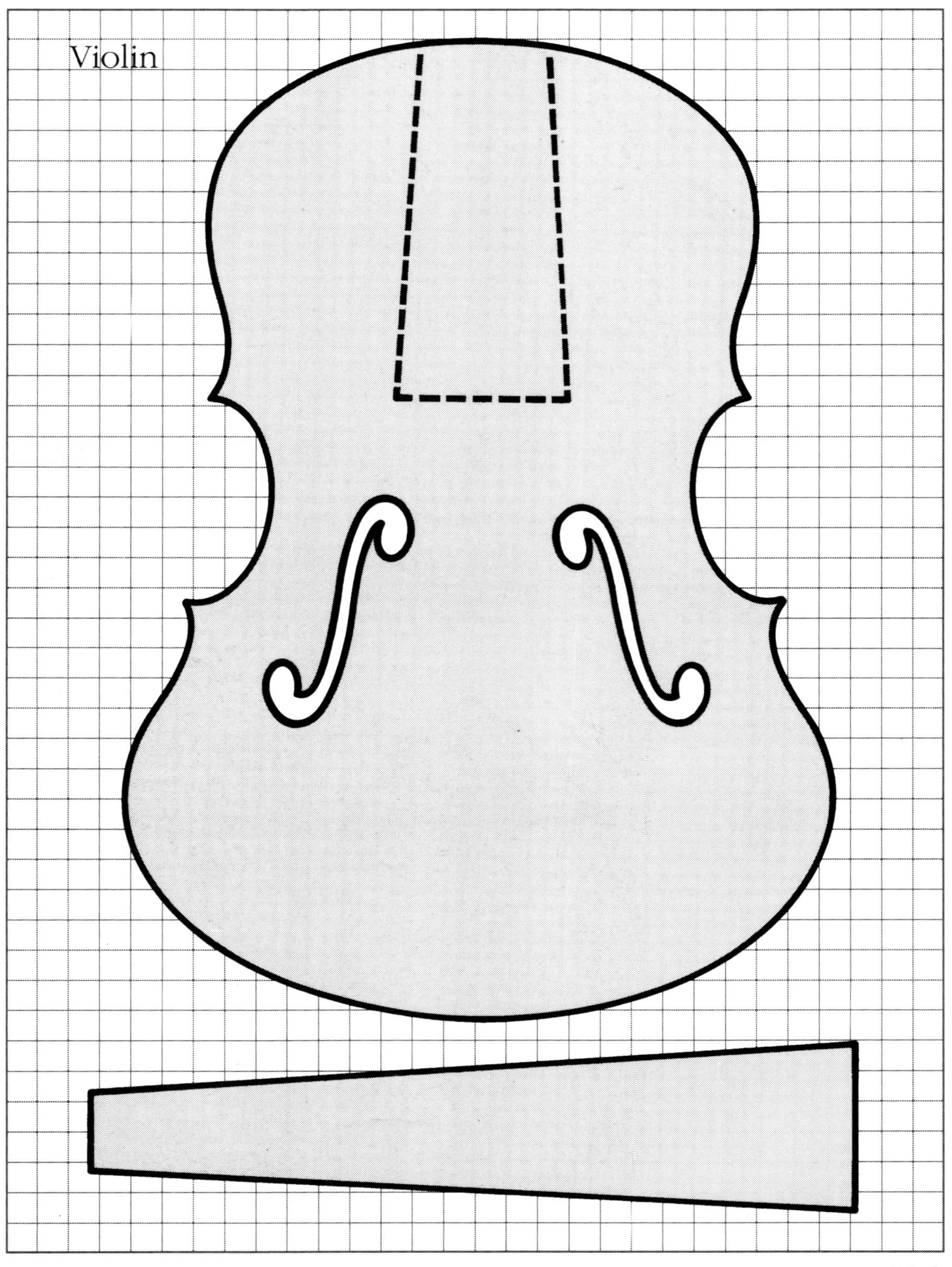

one square = ¼ inch

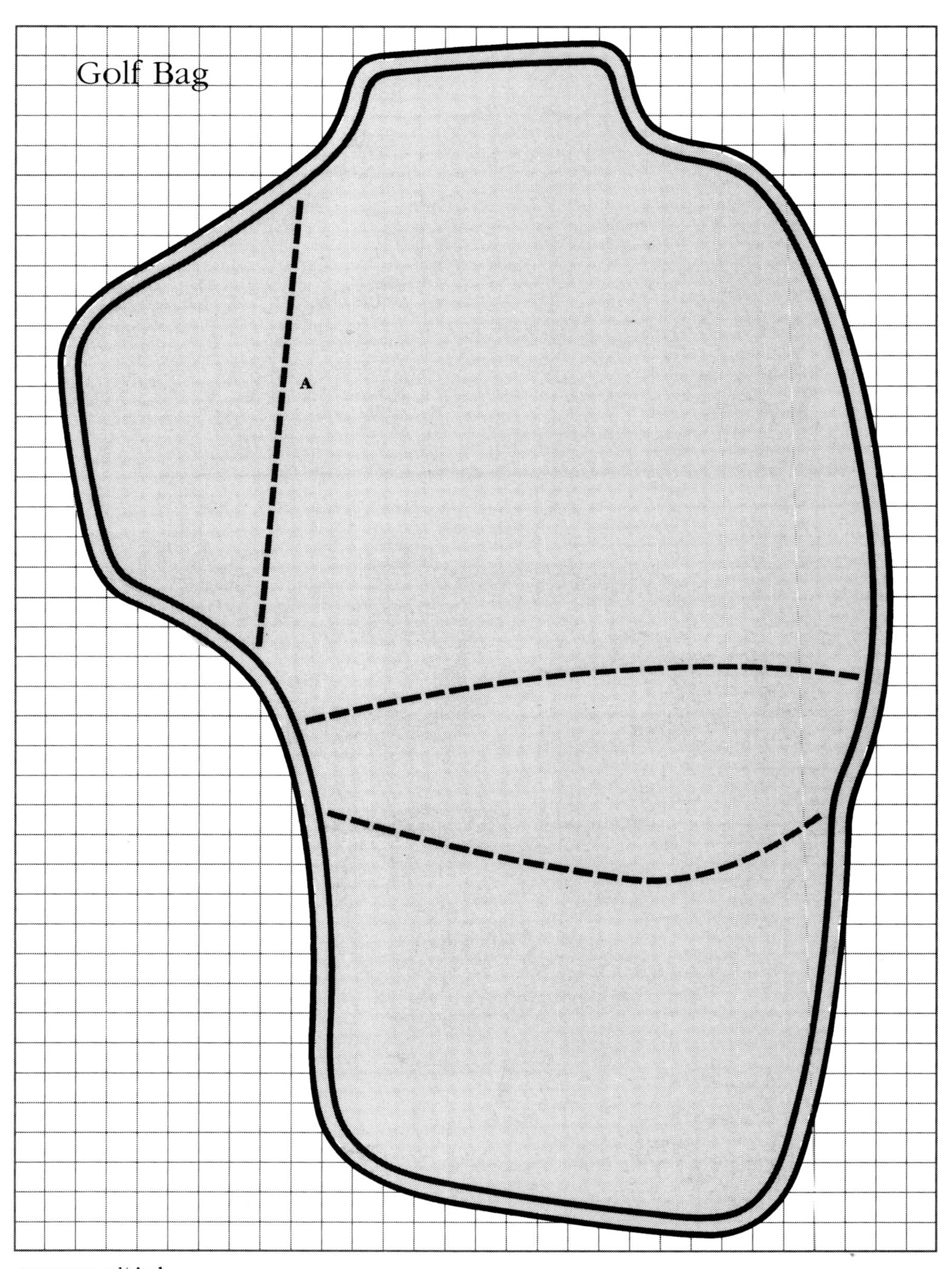

one square = ¼ inch

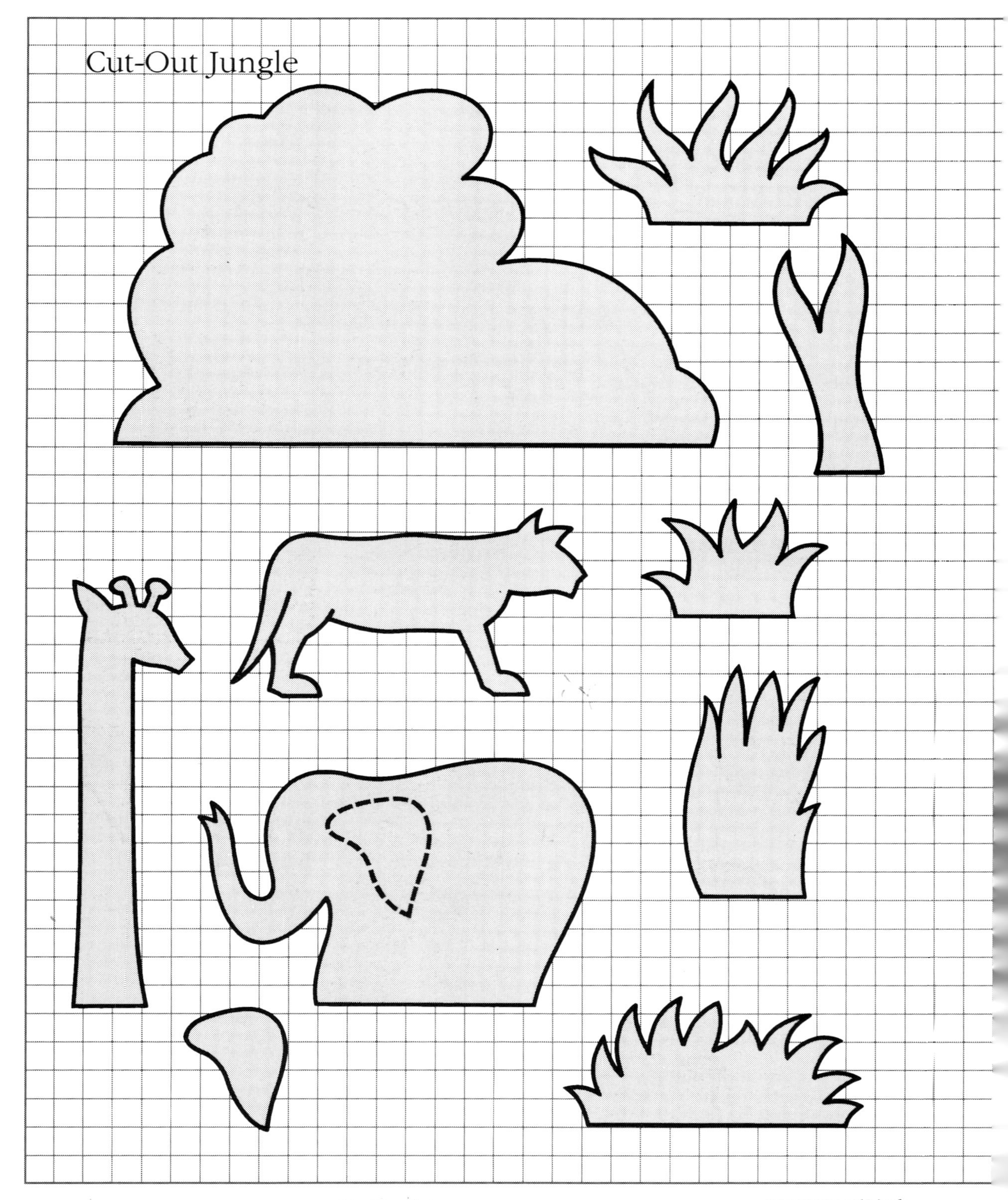

one square = ¼ inch

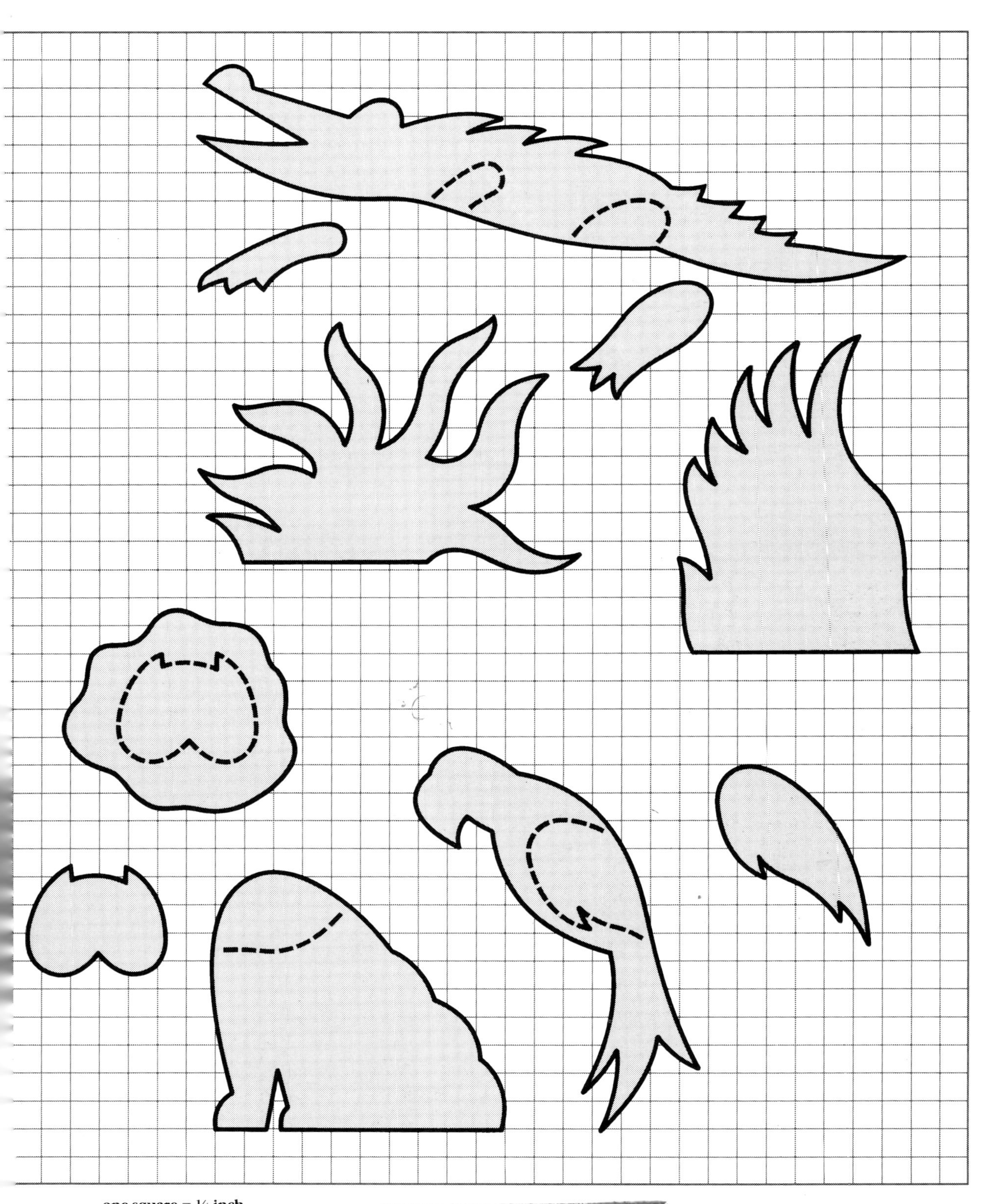

one square = 1/4 inch

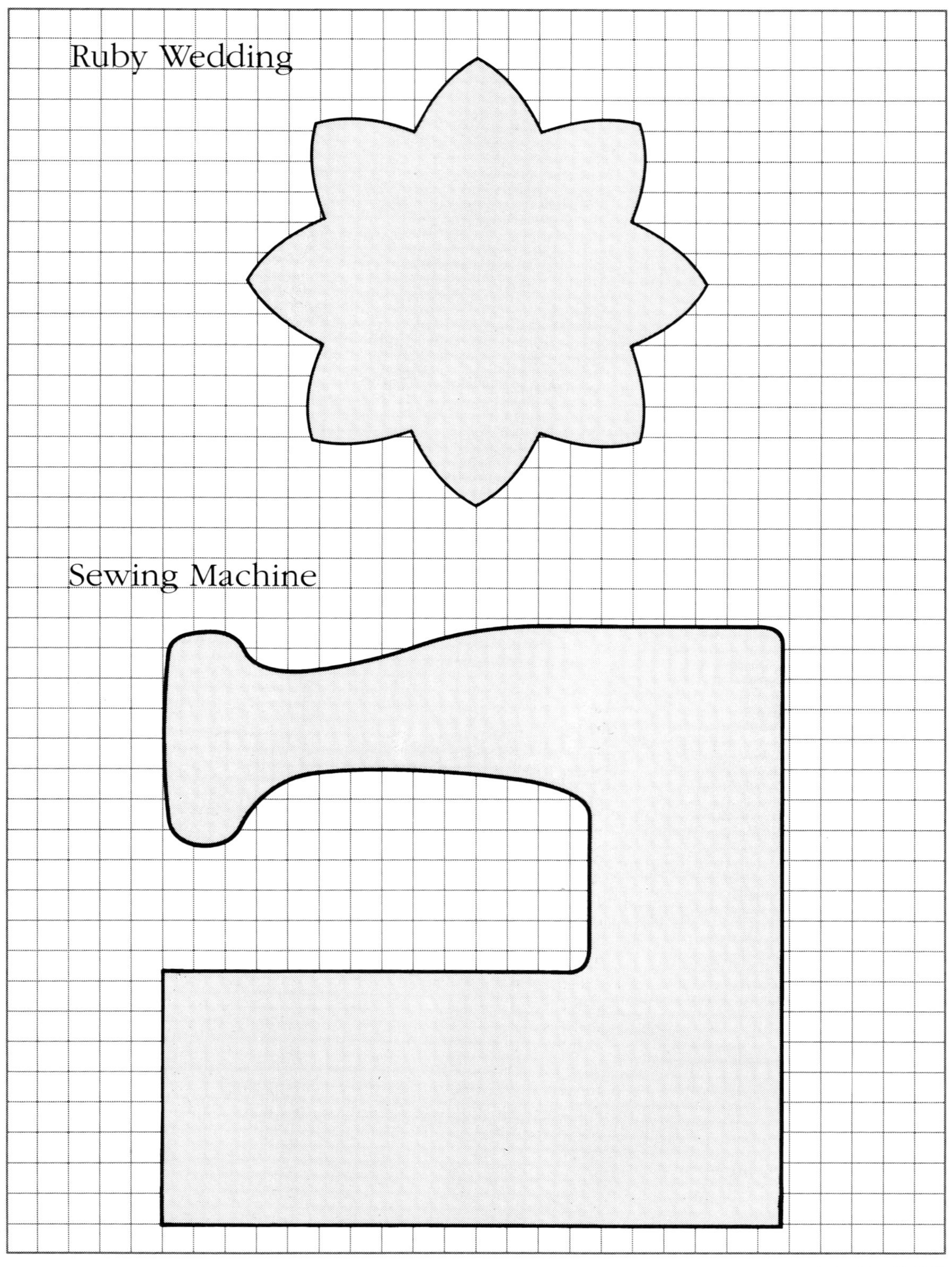

one square = ½ inch

INDEX

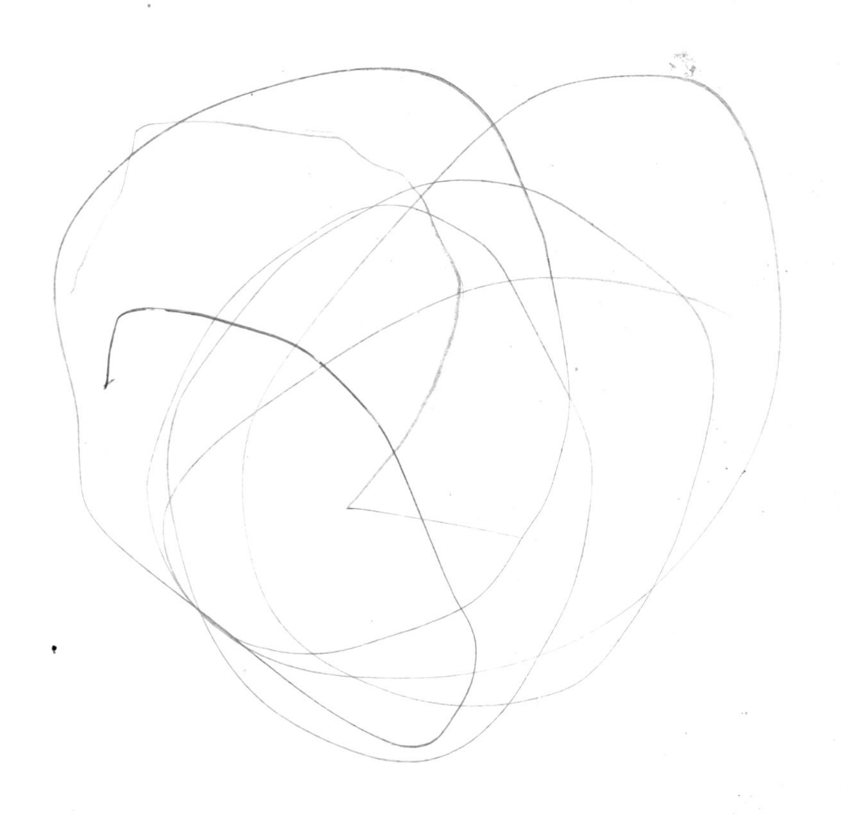